WALTHER RATHENAU

Walther Rathenau

Weimar's Fallen Statesman

SHULAMIT VOLKOV

Yale

UNIVERSITY

PRESS

New Haven and London

Frontispiece: Edvard Munch, *Walther Rathenau,* 1907. Courtesy Bildarchiv Preussischer Kulturbesitz. © The Munch Museum / The Munch-Ellingsen Group / BONO, Oslo 2011.

Yale University Press books may be purchased in quantity for educational, business, or promotional use. For information, please e-mail sales.press@yale.edu (U.S. office) or sales@yaleup.co.uk (U.K. office).

Set in Janson type by Vonda's Comp Services, Morley, Michigan.
Printed in the United States of America.

Library of Congress Cataloging-in-Publication Data

Volkov, Shulamit, 1942–
Walther Rathenau : Weimar's fallen statesman / Shulamit Volkov.
p. cm.—(Jewish lives)
Includes bibliographical references and index.
ISBN 978-0-300-14431-4 (cloth : alk. paper) 1. Rathenau, Walther, 1867–1922. 2. Germany—Politics and government—1918–1933.
3. Statesmen—Germany—Biography. 4. Jews—Germany—Biography.
I. Title.
DD231.R3V65 2012
943.085092—dc23
[B]   2011033169

A catalogue record for this book is available from the British Library.

This paper meets the requirements of ANSI/NISO Z39.48-1992
(Permanence of Paper).

10 9 8 7 6 5 4 3 2 1

CONTENTS

INTRODUCTION

On the morning of Saturday, June 24, 1922, following a busy night of meetings and consultations, Walther Rathenau, foreign minister of the young Weimar Republic, left his elegant villa in Grunewald, an outlying western suburb of Berlin, and was chauffeured in his black open-top coupe along the Königsallee to his downtown offices. On a side street around a curve, his assassins waited in their own car. They overtook Rathenau's vehicle, fired a number of shots, and threw in a hand grenade for good measure. In his memoirs, the literary critic Alfred Kerr, Rathenau's longtime friend and neighbor, described the pietà-like scene that then transpired: a hospital nurse, passing by, gently held Rathenau's head in her lap as Germany's Jewish foreign minister bled to death.[1]

To be sure, every life story is told backward. The past is always revealed to us from a certain present moment, and one's final failures or achievements always color one's view of earlier days. This is particularly so when the end is as startling and tragic as Rathenau's. The storyteller in us wishes to expose a tale that would explain this end, that would lead, as if inexorably, toward it; a tale in which all routes are connected, everything points toward that final scene, rounding up a real-life drama. Walther Rathenau's life was anything but such a clear, one-dimensional tale. In fact, only his death might have been foretold. He had seemed to be moving recklessly toward it. Some of his friends had warned him that his life was in danger. Ever since he had taken office as minister of reconstruction in May 1921, in one of the unstable cabinets typical of the Weimar Republic at the time, he had surely known that the threat was real. Nevertheless, he had ordered his police guards away, had continued to use his unprotected open car, and had remained undeterred in the face of mounting rumors of conspiracy against him. During his last days Rathenau had acted with quiet resolve and self-assurance. But except for this last episode, his life had been characteristically a zigzag course, full of surprising turns, changing directions, oscillating views and intentions. It was the life of a struggling man, beset by inner conflicts, often unable to decide among alternatives, never entirely at one with his own choices, always leaving his options open. Kerr saw in this impressive, powerful figure, a man "not born to resist," one who was "ambivalent by nature."[2]

Rathenau has often been presented as a representative of his time. The part he had indeed played in the various facets of life in Imperial Germany and then during the early years of the Weimar Republic gives credence to such an approach. In another context, his life story can also be seen to contain the essence of German Jewish history, telling the tale of their efforts to combine their Jewish and German identities, at ease with neither of them. As a Jew Rathenau moved between self-loathing and intense inner pride. As a German too, and a committed patriot, he often saw through the nationalist megalomania of his time. And while hoping to fully join his *Volk*, he always treasured his "otherness." Rathenau's was a story of a modernizer who both admired and detested modernity; a man of action who wished to be appreciated for his philosophical reflections; a man of almost unlimited material means who claimed to value soul and spirit above all. He continually socialized, enjoying a huge circle of friends and acquaintances from various walks of life, but remained throughout his life a very lonely man, often withdrawn, even uncommunicative, seemingly preferring the solitude of his country house to the bustle of city life. Finally, his is a story of a man who passionately sought political power but repeatedly drew back from its exercise. When he was finally ready and willing to take on the challenge, this cost him his life. The story of such a life is doubtlessly the stuff of which tragedy is made.

1

A German Jew in the Making

WALTHER RATHENAU was born on September 29, 1867, in Berlin.[1] Later in life he would often mention the hundred years of his Berlin ancestry. But the Berlin to which his grandparents moved from the northern and northeastern plains of Brandenburg in the early years of the nineteenth century was a very different city from the Berlin of Rathenau's own youth.[2] From being a capital strictly oriented toward the Prussian monarchy's military needs, a garrison city only recently adorned with a few royal structures in grand classical style, the Berlin of the 1860s was quickly changing to fit its new role as an imperial seat. The Prussian army won three consecutive wars during that decade. Soon after the first victory, over Denmark in 1864, the town began to experience an unprecedented growth. It attracted new inhabitants by projecting the image of a youthful, energetic metropolis, destined for greatness—politically and economically alike. Following the next victory, over Austria in

the summer of 1866, it was Bismarck's presence in town that
caused excitement among the many newcomers. Himself no
lover of city life, the chancellor was by then seen as the moving
spirit behind Berlin's hectic development. Finally, with the
crowning of the Prussian king as emperor of a new "German
Empire" on January 18, 1871, and in the wake of another spec-
tacular victory, this time over France, it was Wilhelm I, now
both Prussian king and German Kaiser, whose occasional
pompous ride through the Brandenburg Gate was eagerly
awaited by the residents of the new imperial capital. A building
boom, especially the westward expansion of the city, providing
elegant living quarters for the wealthy commercial population,
was now fed by ever more rapid economic growth. The new
Germany was beginning to enjoy the fruits of its industrialization, sustained—at least for a while—by the handsome reparations dutifully paid by the defeated French, and despite the fact
that a financial bubble grew and burst as early as 1873, Berlin
never returned to its earlier provincial self. At the time of German unification the city already had 865,000 inhabitants. It
had grown to more than a million by 1877 and reached two
million by 1905. Of course, Paris, London, and New York
were much larger, but no other city experienced such a dramatic rate of growth at the time. Empire-building was accompanied by economic growth, not without crises or setbacks, to
be sure, but with impressive, lasting consequences. It was an ex-
citing time for Germans everywhere, and Berlin was at the center of it all. Its dynamism was contagious; its achievements—
glorious. It was a propitious time and place to enter the stage,
no doubt.

All the more so if you were a Jew. Discussions of the need
to put an end to the discriminatory legislation that regulated
Jewish life in the various states of the old Holy Roman Empire
had started as early as the 1780s.[3] While the first written statement concerning the so-called improvement of the civil status

of Jews was published in Prussia, in fact in Berlin, early practical reforms were undertaken in the territories under the direct rule of the Habsburg emperor Joseph II. In the rest of the empire, despite a prolonged debate concerning their status, and later on even despite new legislation imposed by Napoleon, most Jews experienced only marginal improvements. Local reforms enacted under French occupation were either entirely withdrawn soon after the defeat of the French in 1814 or were only partially put into effect. Full Jewish emancipation was drafted into the constitution adopted by the National Assembly that met in Frankfurt during the Revolution of 1848–49, but this too never materialized. It was only during the 1860s, at a time of rapid economic growth and liberal reawakening, that opposition to emancipation seemed to fade and one German state after another took the long-awaited legal steps to end discrimination. The matter was finally sealed in the wake of German unification in 1871. A new era for German Jewry had begun.

But legal equality in itself, while surely of great symbolic value, did not always bring about a meaningful change in daily life. From the outset, emancipation was a matter of social integration and acculturation as much as of legal procedure. In France, equal citizenship was conceived as a precondition to integration. It was granted to individual Jews at the same time as their communal rights and what were often considered their privileges were abolished. In Germany, by contrast, a measure of integration was conceived as a precondition for equal citizenship. The conservative regimes that were reinstated in most German states following Napoleon's defeat left intact the old Jewish communal institutions, and individual Jews, striving for "entrance" into German society, could hope to gain equality only on the basis of their good behavior, so to speak, or their special contributions. Jewish "movers and doers,"[4] successful commercial and financial men, took an active part in the construction of the new economic bourgeoisie, while some of their sons gradually managed to enter the ranks of the *Bildungsbürgertum*, the educated bourgeoisie, as well. Thus, change was initiated on both sides: Germans allowed some of the traditional hindrances to Jewish "entrance" to be dropped, and at the same time Jews showed ever-growing interest in achieving such entrance. Limited but noticeable openness on the one side encouraged active striving on the other, and although the process was slow at first, it gradually acquired ever greater momentum and encompassed ever larger segments of the population.

However, the process was made problematic by resistance on both sides. The more cautious members of the rabbinical establishment mistrusted integration in principle and rejected it in practice. Many Germans objected to it on various social and economic grounds, though finally and above all because of a long-lasting and deep-seated anti-Jewish tradition. Conservatives seemed anxious to preserve the Christian character of state and society in Germany; liberals, by then the main spokesmen of a new kind of nationalism too, began to conceive Jews as a foreign ethnic element, constitutionally unfit to become equal citizens in the future German national state. Neither complete formal equality nor easy integration seemed possible under such circumstances. Nevertheless, by the second half of the nineteenth century, German Jews could already point out considerable achievements, both in terms of social and economic mobility and in terms of acculturation. Between 1800 and 1870, they indeed managed to "make it.'" Until the end of the eighteenth century, most of them were poor and lived in relative isolation from their non-Jewish neighbors, whereas by the late nineteenth century they had become, more often than not, part and parcel of the German lower and "middle" middle class. Though the very rich continued to be a small minority among them, the very poor too were relatively few. Within two to three generations Jews had moved from the margin to the center of German society. They were more urban than other Germans, moving in ever greater proportions into the larger metropolitan centers. The range of their occupations was expanding, especially as they entered the free professions. And while they could not become officers in the Prussian army, for instance—usually not even in its reserve units—and their chances of promotion within the bureaucracy, especially within the all important Prussian bureaucracy, were very slim, their voices were now heard more often and more clearly than ever before. All in all, they constituted a very special kind of minority: neither poorer, nor less well-educated than other Germans; no longer marginal in most respects. In fact, they usually did not consider themselves a minority at all. Germany was ethnically heterogeneous in any case, ran the argument, and Jews simply made up yet another "tribe" among many; to be absorbed, like others, into the great German nation-in-the-making.

To be sure, non-Jewish Germans tended to see things differently. While Jews normally endeavored to be socially and culturally integrated without giving up their Jewish identity, Germans all too often expected them to take this last step, too. Even some of the more liberal among the latter, defending emancipation, hoped to see the Jews shed their uniqueness as they entered German society, often simply demanding their conversion. Indeed, some Jews were ready, even willing, to take this step. Heinrich Heine, to name only the most famous example, considered his conversion to Christianity a "ticket of admission to European culture." But with the exception of few big cities and only at particular periods, as for example in early nineteenth-century Berlin, the conversion rate among Jews was not very high, endogamy remained the rule, and Jewish ties, familial and social, were usually very tight.

Thus, while Jews could justly be proud of their achievements in the areas of social integration and acculturation, Germans continued to be skeptical in some cases, and hostile in others. In fact, they were often both skeptical and hostile even when they too appreciated the upward movement of the Jews; perhaps especially when they did so. This created a complex situation. Jews were making significant inroads into German society, but a degree of tension between themselves and other Germans remained and was felt by both sides. Both Germans and German Jews were aware of this tension, and both learned to live with it. Some Jews managed to overlook it more easily and more gracefully than others, though to some degree it remained a problem even for them. Some expected more openness and occasionally found themselves offended and disappointed; others feared more hostility and were favorably surprised by the occasional friendly reception. Some, continuously under pressure, experimented with new ideologies such as Zionism, while others insisted on stretching the bounds of their assimilation. In any case, by the end of the nineteenth century most Jews had reached a measure of contentment. After all, they could only evaluate their newly acquired status by comparing it with that of earlier generations, not with some utopian future state of perfect equality. Alternatively, they could make the comparison with the position of Jews elsewhere in Europe, in Tsarist Russia for instance, or even in republican France, struggling with the consequences of the Dreyfus Affair. Living under a stable regime and within a law-abiding society in Germany, they were confident enough with regard to their own and their offspring's prospects. On the whole, and despite the ever present undercurrent of antisemitism, they usually felt secure, even gratified.

Emil Rathenau, Walther's father, born in Berlin on December 11, 1838, already belonged to a generation of Jews who took for granted their status as emancipated Jews, although the legal process itself was far from completion during his youth.[5] His parents, newcomers in Berlin, were soon engulfed by the brilliance of the city's social life and settled down to the leisurely existence of well-to-do rentiers. His father, wrote Emil many years later in an autobiographical sketch, was "strict and meticulous," while the mother was "clever and witty," an elegant and ambitious lady.[6] Her origins surely warranted such qualities. Therese Rathenau was a daughter of an old trading family, the Liebermanns, whose father had turned to manufacturing, first in calico printing and then in machine building, first in and around Berlin and then in faraway Silesia. Not altogether surprisingly, the familial constellation in Emil's own home, later on in life, seems to have been much like that of his parents. A pattern of distance from the father and closeness to the mother, as we shall soon see in Walther's life too, was clearly a reenactment of an earlier familial situation. Till her death in 1894, Emil visited his mother almost daily, whenever it was at all possible under the constraints of his busy schedule, much as his son Walther did later on with his own mother.

Having graduated from a humanistic gymnasium, Emil was first sent as an apprentice to his relatives' ironworks in Silesia. He spent four and a half unhappy years there, gaining invaluable practical experience, but feeling hopelessly trapped, both socially and professionally. It was a small fortune he had inherited from his grandfather that set him free. He was then able to study, first in Hanover and then in Zurich, acquiring a proper engineering certificate, and then to launch an independent career as a technical adviser at the up and coming Borsig railroad equipment company in Berlin. Though this was clearly a promising post, Emil was not satisfied. Soon he was on the move again, traveling to England, taking on various jobs in a number of industrial firms, learning and observing the political and economic situation in that country, but never entirely happy with himself and his achievements. Finally, back in Berlin, he managed to step forward on two fronts at once. He married Mathilde Nachmann, daughter of a wealthy Jewish banker from Frankfurt am Main, and not unlike his mother a clever and witty, ambitious and worldly young lady. Then, together with an old schoolmate, he took over a small machine-building factory in one of Berlin's industrial districts and established himself as an independent businessman in the technical field of his choice.

Nevertheless, signs of discontent could soon be detected again. Constructing steam engines for heating as well as for urban gas and water distribution was a routine kind of work. At Emil's initiative, the factory took upon itself to provide the Royal Theater of Berlin with all the needed technical fixtures, clearly a job requiring more imagination but rather unpromising financially. And when his partner suggested that they turn their business into a public company, under the favorable circumstances of the economic boom in the early 1870s, Emil Rathenau decided to sell his share. He continued to function as the firm's general manager, but was clearly planning his exit. In fact, as the stock exchange crash of 1873 came soon afterwards, Emil Rathenau's first business enterprise ended in collapse. Thanks to his previous caution, however, his personal financial losses were relatively minor.

Walther was by then eight years old. Though the Rathenaus could maintain their standard of living, the situation at home changed dramatically. The father, till then always busy and rarely at home, was suddenly jobless, living, like his own father before him, the life of a youthful rentier, only this time not really as a matter of choice. In fact, the grandfather's leisurely life had been curtailed quite early in Emil's life, as much of the family property had perished in an accidental fire in 1842. Emil may have had some early memories of these less than glamorous years. In 1870, his father-in-law, Isaac Nachmann, took his own life as he feared the bankruptcy of his bank, a bankruptcy that in fact never occurred. Considering this background, it is hardly surprising to find Emil despondent. For a number of years, he seemed to oscillate between depression and feats of animated activity. He was looking for new employment but nothing seemed to fit his skills, measure up to his ambition, or fulfill his restless personality. He was briefly involved in a real estate business with his brother, but then quickly withdrew, finding it incompatible with his tastes and interests. Then came a series of trips abroad, especially to various international exhibitions, in search of technical innovations, and the accompanying insecurity, intensely felt by the whole family. It was evidence of Emil Rathenau's sure sense of technical potential that he first targeted the telephone as a promising business proposition, but it was also evidence of his lack of confidence in himself at the time that he only sought a bureaucratic concession to install it in Berlin, not the more daring option of building his own factory. Or perhaps he felt that this was not yet what he was looking for. Finally, at the grand Paris exhibition of 1881, he first saw Thomas Alva Edison's new electric bulb, which aroused little interest among others but instantaneously fired his imagination. Emil Rathenau bought the European rights to Edison's patent and thus opened a new chapter in his and his family's life. It was his first step on the road to becoming one of Germany's most successful entrepreneurs, the renowned general manager of the Allgemeine Elektrizitätsgesellschaft (AEG), an innovator on a world scale, a system builder, an enormously rich and powerful man. The journalist Maximilian Harden, whom we shall later meet as Walther Rathenau's friend and rival, saw in this hard-working, cool-headed man "the Bismarck of Germany's industrial empire."[7]

Walther's childhood was practically over as this rush to success began. The father he had experienced during his early years was the unhappy Emil Rathenau, often traveling, rarely at home, for ever searching after some promising opportunity, irritable and less than approachable, surely not very loving. Erich, Walther's younger brother, was born in August 1871, some two months after the death of their grandfather Moritz, Emil's father. He was an adorable little boy, nicknamed "Gold" at home, and from the outset his father's source of consolation and his lifelong favorite. Erich, sickly since childhood, attracted much of the mother's attention too. She was endlessly trying to improve his health and was frequently traveling with him to various health resorts near and far. This life style may have suited Mathilde Rathenau on more than one account. She was not happy in her marriage. While at first a true companion to her husband, she must have soon lost interest in his hectic business affairs and he, in turn, shut her out as the going got rough, disregarding both her need for intimacy and her social and cultural ambitions. Walther's birth provided a temporary relief and Mathilde was enchanted by the handsome, intelligent boy, who remained her favorite and to whom she was deeply devoted throughout her life. Still, with Erich's birth she found attending to the two young boys, one of them often ill, so taxing that she sent Walther to her mother in Frankfurt, at first only for short visits and then to attend school there. This, in addition to the parents' joint trips for business or pleasure, frequently separated the young Walther from them, and he surely experienced this enforced distance as a hardship. It did, however, prove a blessing for the historian. Rathenau's estate includes a letter to his father from as early as June 1871, when he was not yet four years old, and then a trickle of childish, often precocious letters to both his parents, providing a rare insight into the early stages of his life.[8]

From the outset, Walther's letters to his mother were very different from the ones he wrote to his father. He is open, humorous, and chatty with her; formal, orderly, and serious with him. To his father he was forever promising "to do better" and to eventually "bring you joy one way or another."[9] His mother was apparently more easily satisfied, and with her he soon took on a tone of adult responsibility, showing concern and giving advice. When she was away, he reported to her on life at home in great detail, including his and his father's daily menus, invitations to visit relatives, and especially Emil's coming and going, his frame of mind, his angers and worries. The son conspired with his mother to protect the busy father and made some touching efforts to keep his parents' relationship intact. "You should write Papa," he urged his mother, and then described how unhappy and worried his father was concerning Erich's health.[10] Finally, after the birth of his sister Edith in 1883, Walther's letters were also full of loving and amusing details concerning "the child," left with a nanny who was in turn supervised by a bossy grandmother. Meanwhile the mother was always on the move, first in Homburg with her own mother and then in various German and Italian resorts. Walther—almost sixteen by then—was becoming more demanding, more judgmental, sometimes even more critical. He complained when his mother did not write often enough. He worried about her, telling her repeatedly to take good care of herself, and always expressed concern about his brother's health. He wrote often, illustrating his letters with competently executed miniature ink drawings as well as with somewhat less proficient verses and poems. In letters to his mother, humor and irony are mixed with loving care, an easy familiarity, and some direct censure. In writing to his brother, he was protective and always openly didactic. To his father he appeared matter of fact, obliging, even subservient.

The early letters are well written, no doubt, but reflect no particular personal interests at this stage. Walther occasionally reported on evenings in the theater, for instance, but rather laconically and with little enthusiasm. Although he was known as an avid reader, there are only sporadic comments on books, no serious reflections on life in general or his own life in particular, no explicit plans for the future, no disclosure of inner struggle. Walther rarely mentions his school friends or the content of his studies, except to provide some general evaluation of his achievements or to list his grades. More importantly, he is never entirely open in these letters: he is a stickler for good form, anxious to make a good impression, and in the habit of always promising improvement to avoid reprimands. In fact, as a student at the Wilhelm-Gymnasium in the wealthy Tiergarten district of Berlin, he completed his studies with no special distinction. His accomplishments in German and composition were no more than "good," and his other grades were even less impressive. He clearly did not emerge from school with a definite career plan. It was, instead, his father's recent achievements that seemed to have decided his early choices for the future.

By 1883, Emil Rathenau, filled with new vigor and optimism, brought to an end eight years of searching and indecision. Opportunities seemed ripe and he was determined to exploit them. By the mid 1880s, Germany as a whole entered what might be called its Second Industrial Revolution. Its initial take-off occurred in the two to three decades after mid-century. At that stage, building the new railroad network provided an enormous push to the country's economic development, and soon afterwards old and new sources of raw materials, mainly coal and iron, began to be exploited both in the western Prussian region of the Ruhr and in Upper Silesia. Alfred Krupp, the iron and steel manufacturer, August Borsig, the founder of Germany's most successful locomotive factory in Berlin, and Bethel Henry Strousberg, a converted Jew who became "King of the Railroads" before his business collapsed in the crisis of 1873, stood for the vision and drive of industry in this initial stage, while Gerson Bleichröder, Bismarck's Jewish financier, and Adolf Salomonsohn of the new Disconto-Gesellschaft were among the leading names in banking at that time. Clearly, some rich and enterprising Jews were prominent on the list of those who actively modernized the German economy during the third quarter of the nineteenth century. Clearly, too, this modernization did not depend upon them. Nor were they responsible for its failures and crises, as the antisemites so often liked to claim. Just over 1 percent of the overall population, Jews constituted a small minority among German industrialists. They were active primarily in commerce and finance, and throughout the nineteenth century their success usually meant expansion and growth primarily within these sectors. Door-to-door vendors turned into shop owners, small merchants became large-scale commercial men or moved—cautiously—into industries connected with their lines of business. Some, of course, did take more risks even at that early stage. We have previously met the Liebermanns, Rathenau's relatives, operating in Berlin as well as in Upper Silesia in a variety of trades. A few became successful in the newly arising industries. Others managed to turn their small banking businesses into large-scale enterprises. But taking great risks was, as it had always been—and still is—rather exceptional. Such was also the case during the next stage of economic growth, which emerged slowly in the mid-1880s and exploded by the mid-nineties.[11]

Walther's father belonged to a small group of outstanding entrepreneurs, typical of this stage. Industrial business now meant the introduction of new technologies, a great deal of scientific expertise, and an ability to handle large-scale diversified enterprises, often in the form of public companies and in close cooperation with financial institutions that were willing to share the risks. In addition, industrialists had behind them the experience of the economic crisis of 1873 and knew that they must act in cautious and sophisticated ways. Germany had already exploited her "advantages of backwardness," to use Trotsky's apt terminology. Having in the past depended massively on British experience, it was now positioned at the forefront. One could no longer rely on experiments done elsewhere or wait for others to succeed or fail in them. It was a different world now; a brave new world, indeed.

Emil Rathenau's industrial ventures accurately represent this stage. To be sure, he was not the first to enter the field of electric industry. By the 1880s, Werner Siemens was long in this business, head of a huge international firm. His initial breakthrough consisted of developing, improving, and diffusing the technology of the telegraph. But late in the 1860s he was already marketing a new type of generator and using available and inexpensive water turbines and steam engines to produce electric current. Electricity was then quickly introduced into the fields of transportation, lighting, and factory production, practically inaugurating a new industrial age. Soon afterwards, a rush of new technologies opened up further opportunities, and among the first was the one seized by Emil Rathenau, namely Edison's incandescent bulb.

Street lighting was at the time provided by gas lamps, while at home, in the absence of gas, kerosene lamps were still the most common devices. Arc lights were later employed, once again by the enterprising Siemens, for large outdoor public spaces, with generators installed separately for each project. And by the early 1880s, few believed that gas lighting, itself a relative novelty that enjoyed great prestige, would be replaced by electricity in the near future. Since it was impossible to estimate future demand for electric power, it was difficult to trust in the profitability of building huge electric power plants in order to provide it. Emil Rathenau did. In 1888, at the introduction of electric street lighting in Unter den Linden, Berlin's main boulevard, he declared that electricity was "the natural power of the nineteenth century." It would first be used by the bourgeoisie and would later be made available to the entire population. "For the better situated it will be available in the form of bright light, and for artisans as tools for daily use," he explained.[12] Electric lighting, supported by power stations transmitting electricity from a distant source to entire urban areas—this was his vision. It carried democratic and even aesthetic connotations, but above all it had, Emil realized, enormous business potential.

This potential, however, did not immediately materialize. The first ten years were very difficult. Emil Rathenau had to find his own route through the maze of technical, financial, and commercial innovations. When his "German Edison Company for Applied Electricity" (Deutsche Edison-Gesellchaft für angewandte Elektrizität—DEG) was established in 1883, its board of directors included representatives of some of the most outstanding financial institutions of Imperial Germany, a number of fairly small bankers, and, most interestingly perhaps, Werner Siemens himself. Here Rathenau's two main strategic principles were already made apparent. First, since financing would clearly be the major difficulty of the new sector, getting strong, long-term financial backing must be top priority. Secondly, since risks were extremely high, potential competition had to be neutralized from the start, in order to avoid legal hassles over patent rights and to get around the initial problem of limited demand. Thus, from the outset the new enterprise pledged to stay out of Siemens & Halske's business of generators, cables, and electric instruments, while the latter company gave up the right to build central power stations. In fact, Werner Siemens, skeptical concerning the new venture, thought that the DEG would turn out to be an "installation agency for installing the machines and the other materials (for transmission of electric power, etc.) that we produce," as he wrote to his brother.[13] Emil Rathenau, in turn, hoped for great profits precisely in those areas surrendered by Siemens. Unlike Siemens before him or his maternal grandfather Joseph Liebermann, for that matter, and contrary to his initial instinct some ten years earlier, Emil did not establish a family business. AEG, heir to DEG, was always a public corporation, cooperating and competing simultaneously with its various rivals.

To be sure, Siemens and Rathenau did not exhaust the market at this stage. During much of the 1880s and even into the 1890s, Schuckert & Co., yet another electrical firm, built more power plants than both of them together. When the two major rivals became disillusioned by their planned division of labor and annulled all their contractual commitments, Siemens quickly accomplished a merger with Schuckert and thus posed a serious threat to AEG. This, however, happened much later. Meanwhile, in mid-1887, out of the experimental DEG, and following its success in building the impressive lighting system in the center of Berlin, Emil Rathenau established and headed AEG, a public company with a capital of some twelve million marks. And while this was only the beginning of a long and tortuous road to success, he never lost his faith in it. He was completely dedicated to his company, a true "workaholic," cautious but confident, increasingly skilled in all the ins and outs of corporate capitalism.

Surely under the influence of his father's enthusiasm, Walther began his academic career in the summer semester of 1885 at the Friedrich Wilhelm University in Berlin, by studying physics, chemistry, and mathematics, all subjects in which his school grades had been only "satisfactory." He took an intensive course in experimental physics, given by the renowned Hermann von Helmholtz, and, as was common at the time, attended lectures even in fields remote from his own, such as Gustav Schmoller's on economics and Wilhelm Dilthey's on history and philosophy. These three were among the shining lights of the German academic world at the time, so that Rathenau's was not a bad beginning by any standard. But by the spring of 1886, he was clearly unsatisfied, seeking new excitement, somewhat like his father a couple of decades earlier. We find him first on a trip to London, reporting almost daily to his mother on all things great and small, and in May, back in Germany, ready to begin the summer semester at the University of Strasbourg.

Moving between universities was a common practice in German academic life. Credit for courses attended was easily transferred from one institution to the other, and as a rule, regardless of where one studied, one only had to prove attendance and prepare for the final examinations. In the natural sciences one also had to participate in laboratory work, of course, and show some experimental results. Thus, Rathenau was soon busy at work in August Kundt's laboratory in Strasbourg, collaborating with a number of other students, mostly old friends from Berlin. Kundt was among Germany's most important physicists at the time, specializing in various aspects of optics, in particular studying anomalous light dispersion in liquids, vapors, and even metals, by means of a laborious process of electrolytic deposition upon platinized glass. For the first time Rathenau was here confronted with the various methods of electrolysis that would later be of great importance to him. At the time, however, he mostly noticed its dreary, time-consuming side. There was certainly little excitement in this, and he was not long in Strasbourg before he began to send a torrent of unhappy letters, especially to his mother. As usual, his father was spared the complaints, receiving instead detailed accounts of Walther's schedule in and out of the classroom and minute reports of his expenses. Clearly, both were required. The young man was strictly supervised from afar. Nevertheless, when he seemed truly unhappy, even sinking into depression, his family quickly responded. Emil Rathenau, visibly worried, dispatched a warm letter to his problematic son. It was natural to be homesick, he reassured him, but also no more than a temporary hardship. Those at home would make sure he received daily letters and, while Walther ought to continue his studies diligently, he should also take measures to raise his spirits, spend more time with friends, perhaps take a hiking trip to France, and in general make sure to amuse himself.[14] Typically, Walther was quick to calm everyone down. He was only unhappy when he heard nothing from home, he wrote, and in any event, things were really not as bad as they sounded.

In fact, Rathenau did stick it out in Strasbourg, though the overall experience was and remained generally disappointing. In the lab Rathenau was apparently among the less successful students. At least one of his closer friends, Heinrich Rubens, excelled even at that early stage and later became the director of the Physikalisches Institut at the University of Berlin, no less. Others, too, even according to Rathenau's own judgment, were doing better than he. Kundt seems to have taken little notice of him, although they did occasionally interact, even socially, and the pattern that would later become characteristic of Rathenau was now clearly emerging: Being unsatisfied with his own achievements in one sphere of action, he sought to excel in another. He was hanging on to his prescribed task, but at the same time trying his hand elsewhere.

Interestingly, instead of investing more efforts in drawing, having always shown talent in this line of artistic activity, Rathenau now chose to experiment in writing, more precisely in playwriting. *Blanche Trocard* was a play in two acts, written during the first half of 1887, printed at the author's own expense and submitted to the City Theater of Frankfurt am Main. It was a skillfully contrived piece, depicting the misery of the young Madam Trocard in an emotionally barren marriage—reminiscent, at least in theme, of Ibsen's dramas which were shortly afterwards to be much admired in Germany. The theater, however, normally open to works by new and unknown authors, rejected the play without explanation, and Rathenau was too proud to send it elsewhere, nor did he ever try his hand again as a dramatist. He soon plucked up his courage, reengaged in his laboratory work, and finally, moving with Kundt and some of his advanced students back to Berlin, managed to complete his dissertation, receiving his doctorate in October 1889. He kept the final ceremony a secret from his family, arriving late for dinner one evening and excusing himself on grounds that he had just been awarded his degree. Even at that point, he was ambivalent with regard to his achievements in this field.

Soon afterwards, however, we find Rathenau in Munich, continuing his training and making the transition to a more practical line of studies at the Technical University there. He continued to be bored and often unhappy as a student, but persevered against all odds. As before, Walther's main social and emotional contacts continued to be his family members. He corresponded not only with "mama" and "papa" but also, now ever more intensively, with his brother, and occasionally with his younger sister and his two grandmothers. Most of his other contacts were based on family ties, too. Many of his student friends were sons of Jewish families from Berlin, acquaintances and even relatives of the Rathenaus. He still reported almost daily on invitations he was accepting or declining, as he had done in his Strasbourg days, practically all of them at homes of local Jewish dignitaries. The Rathenaus socialized mainly with Jews in Berlin too, of course, but here as in Strasbourg, away from home, this seemed increasingly oppressive to him.

His feelings are exposed especially in letters to his mother. Kundt's laboratory, he told her from Strasbourg, "consist[ed] of the strangest characters: mostly Jews . . ."[15] "Their arrogance [was] colossal," he added in another letter, and "[t]he poor man was completely "in their hands." Moreover, this seemed to be true of the university at large: a third of the faculty, he claimed, were "professors of oriental origins"—almost entirely so in the faculty of law, even more in medicine; only theology was an exception. There, Rathenau noticed, one soon ran into the odd baptized Jew—yet another "convinced Christian," he sarcastically commented. If they had only converted out of political considerations, general caution, or social reasons; but conviction? "This is really beneath the dignity of our time . . . Be sure never to mention all this," he warns his mother: we ought to be seen as tolerant towards these "newly made Germanic youngsters." But clearly, this matter was constantly on his mind. One Jewish friend asked him not to visit while his army comrades were present. "That would have been fatal for him," Rathenau explained. To be sure, "Willi" will have to be baptized if he wants to pursue a military career, Rathenau goes on, though he knows full well that "a baptized Jew is never the same as a baptized Christian." Furthermore, a proper marriage, as Walther apparently had to make clear to his friend, would also be impossible for him. A convert is a marriage candidate neither for a nice Jewish girl with sufficient dowry, nor for a nice Christian one from the right class and rank. "I haven't talked to him about conversion, though," Rathenau adds, "I don't wish to appear as if I so conspicuously prefer either the Jew or the apostate." He himself had no intention of converting, he reassured his mother, but to his "deep satisfaction," the young Valentins, whose parents were old friends of the Rathenaus, were baptized now, as he reported. Finally, he felt compelled to add, "we too should now be able to enjoy some Christian company."

The Rathenaus kept only feeble contacts with Judaism as a religion. We know nothing, for instance, concerning Walther's or his brother's Bar Mitzvah. In a letter of March 1884, Walther quotes a biblical verse, apparently from memory but in uncertain and inaccurate Hebrew. In fact, at a later date he once apparently tried to improve the elementary Hebrew he had acquired during his school days, but this represented no more than a fleeting interest.[16] Rathenau never mentions the High Holidays, not even Passover or Yom Kippur, which were usually observed even by the most assimilated Jews, though we do have at least on one authority that as a full-blown politician during the Weimar Republic, Walther used to arrive in his car at the synagogue on Yom Kippur to say Kaddish for his father.[17] If this is true, it must have been the last vestige of Judaism in his life. The family's social milieu, however, was decidedly Jewish. For many German Jews, being Jewish consisted primarily in living with and among Jews, even late in the nineteenth century. At the same time, speaking disparagingly of other Jews, common for the Rathenaus apparently, was not unknown in other families, while even within that milieu, men seemed less prone to such vulgar lapses than women. Walther's two grandmothers did visit the synagogue occasionally, but at least for one of them, Therese Rathenau, Emil's mother, this gave the opportunity to use scornful language. Walther's own mother was apparently more civilized, but it was not by chance that he sent his reports in matters Jewish mainly to her. He must have felt they shared the same sentiments in this regard. Typical here were the slighting tone, the sarcasm, and the bitter humor.

Antisemitic incidents were treated in a similar manner. One such incident is described in a letter from January 1887. During an evening in the neighborhood bar, someone remarked that since Jews "had made it their habit" to visit it, things there had become "unbearable," clearly targeting Walther and his Jewish friends at the next table. Immediately one of them "demanded satisfaction," ran Walther's report, and finally all of them intervened: the offender must withdraw his statement or face each one of them in duel. "The next morning," Walther concluded, not without a tinge of smugness, the fellow "most solemnly" withdrew.[18] This is a telling episode. Jews were normally rejected as members of the old-style student fraternities, in which dueling was customary, and Walther or his friends were unlikely candidates for the national Jewish groups which sometimes tried to imitate the German associations. Their "feudal" approach to the matter, therefore, re-flected their own individual social preferences: they were will-ing, even eager, to engage Jew-baiters on their own terms, adopting a code of honor that must certainly have been entirely foreign to them both as Jews and as bourgeois Germans. In-deed, young Jews were often attracted by various aspects of the Prussian aristocratic tradition, not least by the notion of an army career and the aura and habits attached to it.

Walther Rathenau was no exception. At the end of his aca-demic training, he was entitled, like all young men who had at least a secondary education, Jews included, to volunteer for a one-year term in the army reserve instead of serving for three years in the regular army. At the end of this year, a select group was made eligible for a period of additional training and went through strict tests and examinations that sometimes ended in a royal appointment to the rank of reserve lieutenant. Jews, however, only rarely managed to win such a privilege. While individual Jews did occasionally become reserve officers earlier in the century, this was no longer the case by the mid-1880s. The last time a Jew received a reserve commission in Prussia prior to 1914 was in 1885, and there seem to have been virtu-ally no such appointments during the five preceding years. To be sure, there was no formal prohibition against Jews in the Prussian army or bureaucracy, but since as a matter of principle Jews could not serve in any position of authority in a "Chris-tian state," the higher echelons of both the army and bureau-cracy were closed to them. In the case of the bureaucracy, dis-crimination could have tangible consequences, because jobs in the administration constituted the main source of employment for men with degrees in law, economics, and a variety of other disciplines. In the case of the army, exclusion was primarily a matter of prestige. Belonging to the reserve corps was consid-ered a prerequisite for becoming a highly regarded person in Imperial Germany, and while officers in the regular army were almost without exception sons of the aristocracy, the reserve officer corps was made up of sons of well-to-do bourgeois families and indicated loyalty and reliability that radiated beyond the military into all spheres of life. Jews could not enjoy this extra bit of status.

Presumably, not many Jews were as deeply hurt by this exclusion as was the young Rathenau. Even while he was a student in Strasbourg, Walther was in the habit of contrasting his exclusively Jewish milieu with that of the landowning aristocracy that he was able to watch from afar. Often enough, his admiration of and attraction to that class became a truly painful matter for him. Thus, against his father's expressed opinion, he managed to be drafted as reservist into one of the most prestigious Prussian cavalry units. Though he could certainly afford the high cost of the uniform and all the accompanying paraphernalia and was physically fit for the task, there was no way he could become an officer in such a unit. It is surprising that a man as sensitive to questions of social status as Rathenau would take such an obviously mistaken step. It points to his ambition as well as to his youthful optimism. And it was soon to cause him a great disappointment.

By August 1891, already a soldier for some ten months, Walther was complaining bitterly, again only in letters to his mother. The performance of the endless military chores, he wrote, which would easily have brought promotion to the "blameless," brought only hard work "for us, of the chosen people."[19] He continued to make every possible effort, but to no avail. "In the early years of every German Jew," Rathenau later wrote, "there is a painful moment that can never be forgotten: [the moment at which] he becomes aware for the first time that he entered the world as a second-class citizen and that no amount of talent and merit would free him of this status."[20] As far as Walther Rathenau was concerned, this evidently occurred during his army service. For the first time, his Jewishness clearly played a role in thwarting his ambitions. A pattern had been established: he was doing his best but was repeatedly failing to live up to his own expectations. The reasons were many, but his identity as a Jew always seemed prominent among them.

2

A Man of Many Talents

By THE FALL OF 1891, Walther Rathenau, twenty-four years old, had completed the preparations for an independent career. It was by no means an easy ride, but—for better or for worse—many crucial decisions concerning his future life seemed to have been irrevocably taken by then. To begin with, Walther was determined to stay within the professional parameters drawn by his father's business choices. This was not self-evident. Firstly, because Emil Rathenau's enterprise was at the time in its infancy and, though its future did look promising, AEG was still far from being the gigantic enterprise that it would later become. Secondly, because Walther clearly had many talents and a variety of career options were open to him. Even his father was by no means insistent upon enlisting him into his business, and while the son may have been insulted by the cool reaction to his show of interest in his father's affairs, he was himself repeatedly plagued by doubts concerning his future. Walther's other interests seemed all too often more central to his life, more fitting to his personality, occasionally even more promising as career paths.

Foremost among these was his artistic talent.[1] During his student days, Walther had been known for his caricatures and pencil or chalk drawings, portraying friends and relatives in letters, postcards, and numerous sketchbooks. Most of the drawings have been lost, but particularly striking among the remaining ones was doubtless a dashing self-portrait from 1888: the young Rathenau half-smiling, with cap and cigarette.

In Munich, his interest in art and artists had seemed to become even more consuming, and he was a frequent visitor to the city's galleries, antique shops, and artists' ateliers. His insistence on participating in the interior decoration of his parents' new home in Berlin was yet another testimony to his attraction to aesthetic matters. In one letter after another he gave his mother detailed instructions concerning furniture, wallpaper,

Walther Rathenau, self-portrait, ca. 1888.
Courtesy Walther Rathenau Gesellschaft.

and various items to be displayed. Some items were actually purchased and sent by him to Berlin, and he either complimented his mother on other items when her taste matched his, or reprimanded her when it did not. At one point he actually wrote to his brother, expressing concern that "they" at home, most importantly his father of course, would think he was "wasting his time," "just playing around," or apparently even worse, "secretly painting."[2] Secretly or not, Rathenau continued to paint from time to time. Later on, he reported a visit by the not yet famous Norwegian painter Edvard Munch, who presumably found Rathenau's own paintings "much better than [Lesser] Ury's"—a well-known local Impressionist—even "before he knew by whom they were painted."[3]

To be sure, it was not unheard-of for sons of successful businessmen to choose a career in art, music, or literature. The scenario was later described in all its glory and misery by Thomas Mann in *Buddenbrooks*. But the Rathenaus were directly acquainted with this option through the case of Mathilde's own cousin Max Liebermann, one of the most renowned painters of fin-de-siècle Berlin. Walther must have been aware of Liebermann's brilliant career, realizing that in its way it added considerable prestige to the family at large. He himself, however, did not dare to follow this route. Perhaps he did not trust his talent. Perhaps he was too often discouraged by his relatives, including Liebermann himself. Nevertheless, for a number of years and especially in gloomy times, his dream of becoming a painter continued to crop up, even in conversations such as one reported by Paul Mamroth, his father's colleague on the AEG board of directors, from the early 1890s.[4] Finally though, it was given up. Rathenau continued to draw and paint occasionally, but this remained no more than a private leisuretime pursuit. Eventually he even seemed to adopt his father's attitude to the "artistic type": "If one meets among the military, politicians, industrialists, or scholars a man who shows more than a conventional interest in the visual or the-atrical arts," Rathenau wrote in 1913, "it is unfortunately to be feared with some likelihood that one has to deal here with a soft, suffering person, unfit for his profession and unfulfilled by it."[5] He himself definitely did not want to be seen as such. In any case, despite many moments of hesitation, Rathenau never went back on his decision to follow in his father's footsteps and become an entrepreneur. He would soon try his hand in jour-nalism and critical writing. He would later on strive to exercise influence in the world of politics. But he never gave up his vo-cation in the business world, never retracted his youthful deci-sion to join his father, to contribute his share to Emil's grand industrial project and thus, indeed, stay within his orbit, gain his respect, perhaps finally also his love.

Walther Rathenau seems to have taken another important decision at this time, namely to remain single. This was an un-spoken decision and its when and why must remain unclear. Rathenau's otherwise informative correspondence is almost entirely silent on the matter. It is possible, of course, that after his assassination, Rathenau's mother made sure that such inti-mate matters would be publicly inaccessible. Walther himself may have acted with a similar purpose in mind even earlier. In any case, we have preciously little information on Rathenau's love life. In the many years of correspondence with his mother there is only one direct reference to marriage. This was in the winter of 1887–88, when Walther was planning his return from Strasbourg to Berlin. He was anxious to secure proper lodgings in town: no longer with his parents, but in a manner that would reflect both his needs and his social standing. He wanted to have a permanent dwelling, he explained, at least till "my bliss-ful eventual marriage."[6] However, no particular candidate for such marriage was mentioned, here or anywhere else. Instead, Walther commented condescendingly on the young women, usually daughters of family relatives or friends, whom he occa-

sionally met. Back in Berlin, following the Strasbourg inter-
lude, he in fact lived in his parents' home in the centrally located Victoria-Strasse and his plans of living independently,
temporarily perhaps with his brother, were discarded, together
with the intention to marry and establish his own family. Alfred Kerr commented in his memoirs that as a result of a
"harmless students' disease," contracted during his Munich
days, Rathenau was "unable to have children."[7] There is no way
to corroborate this single testimony; nor does it convincingly
explain Rathenau's bachelorhood.

To be sure, bachelorhood was not uncommon among successful businessmen in Imperial Germany. In a study of some
400 families of millionaires in Imperial Germany late marriage, or no marriage at all, appears rather frequently.[8] Among
the 115 Jewish businessmen in this sample, 20 remained unmarried. This is surely a high rate. Jewish endogamy provides
at least a partial explanation. It restricted marriage options for
all Jews, in all walks of life. But marriage options for the German upper bourgeoisie as a whole, Jews and non-Jews alike,
were limited too. Generally speaking, their marriage strategy
was mainly directed at keeping as much as possible of their fortunes within their extended families or at joining hands with
carefully selected other families from the same milieu. As a result, consanguinity was far more common among the upper
bourgeois than one usually imagines. Cousins and nieces were
all too often the most obvious marriage choices, not only
among Jews.

Two examples taken from Rathenau's surroundings may il-
lustrate this point. Hugo Stinnes was one of Germany's most
powerful industrialists, both before and after the First World
War. He had multiple contacts with the Rathenaus and could
be considered Walther's main competitor as well as his occasional collaborator. His wife, to whom he was deeply devoted
and with whom he eventually had seven children, was a relative

on his mother's side. The two met while their families spent a joint summer vacation and later on, much of their social life, even when Hugo's business grew to enormous proportions, remained within the family.[9] By contrast, Max Weber, the renowned sociologist, came from a well-established family of the educated bourgeoisie, complementing and constantly interacting with the upper economic elite. It seems that among the *Bildungsbürgertum*, too, family connections were the center of social life, and Max, first engaged to one of his cousins, eventually married another relative of his, Marianne Schnitger, who had been living in his parents' household for a number of years prior to their engagement.[10] There are ample examples to prove the centrality of family ties among the rich and famous in Imperial Germany and the various ways by which marital decisions were inspired by the desire to improve social standing and promote business interests. Examples from among prosperous Jews are particularly easy to come by. Max Warburg, the Hamburg-based Jewish banker, married a relative from the Altona branch of his family and much of his business and social life was conducted in the company of his relatives close and distant. The picture is similar for other wealthy Jews: the Tietzes, the Walichs, and many more. The Rathenaus were no exception. Thus, endogamous habits, Jewish and elite-oriented alike, must have limited Walther's choice considerably. He apparently did not find a proper wife within the proper close circles, and if marriages were arranged in order to keep the family fortune close to home, perhaps there was no point in looking for a proper bride farther away, all the more so if he showed no real interest in marriage in any case.

Rumors of one or another mysterious love affairs that came to nothing do sometimes appear in the Rathenau literature. These were seemingly inspired by information from his mother and were rarely supported by proper documentation. It was Alfred Kerr, again, who mentioned in his memoirs "a woman" occasionally visiting Rathenau, presumably at his invitation.[11] This seems entirely out of character, but can—yet again—be neither verified nor rejected. Walther was surely attracted to female companions in some ways. Early in 1905, he had what appears to be a short intimate relationship with the feminist Julia Virginia Scheuermann, a writer, poet, and sculptor to boot. The tone of Rathenau's letters to her is strikingly unusual for him. Here he is playful, humorous, even provocative. But the affair, if it really was one, ended as quickly as it began. Much later, writing to his Swedish friend Ernst Norlind, he speaks of three women whom he had loved and who had returned his love—not including his mother, he hastens to add—and of another who had loved him, a love that was presumably unrequited.[12] Rathenau's biographers now seem to agree that the last was most probably the journalist Lore Karrenbrock; two of the others were either the painter Minka Grönvold or Lina Oppenheim, later the wife of the philosopher and Nietzsche expert Raoul Richter, and certainly, last but not least, Lili Deutsch, the young wife of his father's right-hand man Felix Deutsch.[13] It was only with Lili Deutsch that Rathenau had a sustained loving relationship. But beyond the luckily extant selection of letters between the two, we know relatively little even about this relationship—one that was from the outset entirely hopeless. At the same time it was also conveniently unthreatening, as far as Walther was concerned.

Despite the scarcity of material, some aspects of Rathenau's attitude towards women emerge directly and indirectly from his correspondence. It was, for instance, only in letters to women that he was capable of opening up, though never entirely, and of reaching out for a measure of intimacy, though always very guardedly. As in his letters to his mother, Rathenau often complained in letters to his women friends of being tired, depressed, unhappy, of his dissatisfaction with work and life. His tone was one of respect mixed with paternalism, again not unlike the tone he had established early in life in writing to his mother. He made a noticeable effort to respond with empathy to both ideas and feelings expressed by his women friends, but made always sure to set clear limits. The two unmarried women with whom he had more than fleeting relationships, Fanny Künstler, especially in 1914, and Lore Karrenbrock, with interruptions between 1918 and his untimely death, were strong and assertive individuals. They openly courted him, while he remained polite, but was only rarely and never for long truly intimate with them. In an exceptionally open letter to Fanny Künstler, dated September 1914, the forty-seven-year-old Rathenau tells of his great desire as a younger man "to live *with* and *in* someone else," as he put it. And while this was not entirely a thing of the past, he explained, he no longer experienced the passion, the excitement or the "joy of communicating" he had known in earlier days. His other self, so to speak, had taken over. He was now more concerned "with his mission" and "his service." "My heart is not cooled down, humanity is closer to me than ever," wrote Rathenau, "but I have nothing more to give to individuals." And then: "Whatever is alive and rings in me are less and less subjective things and more, as in a shell that is almost perfectly happy being pulled back within some kind of a vessel, the echo of the sea outside."[14]

Was this only an excuse, a way of discouraging the advances of his women friends? Was Rathenau a homosexual, as was so often suggested? We do not know. If he was, he must have realized that the combination of being a Jew and a homosexual would be fatal for his career, and he would have made every effort to conceal it. Rathenau's outward appearance, to be sure, was striking. His portraits and numerous self-portraits attest to his impressive looks and commanding posture. In his youth he was something of a dandy, wearing "colorful shirts with matching ties and vests, all well-chosen and inconspicuously elegant," as one contemporary reported.[15] Among his many acquaintances, we find male friends with whom his correspondence suggests very close contacts, at least for short periods. The fact that they were usually married men does not, of course, exclude the possibility of homoerotic relationships between them.[16]

Two additional factors complicate matters for the biographer. To begin with, intimate-sounding correspondence between men was not uncommon at the time. Any casual reading of contemporary letters discloses affectionate expressions that would probably have seemed odd in conversation at the time and are certainly unusual today. The chemists Fritz Haber and Richard Willstaetter, to take a random example, were lifelong friends. In their correspondence, we find repeated expressions of friendship, even love, especially coming from Haber. He painfully missed his friend, he wished for their reunion, etc. In Hugo von Hofmannsthal's correspondence too, one can find such longings, often alternating with critical, even disparaging comments. This is common in Thomas Mann's correspondence, as well as in that of Count Harry von Kessler, as open a homosexual as was at all possible at the time. Kessler himself, in fact, commented in his biography of Rathenau that some of Walther's letters read like love letters, suggesting that even for contemporary insiders their passionate tone seemed extraordinary.[17] In any case, homosexuality was a well-kept secret in Imperial Germany, as elsewhere in Europe of that time. When the journalist Maximilian Harden chose to disclose the homoerotic atmosphere characteristic of the Kaiser's entourage, many, including Rathenau, found his tactics unbecoming.[18] Was this just prudence, even prudery, or were Harden's critics, at least some of them, worried lest a wave of disclosures would eventually engulf them, too? It seems that we shall never know.

In Walther Rathenau's case, a second factor must also be taken into account. Already as a boy and then throughout his life, Walther—like his father—exhibited very poor social skills.

Friends and acquaintances complained of his lack of spontaneity, his insistent and opinionated style, his frequent and pompous preaching. They repeatedly mentioned, for instance, his habit of laying his hand condescendingly on a person's shoulder in conversation.[19] In private talks and letters, the poet and playwright Hugo von Hofmannsthal expressed distaste for what he saw as Rathenau's snobbishness and affectedness, making it finally public in his one-act comedy *Die Lästigen* (The Annoying Ones), in which the vain and empty Adlon was apparently "a caricature of Walther Rathenau."[20] Still better known is Robert Musil's Paul Arnheim, a major figure in *The Man without Qualities*, likewise based on Rathenau, whom the author unquestionably detested.[21] Above all, Rathenau's inability to express emotions caused repeated clashes even with those closest to him. On his twenty-fifth birthday, he responded emphatically to a letter by his mother, in which she must have complained of his distance and reserve. "Don't think that I fight against feelings or affections," he wrote, "but life with passionate people—and passionate we all are, by nature—has taught me to beware of exaggeration . . ." He preferred steadfastness and equanimity to open enthusiasm combined with readiness for self-destruction, as he put it, and disliked outward expressions of passion. He valued true conviction, constancy, and loyalty that required no outward signs, and even this exchange itself went against the grain for him: "That's why I'd never speak about such matters with you again," he concluded.[22]

There is more than one way of interpreting this declaration, no doubt, but its importance cannot be overestimated. Walther Rathenau could not and would not open up. He was determined to do the right thing by his family and friends, but he was unwilling to disclose his inner self or give expression to his feelings, much less be swayed by them. Rathenau was anxious to defend himself against open emotions and their possible

encroachment upon his life. Simply put, he was anxious to protect himself against heartbreak and disappointment. If he was a
self-conscious homosexual he was certainly not going to share
this with others and most likely he would never act upon it.

Be that as it may, by Christmas 1891 Rathenau had completed his studies, fulfilled his army duties, and begun his industrial apprenticeship. Emil had been sent to Silesia at the
corresponding stage in his life, as an apprentice in his uncle's
industrial works; Walther went to Switzerland. There, in the
little town of Neuhausen, near the source of the Rhine, a Swiss
company was attempting to improve the processes of electrolysis for the production of various metals. In fact, the electrochemical industry as a whole was part of the larger industrial
project of generating and applying electric power in a variety
of ways, and it was Emil Rathenau's business strategy to be involved, at least to some degree, in all of this project's branches,
especially in the initial stages. Walther, as we saw, had had
some experience in electrolysis during his student years and did
occasionally express an interest in further experimenting in this
field. He often stressed his desire to move from theory to practice and be given a chance to prove his talent in technical and
business matters. It was thus sensible enough to send him to
Neuhausen as a technical assistant and allow him to amass experience in a situation that was related to, but at the same time
at least geographically removed from his father's direct sphere
of influence.

The choice of location, however, had two main drawbacks.
Neuhausen was far off and isolated, as Rathenau quickly real-
ized. His tight working schedule made even a visit to the rela-
tively nearby Zurich too time-consuming. Moreover, although
AEG controlled the Swiss firm and the chief engineer there,
Martin Kiliani, was a highly valued former employee of his fa-
ther, Walther was given no managerial authority at this point.
He was to be a regular technical hand. Even during his days as

a student in Munich, he was more truly involved in business through his close contacts with local AEG officials. In Neuhausen he felt "uninvited," forced to excel but given no freedom of movement or initiative.[23] As he was soon reporting to his mother and occasionally to his brother too, there was only hard work, an exhausting routine of alternating day and night shifts, boring and unfulfilling. In fact, he complained of loneliness not only during the long, cold days and nights in Neuhausen but even while on vacation in Italy, frustrated at having no one with whom to share his enthusiasm.[24] The family was far away in Berlin and the student milieu that had provided some relief from loneliness in Strasbourg and Munich was no longer at hand. Alone on the industrial front, he felt bored, lonesome, and resentful.

Once again, his parents got the message and reacted. A year after his arrival in Neuhausen, having decided to skip Christmas vacation at home, Mathilde Rathenau tried to convey to him what must have been a joint family response to his plight. Since he was so sensitive, she clearly paraphrased his father's views, and apparently lacked both the energy and the stamina for work in industry, he should consider a change of career. "You could become a professor or a painter," she now wrote, assuring him that "father was not angry. . . . He is worried and does not want you to dedicate your life to something that you find so unappealing."[25] Walther's reaction could be expected: he was insulted. He firmly decided to complete what he had taken upon himself, we read in his reply, and he would do just that with whatever energy or stamina he could muster for the task. Only with great effort, he continued, could he manage to achieve anything at all in this field, for which he was as "untalented as a cow," but he was not going to give up. Here is how he described the situation to his mother: "It makes me desperate to be dependent and to see no end to it, never an end. To be controlled every day, to be given work to do, to be made to ask for it, to be degraded by having to beg where I feel I have my rights, to excuse myself, to act as a colleague with inferior people. . . . After a while it makes one mad, [especially] if one values one's freedom above all else."[26] Nevertheless, he would stick it out. Against all odds, he *would* finally achieve success, ran the subtext.

It must have been his father's silent supervision and his apparent lack of respect that pained the young Rathenau so acutely. He longed to be his own master, but continued to seek independence without breaking away from his father. Becoming a professor, even if in the field of electrochemistry, or switching to art and becoming a painter, only meant more years of financial dependence, he feared. "Should I be thirty years old and let Papa tell me every couple of months that I cost him money and achieve nothing?" "If worst came to worst," he added, perhaps "something could be found in America."[27] Immediately afterwards, to be sure, such far-reaching plans already seemed too radical. In a letter to his brother, he confessed his actual fright at the thought of emigration. On balance, it would have been easier to take up another profession perhaps. But Rathenau was not ready for this or any other fundamental shift.[28] Clearly, he was still uncertain about his future. Hesitations plagued him on and off for at least another decade. But at every junction he always decided to stay put. He would not give up hope of making it in business; he would never despair of gaining his father's approval.

All in all, Rathenau was not unsuccessful in Neuhausen. During his years in Switzerland the plant developed a number of significant electrolytic processes, most particularly for the production of aluminum, that later proved particularly profitable. At the time, however, demand was limited and production costs too high. Emil Rathenau finally decided to purchase from the Swiss company only the rights to the alkali chloride electrolysis process. Then, letting himself be convinced by his son that coal would be a cheaper energy source for the process than water, he invested in a new electrochemical plant in the coal-mining town of Bitterfeld, some hundred miles south of Berlin in Prussian Saxony. He then made another risky decision and appointed his son the general manager of this new plant. Despite Walther's sense of being passed over by his father, the elder Rathenau was willing to give him a chance, and not for the last time.

Emil's choice was not a self-evident one. Walther had no prior managerial experience, and the conditions in Bitterfeld were at first not very promising. The brown coal produced in the neighborhood was expensive, and competition in the field of electrolysis was becoming ever more intense at just this time. No sooner had the new factory begun production than a competitor with greater experience and ample capital entered the scene. It took Walther Rathenau much convincing before the two plants began working together, but even then success seemed far from certain. Rathenau felt an immense pressure. The electrolytic process applied in Bitterfeld was his own development. He alone was responsible for the choice of location, and the conciliatory tactics vis-à-vis the local competitor was his own initiative, too. Failure would be only his. On the whole, however, there was some ground for optimism, too. To begin with, he was now a proper *Chef*, with no one above him. In addition, the atmosphere in Berlin seemed to have changed in his favor. His board of directors, located in the capital, was chaired by Carl Fürstenberg, head of the Berlin-based Handelsgesellschaft, by then one of Prussia's main banks, a loyal friend, close colleague, and one of the most outspoken admirers of Emil Rathenau. From the very outset, Fürstenberg offered Walther considerable practical and moral support. He tactfully supervised the young Rathenau's industrial activities and soon became his chief mentor. As a result, parallel to his work in Bitterfeld, Rathenau now gradually became involved in various other AEG business affairs—technical, institutional, and above all financial. He traveled frequently, established useful national and international connections, and gained invaluable experience. Moreover, Bitterfeld was near enough to Berlin for Rathenau to spend long weekends at home. His social life improved radically, and though his tendency to worry and complain remained unchanged, matters did seem to brighten up for a while, even in his own eyes.

An unexpected testimony to his sense of well-being has recently been discovered.[29] Rathenau's first published essay, in contrast to what was always assumed by contemporaries and historians alike, was a piece entitled "Morality Today," printed in the periodical *Die Neue Bühne* in August 1893 under the pseudonym that Rathenau is known to have used later on, Walther—or sometimes only W.—Hartenau. The essay was a response to an article that summarized contemporary critiques of conventional morality more or less along the lines of Nietzsche's *Thus Spoke Zarathustra*. An editorial comment invited readers to express their own views on the matter, and Rathenau attempted to do just that. Here we find indeed some of his later ideas on morality and its links with religion, philosophy, and everyday life. But most strikingly this little piece provides us with an unexpected and only slightly disguised self-portrait of the young author: a well-balanced, contented, "rather virtuous . . . decent guy."[30] This presumably fictitious "I" was not normally preoccupied with matters of conscience. He felt that morality was a kind of instinct that had evolved over generations, directing human behavior almost automatically. Posing as a paradigmatic average individual, Rathenau confessed to having always felt more pangs of conscience over his stupidity than over cases of cheating, laziness, fits of temper, or selfishness. On the whole, he admitted, moral lapses caused him merely some embarrassment. More importantly, they ran counter to his "sense of personal hygiene." He found himself only rarely disturbed by them. Instead, he was dedicated to the enhancement of his physical and spiritual potential, ensuring that he made his daily choices and decisions according to his personal "taste," independently of any external moral norms.

One could argue that this was a case of the lady protesting too much, or that the text covers up more than reveals Rathenau's actual state of mind at the time. After all, he was a moody man, given to changing fits of euphoria and depression. But, during the summer of 1893, he did have good reason to feel "contented with himself," as he put it. Such positive feelings, however, did not last very long. Despite his hopeful disposition, success continued to evade him, and the Bitterfeld project soon ran into severe difficulties. Stuck there for New Year's Eve, Walther wrote to his brother, complaining of "much aggravation, many worries, lots of work," and a few weeks later added a description of the "nervousness, apathy, fatigue, [and] weariness" that overcame him periodically. Then, perhaps inadvertently, he fell into echoing his father's opinion of him: "I lack the constitution," he concluded dejectedly.[31] Finally, in July 1898 Rathenau was forced to lease out the Bitterfeld plant and its extension in Rheinfelden in order to avoid bankruptcy. At the same time he was also forced to abandon his own electrolysis patent in favor of more efficient processes developed by others. In the end, and despite all his efforts, he could not prevent the collapse of his first independent industrial enterprise.

Once again, due to his father this failure too ended in a promotion. At the request of Emil Rathenau, both his sons, first Walther and a year later Erich, became members of AEG's board of directors. Walther was given the opportunity to work directly at his father's side. He was not made an heir apparent, but neither was he disinherited. Emil continued to do as much as he could to enhance his career.

Walther was not content. As before, failure in his chosen

path caused him to try harder but at the same time to grasp for new alternatives, and this time too, his choice was not painting, despite the fact that it was precisely then that he seemingly strengthened his ties with the contemporary art scene, especially in Berlin. By June 1893, Walther acquired one of Edvard Munch's early paintings, *Rainy Weather in Christiania*, having seen it in an exhibition organized in protest against the artistic establishment in the Prussian capital. In addition to Max Liebermann, he was also acquainted with other Impressionist painters belonging to this circle, and somewhat later, Lesser Ury even painted his portrait. By then the young Rathenau had also become a member of the Pan Club, made up of painters and writers supporting new trends in art and literature. In fact, Rathenau's interest shifted during these days from painting to literature. During the many lonely nights in Bitterfeld he had read a great deal and become acquainted with some of the most influential contemporary authors such as Max Stirner, Maeterlinck, and apparently with Nietzsche as well. In his visits to Berlin, he was increasingly drawn to the literary men of his new milieu and in 1897 met the journalist Maximilian Harden, a major figure within it, well connected, well read, and properly eccentric. Their quickly evolving friendship brought about a significant turn in Rathenau's life.

Felix Ernst Witkowski was born in 1861 into the family of a Jewish silk merchant from Poznań who had moved to Berlin in an effort to improve his lot.[32] He was one of nine children and still a young boy when his father experienced first a financial and then a mental breakdown. The young Witkowski escaped his father's oppressive care and joined a traveling theater as an actor. By the time he was twenty years old, he had converted to Protestantism and changed his name to Maximilian Harden. He then became a freelance journalist, writing political and cultural satire for some of the country's major liberal papers, eventually concentrating on theater and book criticism. Harden soon became acquainted with the entire intellectual elite of the Prussian capital, though his merciless sarcasm and sharp tongue made him always something of an outsider even in this circle. In the early 1890s, as he was moving to the right politically, he became an admirer of Bismarck, who was no longer in office but still drawing much attention to himself, and began to feel constrained in the company of liberal journalists and the literary avant-garde of Berlin. Seeking greater intellectual independence, he was forced, at least temporarily, into financial dependence upon one of his older brothers, who provided him the necessary funds for establishing his own weekly. When *Die Zukunft* (The Future) began to appear in October 1892, Harden quickly attracted a group of like-minded writers, diversely supplementing his own weekly crop of articles, and was now representing a conservative line that grew stronger during the following years. The journal was first published in some six thousand copies; by 1900 it reached the ten thousand mark and, sharpening its critical political profile, sometimes sold as many as twenty thousand copies, especially during the immediate pre–World War I years.

By then there was no lack of demand for Harden's ideological line. After all, the turn away from the short-lived liberal hegemony in Imperial Germany had already been accomplished by Bismarck himself as early as 1879. The enormous economic optimism shared by wide strata of the population in the wake of the industrial take-off during the 1850s and especially the 1860s had come to an end and had eventually brought to the fore intense opposition to economic as well as political liberalism, emanating from both the right and the left. Social Democracy and its trade union movement could no longer be checked, neither by sticks, in the form of Bismarck's anti-Socialist legislation, nor by the carrots that he offered of state-supported social benefits. Exhausting the possibilities of further parliamentary manipulations, Bismarck concluded that revolution could only be prevented if the constitutional arrangement that he had himself constructed two decades earlier were thoroughly revised. By then, however, he no longer had the Kaiser behind him. Wilhelm II, who came to the throne late in 1888, felt he could do a better job himself, even without shaking the whole system, and decided to bring about the aged chancellor's resignation.

While Social Democracy was attacking the emerging "organized capitalism" typical of these years for its inherently unjust system of distributing wealth, conservatives objected to its mode of producing this wealth and the results consequent upon it. In fact, the German economy was meanwhile undergoing a rapid and effective modernization, even though politicians and intellectuals were still debating the pros and cons of this very process. Aristocratic large landowners found ways of defending their interests, often in cooperation with heavy industry, while the debate on the relative value of their respective sectors for the future of Germany continued to rage. In fact, the matter had by then been decided and modernization could no longer be checked or reversed. Its social aspects and cultural implications became quickly apparent, too. There were, to be sure, scholars and intellectuals who accepted this onward march, and some of them were ready, even eager, to embrace its full consequences. Many, however, faced modernity with growing unease. Group interests were surely involved. Aristocrats dreaded the loss of their social and political supremacy in the wake of agricultural decline. The lower middle class of artisans, shopkeepers, white-collar workers, and the lower echelons of the bureaucracy feared decline into the proletariat. In a rapidly changing social order, educated people faced the danger of losing their livelihood, too. But anxiety in the face of rapid change had not only economic and social causes but also political and cultural ones. Democratic trends, gradually unfolding in Imperial Germany even under its semiauthoritarian state system, aroused deep apprehensions. The evolving faceless, homogeneous mass society seemed a tangible threat. Individuality was here at stake, it was argued, and as a reaction, various solutions were formulated, experimented with, and often rejected as quickly as they were put forward. A longing for a new Caesar became widespread among the conservatives. Bismarck was ranked with Friedrich II, the Hohenstaufen, Napoleon in the sphere of politics; Dante, Beethoven, Rembrandt were the most commonly mentioned cultural heroes. Poetry, music, and the fine arts could not flourish without such Great Men, ran the argument. But in order to uphold culture, individuality was not enough. Equally important was a stress on subjectivity as against objectivity, on emotion against rationalism, spirituality against materialism, the human soul against the intellect. Metaphysics and neo-Romanticism were lined up against the values of the Enlightenment.

This cultural bias was clearly apparent in the pages of *Die Zukunft*. In literature and theater Harden and his co-writers came out against naturalism and for an elitist, antidemocratic, anti-egalitarian, and antibourgeois subjectivism on all fronts. To be sure, they were not acting alone but as part of a general European movement. The Italian Gabriele d'Annunzio wrote for Harden's journal, as did the Belgians Maurice Maeterlinck and Emile Verhaeren and the Parisian Anatole France. Ibsen and Strindberg would soon become Harden's literary heroes; Nietzsche, Julius Langbehn, and the new prophets of Social Darwinism his philosophical guides. But despite this apparent cosmopolitanism the tone of *Die Zukunft* consistently became more nationalistic. German chauvinism was joined to racism and imperialism, and these in turn were made to reaffirm Germany's superiority, stress its unique culture of "inwardness," and celebrate its artistic, primarily musical "soul."

This was Rathenau's intellectual nourishment during the years of what he sometimes called his "Bitterfeld exile." And by

1897 it was natural for him to choose Harden as the publisher of his next journalistic attempt. At this point he no longer relied on his technical or business expertise, nor did he seek to reproduce the good-natured, conciliatory tone that had characterized his "Morality Today" four years earlier. The piece he now handed in was very different. Both its content and its style were unexpected; both no doubt were meant to shock. Rathenau must have known it would elicit a widespread response and bitter criticism. But by then he was apparently ready to enter the public sphere as an accomplished intellectual in his own right, take the heat if necessary, and hopefully get the credit when it was due.

"Hear, O Israel!" is a short piece, consisting of a frontal attack against Germany's Jews for failing to fully assimilate, for living "in a semivoluntary, invisible ghetto" and making up "a foreign organism" within the body of the German nation, "an Asian horde on the soil of the Mark-Brandenburg . . ."[33] The essay opens with a confession, of the kind that would later become characteristic of Rathenau: "I want to profess straight off that I am a Jew," he writes and then provocatively adds: "Does it require justification if I write in a spirit other than that of defending the Jews?" Surely, he immediately attracts our attention, but also arouses our unease. Moreover, this opening represented a milder version. In an earlier draft, now available in Rathenau's archive, we read: "Does it require an explanation if I tend towards antisemitism?" And, indeed, he does sound here sometimes like a full-fledged antisemite. In long passages he laments the fact that all Jews look "frighteningly alike," describes their "East-Mediterranean appearance," their "unathletic, sloppy shape," their "loose and lethargic manner," offering petty advice on how they should dress up and behave if they were to achieve "full adaptation . . . to the expectations of the Gentiles" so as to become true "Jews of German character and education." Nothing less than a complete metamorphosis is required, he claims. Neither acts of self-defense nor cries to the authorities would cure the widespread antipathy felt by non-Jews towards Jews. Rathenau clearly, though never openly, argues against the antidefamation campaign of the newly established Central Association of German Citizens of the Mosaic Faith, and perhaps also against the early stirrings of Zionism. For him, such joint communal efforts were clearly destructive.

Baptism, however, a possible solution for individuals, was equally detested by him. Even "if half of all Israel converted," he wrote, "it would create nothing other than a passionate anti-semitism against the baptized." The result would be "prying and suspicion" on the one side, "hatred and mendacity" on the other. It was, in fact, a year earlier that Rathenau had filled in the form announcing his withdrawal from the Jewish Community of Berlin, but true to his convictions, he never followed it up with the expected conversion. He may have even retracted the initial step, since at a later date he claimed to have actually remained in the congregation.[34] In any case, at the time of "Hear, O Israel!" he must have still believed that a true "Jewish patriarchy" would soon emerge; a patriarchy "not of property, but of intellectual and physical culture," one that would in time manage to "absorb all the material that is digestible and capable of transformation" in German culture and make it fully its own. And apparently, no one could be more fitting to join this patriarchy, in his eyes, than himself. It is curious that Rathenau chose to open his serious literary career with this piece. After all, regardless of its actual content, it marked him first and foremost as a Jew, albeit a rather unusual one. Furthermore, some of Rathenau's other pieces, written for *Die Zukunft* soon afterwards, likewise stressed this side of his identity. By mid-1898, Harden was publishing Rathenau's five "Talmudic Folktales," intended as current political commentaries in the guise of Jewish legends. These too appeared under the pen name W. Hartenau, a rather poor cover-up, providing only minimal defense for one intent on attacking his own people. In fact, these pieces already indicate the beginning of a change in their author's attitude, moving slowly now towards a more favorable approach to Judaism and using a milder, more generous tone. Thus self-hatred, an accusation often hurled at Rathenau on account of "Hear, O Israel!", surely does not exhaust the matter. Rathenau was attacking those Jews whom he considered as fundamentally different from himself in every meaningful aspect. He did give vent here to his urgent need to "pass" and to his frustration at remaining an outsider despite all efforts. But he clearly did not despair of breaking through. He blamed the Jews rather than the Germans for what he considered his misfortune, but interestingly, his insistence on remaining Jewish seemed unshaken. He was torn between self-pride and self-loathing, not an uncommon combination, and it would take him at least another decade before he could even begin to clear up this confusion. Being Jewish was a tormenting issue for him, emotionally and intellectually, and he was facing it passionately, often aggressively, as he did all other points of conflict and contradiction in his life.

Meanwhile, the publication of "Hear, O Israel!" had a number of direct and indirect consequences for him. First of all, it marked the beginning of an intense, though volatile friendship between himself and Maximilian Harden. Harden was delighted with Rathenau's essay. It must have expressed some of his own feelings, though matters seemed less complex for the successful journalist, who had converted early in life and was never in any way attracted by his Jewish origins. Upon receiving Rathenau's manuscript, Harden not only announced his intention of publishing it in the next issue of *Die Zukunft*, but also warmly congratulated the author on content and style alike. "It doesn't happen often that one encounters such a powerful literary talent," he wrote to Rathenau in a letter of January 15, 1897, expressing his heartfelt hope of meeting him as soon as possible.[35] For his part, Rathenau, who always needed reassurance, needed new friends too. Soon after publication, on March 6 of that year, the two men met and took to each other immediately. "Stay well," Harden concluded one of his early letters to Rathenau, in May 1899, "You should know how much I like you."[36] They then remained in close, even intimate contact for more than twenty years, and their correspondence during this long friendship attests to its many ups and downs. Indicative of its complexity is the fact that while they often began their letters with "Lieber Freund" or with first names, expressing warm feelings towards each other in many different ways, they kept to the third-person form throughout their friendship. This, to be sure, was not uncommon at the time, but both Rathenau and Harden are known to have dispensed with such formalities in several other cases. Apparently, that extra feeling that was the precondition of transcending conventions was missing between these two highly strung men. Harden insisted on seeing Rathenau as his protégé, while Rathenau, admiring his friend, did not always see eye to eye with him with regard to both public and private matters. The two would soon become bitter rivals, but meanwhile, conflicting emotions were here constantly at play: love and hidden distaste, admiration and envy.

Rathenau continued to write for *Die Zukunft*, sometimes even in response to Harden's direct suggestions. On the whole, he seemed to share in the spirit that animated his editor-friend and the men of his literary circle. Furthermore, at Harden's instigation, Rathenau also began to move socially among his new colleagues. It was through Harden that Rathenau first met Hugo von Hofmannsthal and Graf Harry von Kessler, his later biographer; both outstanding figures in Berlin's intellectual and artistic elite. He then met some of the most renowned German poets and playwrights, such as Frank Wedekind and Gerhart Hauptmann, as well as visitors or newcomers from far-off Vienna, such as the author Stefan Zweig and the theater director Max Reinhardt. He was now gradually becoming a full and legitimate member of Berlin's most respected milieu, as was his due both as the son of a wealthy and prominent industrialist and as a budding intellectual in his own right. Though fully independent neither of his father, Emil Rathenau, nor of his mentor, Maximilian Harden, Walther could now take his place in the Berlin-based German elite of his time.

Surprisingly small and close-knit, this elite depended on status achieved through exceptional wealth—old and new—as well as through *Bildung*, that special German combination of culture and a correctly formed character. This milieu was identical neither with the aristocracy nor with the upper economic bourgeoisie, and surely not with the German middle class as such. It was a social and cultural upper crust joined to elements of the urban nobility of government service and the officer corps, accepting into its ranks exceptional individuals at its own discretion and permitting social intercourse almost exclusively within itself. With few exceptions, old-style aristocrats, often living on the land, were notably absent, as were men of academic standing, who otherwise seem to have been so prominent in the public life of Imperial Berlin. And interestingly enough, being Jewish was no hindrance to membership in this elite. In fact, many of the most coveted salons in Berlin were presided over by the wives of wealthy Jewish businessmen, such as Aniela Fürstenberg and Lili Deutsch. Confessionally this was truly a mixed society, though—like every nook and cranny of Imperial Germany—not entirely free of some forms of antisemitism.

Most Jewish members of this elite, that is, those who did not convert, had—like the Rathenaus—little interest in Judaism. But for many, like the Rathenaus again, baptism was out of the question, sometimes precisely because of hidden antisemitism. At the time it was common to talk of "Trotzjudentum," of "defiant Jewishness," on the part of those who found it unbecoming to desert the weak, shameful to convert without true faith, indecent to try to "pass" so eagerly. Like the older Rathenau, most Jews who shared these feelings took cases of prejudice and minor exclusion, say from some of the most highly aristocratic circles, in their stride. They enjoyed their reputation as industrialists, commercial men, or financiers; consumed and sometimes participated in the production of German culture goods; and cherished their well-deserved social prestige. It was slightly lower down the social ladder that socializing between Gentiles and Jews outside the business sphere remained so rare, according to many testimonies. Among the elite this was not the case. Enjoying such social ties was yet another of the privileges enjoyed by its Jewish members.

For Walther Rathenau, staying Jewish while climbing to the top of the social ladder was from the outset a matter of honor. But he did more than that. Unlike many assimilated Jews, Rathenau always felt obliged to make his Jewishness public, carrying it up front, so to speak. Despite the repugnance he often expressed for other Jews, sometimes even for his own relatives, he did not hide his Jewish identity, made sure all his friends and correspondents were aware of it, and with time seemed to consider it a sign of distinction. This did not come easily to him. He fought with himself repeatedly in order to construct the complex identity of a German Jew that seemed both true and honorable to him, and this always remained a major theme in his life.

Meanwhile, being both German and Jewish was only one aspect of his curious double-life. In 1899, coming back from Bitterfeld to Berlin to take up his post in the AEG board of directors, Walther Rathenau was split between his role as an "industrial organizer," as he himself liked to call his line of work, and his position as a freelance writer and intellectual. From the outset, however, there could be no doubt as to which of his two careers was more important to him. Despite the excitement associated with being published repeatedly and moving freely within Berlin's intellectual circles, Rathenau's business activity was clearly uppermost in his life.

To begin with, his income was now beginning to grow substantially. He was finally not merely financially independent of his father, as he had always wished to be, but truly a rich man himself, heavily involved in efforts to coordinate production in the electrical industry, inside and outside the immediate sphere of AEG. Since 1896 and in addition to his role in Bitterfeld, he also took part in a number of projects in Poland, France, Norway, and Austria. Then, moving to the AEG central office in Berlin, he was made head of the department of power stations, as such initiating and managing projects in and out of Germany, and working in dozens of locations. During that time he likewise introduced a new kind of light bulb, the "Nernst lamp," initiated the establishment of the cable cartel with Siemens and others, and was made a member of the so-called Electro-Bank in Zurich. By the early twentieth century, then, Walther Rathenau was a prominent figure in the business world. A lecture series on the achievements of the electric industry made him known in wider social circles too, and on one occasion he was asked to repeat a lecture before the Kaiser himself. Stressing German superiority in this field and explaining it by the superior features of Prussian tradition, he gained the Kaiser's favor and received a minor imperial decoration.

Times, however, were hard. At the beginning of the twentieth century the entire electrical industry suffered a severe crisis. Eventually, both AEG and Siemens emerged larger and stronger, but for a while the riding was rough. The big companies learned to improve their position by cooperating with municipal and state authorities that were often initiators and partners in large-scale electric power projects, and by taking over weaker competitors if other arrangements with them proved impractical. It is not always possible to determine the extent of Walther Rathenau's contribution to the success of AEG during this period. In the end, however, it was a major failure that led to his resignation from its board of directors. Early in 1902, one of Germany's main electric concerns, Schuckert & Co., experienced severe difficulties. Walther Rathenau and Felix Deutsch, Emil Rathenau's chief executive, investigated the matter and came to the conclusion that a "combination" with Schuckert would be in the long run beneficial to AEG. Their suggestion was rejected by the majority of the AEG board of directors, with Emil Rathenau abstaining in the final vote. In addition to his apparent dislike of Schuckert's management, the older Rathenau was reluctant to spend the necessary money on saving the failing firm and was by this time not entirely averse to using this opportunity to openly oppose his son's suggestion. Complaints against dynasty building, directed at him since both Walther and Erich had become board members, seemed to undermine his authority in the firm and as far as he was concerned, Erich—a simpler man, more technically oriented, and always much loved by his father—was indispensable. Walther handed in his resignation.[37]

It was often speculated that additional ill feeling between father and son was caused by the publication of Walther's first volume of collected essays, *Impressions*, at that time. Emil did not appreciate his son's intellectual ventures. "He is a tree which bears more blossom than fruit," Emil once said of Walther, and his essays were "easier to write than to read."[38] But now "Hear, O Israel!", reprinted under its author's real name, apparently made things much worse. The older Rathenau was furious. It was said that in his rage he had all copies of Walther's book removed from the bookstores, and—whether the allegation is true or false—this episode surely aggravated his frustration with his son's literary pretensions. Thus once again, this chapter in Rathenau's life came to an unhappy ending in connection with his position on the Jewish issue. By then he may have already begun to change his mind, but this could not avert the problem. He was forced to pay the price. It was the outside world that had denied him success in the military. This time he was held back by forces at home.

3

Incursions into Politics

ONCE MORE, it seems, partial failure did not hinder Rathenau's further advance. In fact, the last setback found him stronger than ever. Immediately after his resignation from the AEG board of directors, he was asked by Carl Fürstenberg to join the board of the Berliner Handels-Gesellschaft (BHG), one of Germany's major banks at the time and the main financing institution of AEG. "Alone at last!" commented Harden in a letter of May 15, 1902. But this was probably not how Rathenau himself saw it.[1] On the one hand, leaving AEG must have felt more like an expulsion than a liberation. No one, not even his father, or rather most particularly not his father, fought to keep him. He had hoped to be a success there even if it left him in his father's shadow, but now he had been practically ousted. On the other hand, working for the BHG did not mean a complete break with AEG, nor did it represent a final release from his father's supervision. Still, the BHG was important enough to make Walther feel he was advancing in the world, and the years in that institution proved profitable for him in every sense. To begin with, his income as much as doubled at once and from then on only continued to rise. More importantly perhaps, he was now in a position to experience ever more intensively the financial side of large-scale industrial affairs, amass new experiences, and prepare for greater things to come. In his new post Rathenau got involved in establishing and managing many different firms, and soon he was on the boards of no fewer than eighty-six German and twenty-one foreign companies. By 1904 he was also officially involved in running AEG again, this time as a member of its influential supervisory board. His correspondence from these years attests to his many complicated business affairs, to his keen perception of financial problems, and last but not least, to his evolving talent as a negotiator.

As he did during his short time on the AEG board of directors, Rathenau continued to prefer cooperation to what he considered "unchecked competition," particularly in times of crisis. While Siemens managed to reach an agreement with Schuckert & Co., AEG, at the initiative of Walther Rathenau and this time with the active support of his father, achieved a fusion with another large-scale firm in the electrical sector, the Union Elektrizitäts-Gesellschaft, and the result—also a function of the upward turn of the economy—was a doubling of AEG's turnover. It also meant a significant rise in dividends, especially between 1901–3 and 1906–7, to the great satisfaction of the shareholders and the delight of his father, who was always most loyal to them. Emil's trust in his son's business acumen grew by leaps and bounds. In a letter of August 21, 1903 to a banker colleague in Switzerland, he recommended Walther for both his financial talents and his technical expertise, describing him simply as "an authority in this field."[2] Distance, even just relative distance, seemed to have created a new bond between father and son.

Distance, however, may not have been the main cause of this rapprochement. Less than half a year after Walther's resignation from the AEG board, his younger brother Erich, who had suffered from a heart condition since childhood, died while on a pleasure trip with their father in Egypt. Emil managed to return home safely, but suffered a severe mental breakdown. He was unable to conduct his business affairs for weeks, and under these unexpected circumstances experienced the helping hand of his elder son. Walther, overcoming his own shock and grief, seems to have been a tower of strength to both his mother and his father in these trying times. This demanded a great deal of patience and sympathy on his part. His father's partial loss of orientation and his mother's bitterness and desperation must have created a very stressful atmosphere. It was made worse by the morbid efforts of both parents to commemorate Erich in various ways, most particularly within their home. Finally Walther was brought to observe in a letter to his mother that remembrance was not a "cult of departed spirits," nor did it require constant "self-castigation."[3] In any event, Erich's death markedly changed the family situation.

At about the same time, Edith, the Rathenaus' only daughter, twenty years old by then, married Fritz Andreae, an offspring of a banking family from Frankfurt, ten years her elder and, though from a partly Jewish family, a practicing Protestant. Despite the fact that her wedding was celebrated in church, Edith did not convert till 1911, apparently because of her father's opposition. As a child, she had suffered both from her mother's frequent trips and from her father's obsessive devotion to work, his stinginess, and his aloofness.[4] An early marriage granted her a measure of independence from her parents, while she continued to keep close contact with her brother Walther. The two often met, usually outside their parents' home and sometimes even despite their mother's inexplicable opposition. Thus, by the early years of the twentieth century, the two remaining Rathenau children, now adults, had each re-asserted their own individuality in opposition to their parents, and at least to some degree managed to achieve this feat by joining a kind of substitute family—an extensive one, indeed, in the form of the Berlin-based social elite. Edith entertained lavishly in her elegant villa, holding open house on Sunday afternoons, where the entire economic and cultural elite of the capital, and later also the political elite, gathered for food and drink, but more especially for lively and brilliant conversation. Her brother was a welcome guest on these occasions, of course, as well as in the various other salons in town.

During all these tumultuous years, Rathenau also continued to write extensive essays on various topics, publishing them usually, though no longer exclusively, in the pages of *Die Zukunft*. Some of these pieces were entertaining and satirical, such as one on his hometown Berlin, characterized by him as "the parvenu of great cities and the great city of parvenus."[5] Others were more serious, despite their feuilleton-like style, and some gradually began to point to Rathenau's later, more mature and more philosophically oriented writings. Particularly telling in this respect was his "Ignorabimus" from 1898, stressing spirit and soul against intellect and rationalism.[6] Writing on modern art, Rathenau repeatedly revealed his ambivalence toward both Impressionism and Expressionism, as well as his search for what he considered more purely "German" art-forms. And some of his many aphorisms written during these years pointed to the topics that would eventually preoccupy him in his later full-length books. Rathenau was going through his literary apprenticeship.

For a while, he continued to publish under a number of different pen names. This, however, became absurd after the publication of his first book of essays in 1902. By then, his work was being reviewed and commented upon ever more intensively. Rathenau's correspondence attests to his new status. He was now gradually entering into intellectual exchange, sometimes outright controversy, with various literary colleagues and an assortment of dignitaries from all walks of life. A curious correspondence between him and Theodore Herzl, for instance, began at about this time. In response to Herzl's enthusiastic review of Rathenau's "Physiology of Business" in the pages of the Viennese *Neue Freie Presse* in mid-1901, Rathenau saw fit to disclose to him his identity as the author of "Hear, O Israel!" too. Herzl was clearly embarrassed. He first tried to avoid the issue, then admitted that the essay had angered him, and finally decided to settle the matter by arguing that he did in fact share some of Rathenau's premises, though by no means all of his conclusions. On the basis of these presumably shared premises, Herzl went on to try and enlist Rathenau for the cause of Zionism. He offered to send him regularly the central German-language Zionist paper *Die Welt*, though he did not go as far as to send him a copy of his own new book, *Altneuland*. This gave Rathenau the opportunity to confess he was still "far away from Eretz Israel" (written in Hebrew in the original) and to promise that he would order Herzl's book from his bookseller. In any case, the tone between them remained distant. Herzl did not intervene to mitigate Rathenau's critique of Zionism and Rathenau never really changed his mind and never took more than a fleeting interest in the movement.[7]

Others, too, reacted to Rathenau's writings. Fritz Mauthner, for instance, a linguist and philosopher of Jewish origin, like Rathenau, wrote from Vienna, thanking Rathenau for the pleasure of reading his book, and comparing him with Montaigne, no less.[8] But as a whole, Rathenau's *Impressions* did not leave a lasting mark. He was still groping for recognition. Success as an author and intellectual was not yet forthcoming.

Of the essays published during this period perhaps the most interesting, a true milestone in the development of Rathenau's *Weltanschauung*, was his "On Weakness, Fear, and Pur-

pose," first printed in *Die Zukunft* in 1904. It clearly demonstrated Schopenhauer's and Nietzsche's influence, though it
was perhaps Julius Langbehn—by every standard a lesser light
—who seemed to have an even greater influence upon him at
this stage, together with the French racial theorist Gobineau
and the British-born best-selling German author Houston
Stewart Chamberlain. Men are divided into two groups that
reflect the fundamental split within humanity based on the opposition between Fear and Courage, ran Rathenau's argument:
the Wise and the Strong. Though his admiration was clearly
reserved for the latter, it was to the former that Rathenau dedicated most of the essay. Out of fear and inherent weakness
arise the need to lie and flatter, he admits, but also the urge to
invent, amass property, reach for power, enjoy human accomplishments, and seek the praise of one's peers. Here also lies the
source of human ability to reason, to act with alacrity and es-
prit, even to take pleasure in humor. And while all these might
be admirable, each in itself and all together bring neither freedom nor true aesthetic enjoyment; neither happiness nor relaxation. These come naturally only to the Strong, Rathenau insisted, especially to the offspring of that "ancient people of the
North . . . whose fair-haired heads we would so much like to
crown with the glory of Mankind."[9]

Rathenau's unabashed use of racial categories, most emphatically his repeated use of physiognomy, is characteristic of
his thought at the time. It is reminiscent of his "Hear, O Israel!," reflecting a curious mixture of Nietzschean categories
with antimodern sentiments, common in fin-de-siècle Germany. In addition, as in the case of many of his non-Jewish contemporaries, the Jewish issue was for Rathenau too, always at
hand, even if sometimes in disguise. The Weak and the Wise in
his world were most particularly the Jews, especially those occupied in commerce and finance; the Strong and the Happy
were the *Germanen*. His contempt, then, sometimes even his

wrath, was directed at those who populated his life, at friends and relatives. The ones for whom he apparently had only love and admiration were sadly beyond his reach.

This was a position fraught with ambivalence. To be sure, Rathenau never retracted the views expressed in "On Weakness, Fear and Purpose." He revised the text several times, cut out a few passages, but then had it reprinted more than once, including in his collected works as late as 1918. From the outset, however, he was less than completely at ease with this piece. A week after its first publication, on November 19, 1904, Frank Wedekind sent the author his reactions, and Rathenau's reply followed swiftly. He answered Wedekind's commentary point by point: "Wise" and "Strong" were not really the appropriate terms, he admitted, and in any case "Wisdom is naturally more 'prudentia' than 'sapientia,'" while Strength was meant to be "more 'virtus' than 'fortitudo.'" Moreover, both were only "ideal pictures," to use his fashionable terminology, reminiscent of Max Weber's "ideal types." Against what might appear from reading his text, Rathenau rather uncharacteristically admitted, his heart went out to the fearful, the suffering, the unhappy. After all, isn't it true, he asks while throwing in for good measure a phrase from Baudelaire, that "pain is the only nobility"? "In confidence" he is willing to admit that genius can finally arise only from a mixture of the two elements he depicts and it is not the sole reign of the Strong that he strives for. In the immediate context, he too knows that "if the strong is foolish, then he is a Junker." Still, the problem of the age is the superiority of the Wise and the reign of the Fearful. They rule the fate of the earth, decide over economic matters, war and peace, right and wrong. Rathenau may be ready to assault them, but he recognizes that they are indispensable and are surely here to stay.[10] With all his aversion to the "rule of slaves," Rathenau could not but acknowledge its inevitability, even its necessity. By then it was clear to him that industry was dependent upon rationalism and science and that the Wise and the Weak offered the only solution to the basic needs of modern society. In one of his earlier letters to Harden, Rathenau had already stressed this point.[11] From the very outset he argued against his mentor's utopian attacks on modernity. For sheer livelihood, he always knew, humanity depended on increased production, on the rational organization of this production, and on the tools that enabled man to provide for himself even in modern times, in the face of population explosion, rapid urbanization, and the demand for an ever improving standard of living.

In fact, Harden was later persuaded to accept this side of modernity too, embracing it as an inevitability. From around the year 1900, he too moved among bankers and industrialists and on many issues chose to accept their point of view, sometimes even to advance their interests. A prosperous economy, he knew by then, was not only a social prerequisite. It was a precondition for achieving Germany's imperial ambitions and for turning it into a world power. Thus, the tone of the entire antimodern movement, romantic and reactionary during much of the last decade of the nineteenth century, gradually changed in later years, and Rathenau's stand, unique at first, became typical for a growing number of intellectuals. The mixture of accepting modernization, enjoying its benefits, even basking in its glamour, while at the same time despising and depreciating it, fearing its presumably unworthy social and cultural consequences, became common currency.[12]

For Rathenau, moving among such comrades in arms, sharing beliefs and a community of spirit with like-minded men was an obvious relief. To be sure, racialism, even antisemitism, were often part of this ideological package, but even that did not cause him to hesitate. Joining in the changing antimodern movement eased his stressful life. And as a rule his was indeed demanding and extremely hectic. In addition to his unavoidable professional duties and his self-imposed writing tasks, he participated in the social life of Berlin's cultural elite to the full.

Even just keeping a functioning network of relationships within this exclusive milieu and upholding it on a long-term basis was a full-time job. There is no better contemporary witness to this life-style than Count Harry Kessler, whose detailed diary is crammed with descriptions of endless breakfasts, dinners, and after-show or after-concert soirées that often continued until the early hours of the morning. People met tête-à-tête or in groups of ten or even twenty; in the Automobile Club, in the Hotel Adlon, in the best restaurants in town, and especially in the homes of friends and acquaintances; discussing politics, arts and the theater, speaking ill of those not present, flirting, arguing—often humorously and sometimes brilliantly.

One wonders how men with work to do were able to manage such a schedule. Naturally, not everyone who belonged to these circles was as active socially as Kessler and Rathenau, both young and unmarried. Money was not a problem for most; but surprisingly, there was also plenty of time. Long vacations must be added to this leisurely routine. We have seen Rathenau's mother constantly traveling in and out of Germany. Other women, not burdened by a sick son and perhaps less unhappy at home, may have traveled somewhat less, but the business of arranging vacations and then going on them was a major preoccupation of the female members of the elite. Men traveled incessantly, too. In addition to their job-related trips —a routine for industrialists or bankers, but also apparently part of the life of the more or less successful artists, authors, and musicians—they all enjoyed at least one summer month away from Berlin in various elegant spas and resorts. Families traveled together to the North Sea, to Italy, to Switzerland, sometimes to Paris, London, even New York. Single men took longer trips, often with male friends, to Egypt, Greece, or

Scotland. Many of the magnates had weekend and summer villas near and far. And the younger generation often came too, meeting among themselves, sometimes in preparation for marriage—partly freely chosen and partly arranged. Extended families often vacationed together but such summer trips were also opportunities for carefully widening one's social network. Less wealthy people had their meeting places in and out of town too, to be sure, but the exclusivity of the elite was never in doubt. Different classes may have all visited the theater together, but they then dined in their separate eating places. They went to the same concerts—but talked about them and criticized them separately. They may have even taken the waters together, but lived in separate hotels and only rarely met each other.

Rathenau entered into this life with a vengeance. In letters to his mother, herself so often away in this or that resort, he lists his social obligations one by one. The routine of daily gatherings, cultural consumption in public and in private, as well as endless conversations, are major themes in these letters. Rathenau was everywhere a frequent guest, it seems, especially during the first decade of his adult life in Berlin, and particularly after resigning his post at the BHG in mid-1907. As a matter of fact, a year earlier Rathenau had announced his intention to quit his business career and become "a private person," as he put it. Always keeping his literary options open, he was in the habit of periodically mentioning to his various friends that his real wish was to leave the "life of the world" and abandon industry for philosophy, business for literature.[13] Clearly, neither the short episode on the AEG board nor the years at the BHG met his expectations. In both cases, Rathenau was acting as his father's son in the interests of AEG, in partial independence but also with partial success. This must have been both psychologically and intellectually unsatisfying, even frustrating. In fact, one is reminded of Emil Rathenau's midlife crisis. He too, not yet forty, had left all previous occupations and for a number of years sought out a new beginning. Emil, though, had been entirely devoted to his technical interests. In contrast, Walther's many talents pulled him sometimes in this direction and sometimes in that. Meanwhile he was a rich man and, in contrast to his father at this stage in life, had no family of his own and could more easily allow himself to take time off, experiment, and even take risks. Spending many evenings in conversation with Rathenau, Harden was perhaps the first to sense the direction of his friend's new ambition. Observing him in his various capacities, he came to the conclusion that Rathenau was ripe for a junior political or diplomatic post, and being a journalist, he hurried to make his views publicly known.

Things then happened faster than was to be expected. A sign of the fact that Rathenau's political ambitions may not have been entirely unrealistic was the appointment of Bernhard Dernburg first to the post of deputy director of the Colonial Department in the Foreign Office in September 1906 and then as colonial secretary in May 1907. At the time, the entire political system was inflamed by a controversy over the colonies. Years of continuous scandals and corruption, and finally the brutal massacre of the Hereros in the German colonial protectorate of Southwest Africa, brought matters to a head. Prince Bernhard von Bülow, chancellor since 1900, attempted to quiet things down by appointing a new person to head colonial affairs, and was persuaded, not least by a press campaign in which Harden played a major role, to choose an active businessman with a fresh approach. Presumably he had considered Rathenau among others, but finally chose Dernburg, a director of the Bank for Commerce and Industry in Berlin. In addition to the fact that Dernburg was a complete outsider as far as the bureaucracy was concerned, he was also from a Jewish background. Both his parents were already Christians and he himself had grown up as a Protestant from birth. Still, as was common at the time, Dernburg was generally referred to by high and low as a Jew, and his appointment to such an important and visible post was considered unprecedented. In the end, even Dernburg's energetic efforts and his ability to gain the support of the most unlikely allies, such as the representatives of the antisemitic splinter parties in the Reichstag, did not prevent the coming political crisis. By December, the government was unable to pass its budget and Bülow chose to dissolve the Reichstag and revamp his coalition by replacing the Catholic Center with the left-liberal Progressive Party. Following a general election in February 1907, the so-called "Bülow Bloc," composed of Conservatives, National Liberals, and Progressives, attempted to give Germany's domestic as well as foreign policies a new face. On the one hand, the bloc was meant to isolate Social Democracy and remove the Catholics from power; on the other hand it seemed to give the Reichstag, often considered impotent, a new authority. The cabinet was now handling its affairs as if it were a constitutionally constructed coalition government, de facto if not de jure, presumably acting under the authority of the parliament. Some very crucial principles were involved in the ensuing changes and a heated public debate was aroused.

Harden and Rathenau found themselves in opposing camps. Rathenau, previously a champion of aristocratic rule, was now in the process of changing his mind. In Bülow's rather flimsy parliamentary reconstruction he saw a desirable shift in the balance of power between the Junker aristocracy and the upper bourgeoisie. There was a chance now, he thought, to invigorate the state with fresh blood from a particularly capable and particularly willing new social element. And in a detailed article on this matter, first intended for *Die Zukunft* but then published by a provincial National Liberal paper, the *Hannoverscher Courier*, he expressed his hope that the new alliance would manage to lead the failing German political system into the modern age.[14] Harden, on the other hand, considered it a dangerous gamble. The two had disagreed before on matters related to the primacy of the Junker and the significance of modernization. Now, however, Rathenau, apparently no longer enamored of the blond Prussian nobleman, was willing to see the benefits of a mild liberal turn, while Harden held on to his fundamental suspicion of any sort of liberalism. A compromise between them seemed beyond reach, and in addition, Harden suspected Rathenau of defending the new government out of sheer personal ambition and of concocting an elaborate political argument in order to serve his petty goals. On a still deeper level, he seems to have resented the newfound independence of his protégé. By then, though often through Harden's mediation, Rathenau was moving on his own in the highest circles, reevaluating his previous alliances and tasting the pleasures of budding political influence.

Dernburg was among Rathenau's new acquaintances at that time. In a diary entry from mid-October 1906, Kessler described a dinner at Rathenau's, in which Dernburg, recently installed in his new position, was among the few select guests. "A cross between a bank clerk and Heinrich Heine," he jokingly commented.[15] Bülow himself recorded that during these days Dernburg recommended Rathenau to him as "his best friend" and somewhat later managed to bring them together. It is worthwhile recalling Bülow's description of this scene in his memoirs: Rathenau "was about forty at the time," he writes, "but looked older, a very pleasant figure and impeccably attired. He approached me with an equally impeccable bow and said in a resounding voice, with one hand resting on his chest: 'Your Highness, before I am granted the honor of speaking with you, I wish to make a statement that is also a confession: Your Highness, I am a Jew . . .'"[16] This was as typical of Rathenau as it was unnecessary, even embarrassing. His "confession" could hardly have come as a surprise to the chancellor. After all, he was known by all as the son of the famous general manager of AEG, Jewish by origin if not by ties to the community. And at this juncture, his Jewishness in fact was of no significance to Bülow. He seems to have taken to Rathenau: he invited him to his home and spoke with him openly, showing uncommon trust and a measure of warmth and friendliness. Rathenau on his part was properly impressed. He made sure to report every detail to his father—in confidence, of course—including all items on the menu and the eating habits of both the chancellor and his wife.[17] And it was thereafter easy for Dernburg to convince Bülow to let him invite Rathenau to join the two official tours he was about to undertake, first to the German territories in East Africa and then to Southwest Africa. On both occasions Rathenau served as Dernburg's unofficial adviser, even paying his own fare. Nevertheless, upon his homecoming, he was expected to report on his impressions and suggest plans for reform to the highest political echelons, including the Kaiser. Harden, who had originally hoped for Rathenau's success precisely on some such course, was no longer supportive. He was now watching his friend making his way up into the world of politics and resented it.

Immediately after Rathenau finally resigned from the BHG on July 1, 1907, the new adventure awaited him. Ten days later he was on his way to Marseilles, where he embarked on a German East Africa Line steamer that then picked up Dernburg's expedition in Naples and headed to Port Said and from there southward to the German colonial lands in East Africa. On board were a number of experts accompanying the colonial secretary, a few businessmen, seven journalists, and one landscape painter, whose trip was jointly paid for by Dernburg and Rathenau. The trip lasted almost three months and opened up a new world for Rathenau. On July 15 he began to write a diary.[18] At first his entries contained only descriptions of the natural scenery and of the great human variety that he was suddenly encountering. He was impressed by the different African skin colors, their costumes, their habits, their striking characteristics. His power of observation and his empathy stand out unmistakably in these pages; he is occasionally even poetic. Approaching Port Said in the evening, Rathenau's visual sensibilities came to the fore: "Network of moonlight on the water," he wrote. "Ships with searchlights far off in the bosom of the canal: drawing near, moving away." Or notice his description of the vegetation: "Round blackish-green mango trees, from a distance like chestnuts, in groups, in perspective . . . Trees with yellow blossoms. Bluish-red rivers of bougainvilleas . . ." Likewise of living creatures: "Lone hyenas. Gazelles in pairs. Herds of gnu and hartebeest"; "In the evening sun a reflection of the lake appears. Herds of zebra grazing . . ."; and then of the human landscape: "Covered market. Comparison of the black crowd clothed in white and white men clothed in black. Favors the former." Echoes of his Jewish identity could also be heard here: "Old Testament scene . . . The image of the Arabs of old . . . Heads of prophets. Next to me Isaiah—little, sharp, dark . . ."; and then rather cryptically: "Youth, old age, and death for thousands of years. Without tradition and history. Contrast with the Jordan tribes whose names, traditions, songs, and laws still rule the world today."[19]

Interestingly, more practical notes that could thereafter help him in writing reports on both trips were few and far between in the diary. If he wrote such notes separately they were lost. Still, both his later reports convey devotion to the task at hand, attention to details, a deep personal involvement, and a genuine effort to observe the situation open-mindedly. They reflect both his strengths and his weaknesses in his unfamiliar role as an up-and-coming political man.

Rathenau's first report, entitled "The Development of the German East African Colony," was presented to the Kaiser on November 28, 1907 and gained him, at the initiative of both Dernburg and Bülow, an "Order of the Crown, Second

Class."[20] It included an overview of the conditions in the colony, the chances for its economic growth, the situation of its inhabitants, and finally a discussion of the achievements as well as the failures of the German administration. Rathenau made recommendations for improving the natives' agricultural production and remarked on the need for better legal and transportation systems. Despite his criticism of existing conditions, he felt that "on the whole, the work of colonization demands qualities which the Germans possess in rich measure," and that "education for colonization will eventually open for the German soul a field that corresponds to its earthly mission."[21] He went on to explain the reasons for the many instances of misconduct by the colonists, sometimes even justifying the application of their peculiar "racial justice" as a matter of life or death. But one could sense his unease with the treatment of the African population. He would have preferred to achieve total submission "through exemplary leadership" and not by the brutal use of force, he wrote, and the fact that "judicial action against such transgressions rarely takes place or is ineffectual" only intensified his uneasiness.[22] He was clearly vacillating between outright condemnation of the treatment of the "natives" and his sympathy for the colonizers and their difficult, "almost inhuman task." In addition, he was apparently uncertain whether an open critique on his part would be appreciated or simply bring to an end his first inroad into the world of political affairs.

These doubts were all the more pressing as he composed his second report, following the trip to Germany's Southwest African territories a few months later. This had been the site of horrific atrocities only a short while earlier, the most disastrous of which was the killing of some 80 percent of the Herrero tribe— men, women, and children. The Herreros, a cattle-breeding nation, complained of land seizure by German settlers and by the early weeks of 1904 many of them took up arms. When the civilian governor of the colony asked for military reinforcement from the homeland, Lieutenant-General Lothar von Trotha was sent over, and introduced a policy of not merely subjugating the Herreros but of eliminating them. In battle and then through starvation in the desert, confinement in concentration camps, and forced labor, this aim was almost completely achieved. Another wave of revolt later the same year, this time of the Nama tribe, often known at that time as the Hottentots, was crushed by similar means. From Berlin Bülow made some efforts to restore civilian control and stop the atrocities, but the situation in Southwest Africa only gradually, and never completely, calmed down. While the Dernburg-Rathenau trip to East Africa was intended primarily to evaluate the economic potential of the colony, the burning issue in Southwest Africa was the need to review the consequences of the massacre and weigh the chances of reestablishing a measure of normal life there. It is to Rathenau's credit that this time he did not retreat into middle-of-the-road verbiage, trying to please everyone. To be sure, he did attempt to avoid moralizing and refrained from naming the culprits. But he clearly felt compelled to voice his practical political reservations and, if somewhat less outspokenly, his moral unease as well. The handling of the Herreros, he wrote, involved "the greatest atrocity that has ever been brought about by German military policy." He condemned "the system of deportation and concentration camps" created in the wake of the military campaign, as well as "the present position of the native" as helot, having "the outward appearance of slavery."[23] Rathenau did not mince words. He criticized German policies, compared them unfavorably with those of the British in the nearby South African territories, and insisted that they were contrary to the real interests of the Reich. Without an energetic reform of local legislation and an overhaul of the defense establishment, the judicial system, and credit practices, "our only white colony," he declared, could not be properly ruled.

And rule it we must, he added. "The question whether the pos-
session of Southwest Africa means good or bad business for us,
whether this country should be retained or given up, must never
be considered again," Rathenau concluded with his characteristic pathos. "Through German blood spilt on its fields," the
colony "became a part of our homeland, and German land must
remain sacrosanct."[24]

It is hardly surprising that Rathenau's second report was received less than enthusiastically by the powers that be. It was
handed to Bülow, who showed it to the Kaiser at the beginning
of October 1908, and was then simply passed over in silence. By
then the government was having worse troubles to deal with.
In the fall of that same year, the Kaiser was heavily compromised by the "Daily Telegraph Affair," in which both his arrogance and his lack of tact were revealed in a press interview,
causing an international scandal and eventually bringing about
the end of Bülow's coalition. In fact, Wilhelm II's "personal
rule" had been undermined even earlier. It was Harden who
had launched a public campaign against the Kaiser and his entourage as early as the beginning of 1907. In a series of articles
he lashed out at the monarch's incompetence and his unconsti-
tutional interference in foreign policy, attacking the corruption of his so-called Camarilla and especially its homoerotic,
"effeminate" habits, to use his favorite term. We have already
seen that like many in the Imperial German elite, Rathenau felt
uneasy at Harden's merciless blows. While he too was critical
of the Kaiser's irresponsible behavior, Harden's tactics embarrassed him, and he may have felt threatened by their mixture of
political accusations with sexual allegations. When matters
then came to a head in April 1907, he could no longer allow
himself to be too closely associated with the compromised editor of *Die Zukunft* without risking his budding political career.
Possibly he was also under pressure from his father, whose contacts with the Kaiser were by then at their peak.

Meanwhile, although Rathenau's relations with Bülow remained amiable enough, the latter was forced to postpone suggesting him for decoration for his service to the crown in his second African journey. Bülow was apparently eager to do so, as he had explained to a top administrator in the chancellor's office, both because he considered Rathenau "a very capable, useful man" and in order to show "that we don't always treat unbaptized Jews as pariahs."[25] Postponement, however, seemed unavoidable. The situation was made even worse by Dernburg's intervention. Annoyed now by Rathenau's behavior and his newly found independence, he prohibited the publication of Rathenau's second report, so that the latter was practically silenced: his most extended critique of imperial policies was only published posthumously, in 1927. Though he was finally invested with the "Order of the Red Eagle, Second Class," in January 1910, this too turned out to be a bitter disappointment. The *Berliner Tageblatt*, reporting on the ceremony, stressed the decoration of Dernburg with the more prestigious "Red Eagle, First Class," while Rathenau, receiving the lesser award among some three hundred representatives of commerce and industry, was merely mentioned as "the son of the director general of AEG."[26] The decoration may have still boosted his prestige in a society that gave so much weight to such presumed signs of proximity to the court, but it could not hide the fact that the young Rathenau's political ambitions were yielding meager results at this stage. His chance of advancement upon this route no longer seemed real.

This was not entirely his fault. To be sure, Dernburg's exasperation with Rathenau was not unique. People who appreciated Rathenau and trusted him at first often lost interest or turned against him later on. Neither was it always his Jewishness that brought about such disappointments. As we saw, Bülow would have made him an example of the government's honoring a useful unbaptized Jew. But timing was unfortunate and on the whole, Rathenau, despite his achievements, was apparently still seen as no more than his father's protégé. While Walther's personality surely had something to do with it, matters were made difficult for more general reasons, too. In the eyes of the conservative government that ruled Germany at the time, even from the point of view of the Liberals belonging to the Bülow Bloc, Rathenau had the wrong friends and on too many occasions voiced the wrong views. On balance, being Jewish did not help.

Coming back from Africa and for the time being unable to pursue an active political career, Rathenau set out to resume his journalistic work, now giving it a decidedly political twist. Since one of the official reasons for the second trip had been to compare British and German colonial policies, the members of Dernburg's expedition had first sailed to London and spent a few days there discussing common issues with their local counterparts. Back on board, Rathenau summarized his impressions of these discussions in a memorandum entitled "Concerning England's Present Situation," which he chose to publish only later, in 1912.[27] His point of departure was the critical link between politics and economics. In both domestic policies and in foreign and imperial matters, economic considerations were paramount, he argued, in England as well as in Germany. In fact, England's industry had already been the topic of one of his earlier essays, written in 1906, together with a piece on the German economy and another one, dealing with the causes of economic crises in general. Later on, in January 1908, he added to these a longer essay, comparing the "economic meaning," as he put it, of four nations: England, France, the United States, and Germany.[28] "England bears the burden of its best qualities," Rathenau was arguing. Having been the pioneer of industrialization, it was now paying the price for the complacency of its businessmen, the potency of its trade unions, and most importantly, its slowness and caution in applying newer and more efficient technologies. Being themselves aware of these failures, the English were now worried about their competitors, Germany in particular, Rathenau claimed. It is "a rivalry between the workshop and the arsenal," made all the more difficult for the English because their colonies were, in fact, nothing but "millstones around their neck."[29] And this was why, he concluded, Germany must tread lightly. Gestures of friendliness were not enough. A policy of overall reconciliation was needed, reassuring England in order to prevent a European flare-up.

Writing, however, was a poor substitute for exerting more direct political influence, and Rathenau continued to seek opportunities to flex his muscles in a variety of ways. In May 1910, he was able to try his luck again, this time as a negotiator. The Mannesmann Brothers, a large German mining company, asked him to mediate between themselves and their French counterpart, the *Union des mines*, regarding mining concessions in Morocco, a matter that had quickly been politicized in the aftermath of the so-called first Moroccan crisis. Failing to prevent the French from turning the country into their protectorate, Germany was trying to save at least some of its economic and financial interests there. Thus, vital state matters were involved in the Mannesmann issue, and Rathenau was asked to act in a highly charged atmosphere, performing, in fact, a kind of diplomatic mission. Against all odds, he managed to reach an agreement with the French on dividing Morocco's ore mines, but it then became evident that the men who had sent him over were not really interested in a compromise. Guided by their Pan-German imperialist views, they preferred to sharpen rather than neutralize the conflict. Rathenau, acting as a private negotiator, despite being supported by the Foreign Office or even by the Kaiser, did not have the needed authority to force the issue. He resigned and returned to Berlin empty-handed.

Political influence, he must have now realized, could only be truly exercised either through full-fledged public office or through long-term party-political activity. Rathenau had claims to neither. A few months later, in mid-1911, he was in fact asked to run for a Reichstag seat on the National Liberal ticket. Characteristically, he insisted on being jointly nominated by the National Liberals and the other liberal party, the Progressives, presumably in order to remain outside and, as he perhaps saw it, above routine party strife. But then matters dragged on for months and came to nothing. Rathenau's dealings with the local party activists in the Frankfurt on the Oder, the electoral district concerned, turned out awkward, and, fearing the humiliation of losing at the polls, he decided to withdraw. Once again, his failing social skills stood in the way. Once again, he could blame his Jewishness, though it was clearly not a major factor. In any case, the doorway to the corridors of power continued to be closed to him.

Given the special characteristics of Imperial Germany, however, he could still hope to gain influence through indirect routes. After all, he was by then safely ensconced as a member of the small elite of businessmen and intellectuals that interacted intensively with high officials, ministers, chancellors, and even the Kaiser. Rathenau was, as we saw, on friendly terms with Chancellor Bülow till the latter's fall from office in 1909. He then hastened to congratulate Bülow's successor, Theobald von Bethmann Hollweg, on his appointment and soon became a more or less regular guest at the new chancellor's home. In a diary entry of July 25, 1911, Rathenau reported a two-hour "tea" with Bethmann, during which they talked about all current political problems. They discussed the Hansabund, a left-liberal association of big and small industrialists that attempted to counteract the general political turn to the right after the collapse of the Bülow Bloc. They examined "exhaustively," as Rathenau noted, the new constitutional arrangement for the province of Alsace-Lorraine, conquered from France in the war of 1870–71 and at the time suffering endemic public unrest. Finally, they dealt with the so-called second Moroccan crisis, which was reaching its climax during these very days.[30] The Germans were by then trying once more to put a halt to the creeping French takeover of Morocco, using a combination of diplomacy and military threats, and repeatedly heating up the international situation. Matters were complicated by the fact that Germany was clearly trying to use the conflict to break up the Triple Entente between Britain, Russia, and France. It was a sensitive political situation and matters were only discussed within a select circle of people. Rathenau was apparently among them. A few days later, he was dining with Bethmann, "on the balcony in the dark," discussing first the stock exchange and then the deteriorating Moroccan affair. "I commented in detail," Rathenau wrote in his diary, referring to his suggestion of quickly negotiating a compromise with France. Bethmann on his part was seeking information on the interests of the industrialists involved, who were all worried by the volatile reaction of the stock market and anxious to calm the situation. He then accompanied Rathenau to his car, using this courtesy for a further exchange of views in an intimate and friendly fashion. Coming home, Rathenau wrote Bethmann a letter on points he had apparently omitted during their conversation.[31]

Nor were such meetings rare occasions. On December 27, 1912 Rathenau spent another long evening alone at Bethmann's estate talking politics. They discussed naval affairs, by then a cause of growing tension with Britain; matters related to the then-raging Balkan war; Austria's risky political maneuvering—in fact world affairs from Korea to Mexico as well as various domestic issues. At the end Bethmann even asked Rathenau "to sound out Erzberger," the Catholic Center politician, who was endangering the government at the time by his insistence on the repeal of the draconic Jesuit Law forbidding the order from operating in Germany, and to report back to the chancellor.[32] In addition to such informal discussions,

Rathenau was composing semiofficial memoranda from time to time, sending them either directly to the chancellor's office or to various ministers and other leading officials.

Of course, Rathenau was not alone in wielding this kind of influence. Government officials at the highest level participated actively in the life of Germany's highest social circles. The Kaiser, too, appeared at some of their lunches and dinners, sometimes—as for instance on February 13 and June 6, 1912 and again on July 8, 1913—engaging Rathenau alone or with others in long conversations on various topics of the day, participating in their gossip, and joining in their jokes.[33] Lesser people too—ambassadors, Foreign Office officials, and the like—repeatedly appeared on these and other occasions. Rathenau enjoyed a measure of familiarity with them all, like other powerful industrialists and financiers. He might have had occasional influence on their deliberations, but such influence was marginal and it did not lead to a more significant political engagement on his part.

Possibly this was all he wanted. Under such circumstances he could offer his advice but also decline further involvement if he so wished. On July 25, 1912, following a long conversation with Bethmann, Rathenau reported that "Bethmann urged me three times, the last time as he accompanied me to the car, to elaborate for him my ideas regarding electoral reform. Each time I declined: he has better people for that among his staff."[34] In private conversations Rathenau must have taken a stand on this issue, the main domestic one in Prussian politics throughout the late imperial period, but he was not ready to spell it out publicly. He preferred to stay uncommitted at this point, though he did put pen to paper in order to get his views across somewhat later on.

In an essay entitled "Parliamentarism" Rathenau weighed the pros and cons of a full parliamentary system.[35] Clearly, neither the Reichstag, based upon universal male suffrage, much less the Prussian Diet, based on the three-class system of voting, represented true parliamentarism. And it was in this semi-parliamentarism that Rathenau now saw the source of Germany's lack of political direction and its relative weakness as a world power. In the modern world, he argued, governments need to achieve more than purely administrative tasks. Having to take the lead, they require the best minds of the nation, emerging out of the party-political contest and acting according to the will of the people. In a country that excelled in economics, science, and technology, indeed in culture as a whole, the lack of a gifted political elite was incomprehensible. It indicated a general paralysis induced by a system that excluded talent and left politicians to act within parliaments that lacked concrete responsibility, providing its members no chance to experience the workings of real power. Rathenau seemed to be taking a clear stand, but—like Max Weber and Friedrich Naumann, for instance, and like many other moderate liberals in Imperial Germany—while he did argue for political reform he did not consider it urgent. Neither Rathenau nor any of his like-minded members of the Imperial German elite took a truly oppositional stand at this point. They favored change, but only if it proceeded cautiously and did not rock the boat too much. They realized reform was needed, but would easily be satisfied with less than its full measure. They wanted improvement, but without endangering existing achievements. Protecting the status quo was clearly more important a goal for them than experimenting with seriously improving it.[36]

Rathenau, still hoping for a personal political breakthrough, was perhaps particularly cautious. His piece on parliamentarism was published only in April 1914, though it was dated 1913 in his collected works, and that too in the pages of the faraway Viennese *Neue Freie Presse*. He was probably "seeking to restrict readership as far as possible to those who [were] really interested," we read in one of his private letters regarding an earlier piece.[37] And the opening lines of the article explained why. In present-day Prussia, according to Rathenau, one could express one's views on all matters, except parliamentarism. "Whoever does not conform with what exists remains for ever outside; he is no better than a supporter of free trade, a republican, a Social Democrat."[38] In order to avoid exclusion, particularly as a Jew, Rathenau had to tread lightly. While he called for reform, this was a matter for the future, "perhaps within fifteen years"—a delay that was acceptable because conditions in Germany, far from being badly flawed, were on the contrary "so agreeable." The German Volk, he thought, was only concerned with its economic well-being. It declined to see the growing political problems within and without. It needed a veritable shock before it could truly assess the situation and before a new era of reform could finally come about.[39]

This was true of Rathenau himself, too. After all, he was more often than not in basic agreement with the powers that be, and even when he found himself in opposition, he moved cautiously, expressing his views, if at all, in ways that would not cause him loss of favor. Thus, he may have managed to keep his various personal ties intact, but was bound to remain politically feeble. In the end, not achieving what he set out to achieve, he turned back to his familiar safe haven in the world of industry. This was a recurrent pattern in his life. Rathenau was never truly prepared to leave his business career in order to become a full-time writer, as we saw and shall see later again. He had rejected painting even more definitely earlier on. During the prewar years he was likewise never prepared to take the full risk of plunging into politics. As long as he could fit everything in, he was ready to try his hand at new ventures—but no more than that. In business, after all, he could always fall back on his father's eminence. For some time he could rely on Harden's support in his literary ventures, too. In politics, he knew, he would have to act on his own. But the risk was too great. After all, he had always relied on family ties, and while this was a common pattern of action within Germany's uppermost elite at the time, for a Jew it was a particularly crucial prerequisite for success. Evidently one could "make it" only if one had proper backing. For men in lower social strata, the situation was different. Taking a risk was unavoidable for them. For Harden, for instance, letting go of his Jewish ties proved an advantage, even a precondition on the road to success. For Rathenau such a step was unthinkable.

4

Captain of Industry, Literary Star, Lonely Man

DESPITE HIS MANY interests and ambitions, Rathenau held on to his secure position as an industrialist and business-man. While he did resign from active duty in the BHG, he re-mained on its board of directors and continued to be involved in the business affairs of AEG as well. His incursions into pol-itics came to nothing and his often expressed wish to dedicate himself completely to a literary career remained rhetorical.

In fact, despite its difficult beginnings, Rathenau's business career quickly took off again. By 1904, as we have seen, he was a member of the supervisory board of AEG and while this might have been no more than a conciliatory gesture on the part of his father at the time, in 1910 Walther was nominated as the board's deputy chairman, thus being once more fully in-tegrated in the concern's major business activities. The promo-tion followed a successful negotiation, led by Rathenau, for the AEG takeover of a majority holding in the metalworking firm

AEG's Berlin small motor production plant around 1900. Courtesy Bildarchiv
Preussischer Kulturbesitz, Georg Buxenstein und Co.

of Felten & Guilleaume. By then AEG was in the process of acquiring its own iron and steel plants, enlarging its cable production operations, establishing automobile factories, glass
and brass works, and more. Such expansion fitted the economic
style of this era, sometimes called organized capitalism. Accordingly, the economy was dominated by large-scale cartels
and huge vertical firms, requiring for their smooth functioning
a great deal of internal coordination and at least some measure
of outside control or supervision by the state and its agencies.
The system first evolved in the coal mining sector, but was later
proven particularly effective in the electrical industry. Whereas in the coal industry, syndicates and even trusts were needed
for maintaining prices and controlling the market, cooperation
and coordination became essential for the very existence of the
electrical branch; its long-term development and its profitable
expansion depended on such tactics. In fact, by the beginning
of the twentieth century the electric industry in Imperial Ger-

many was considered a duopoly, since it consisted of two major players: Siemens and AEG. Nevertheless, even as late as 1914, roughly four-fifths of German electrical power was produced not by these two giants but by other large- and medium-scale companies, above all by the various mining firms, who, having learned to supply their own needs for electric power, set out to compete with the experts over the right to expand this supply to their entire regions and beyond. The first contact and eventually also the first conflict between Walther Rathenau and Hugo Stinnes, the legendary industrialist from the Ruhr, involved their competing interests in this field.

It all started well enough. Stinnes, visiting Berlin in September 1905, attempted to negotiate with Emil Rathenau a settlement that would allow some sort of division of labor in producing and distributing electrical power in the Ruhr. When he was frustrated by the older man's unyielding opposition, it was Walther who seemed more amenable and, acting from his post in the BHG, managed to suggest a compromise and even sign a preliminary agreement. He then visited Stinnes in Mülheim, his hometown, and although he later reported to have been "completely appalled" by the local *Unkultur*, he did continue to prefer peaceful coexistence with Stinnes.[1] Despite his efforts, the original agreement eventually ran into difficulties. AEG used the first opportunity to free itself of prior commitments, established its own electricity plant in the Ruhr, and then, adding insult to injury, appointed Walther Rathenau as chairman of the plant's supervisory board. At first Walther seemed to be able to defuse the situation. He invited Hugo and Cläre Stinnes to Berlin, treated them to a fancy dinner at the Automobile Club, and tried to resolve matters in a moderate and conciliatory fashion. As we have seen before, he really did not believe in competition and his business strategy had always been that of striving for cooperation. Afterwards, the situation did seem to be cleared up and business took its successful course, despite occasional vexations and disappointments. But when matters went truly astray once again, while Rathenau was on his first African trip, he lost interest, claimed to have no mandate to deal with the issues involved, and withdrew. "The Jews of Berlin finally unveiled themselves" was Cläre Stinnes's verdict.[2]

In any case, Walther Rathenau's overall record in this world of high capitalism and complex systems was somewhat mixed. As in other spheres, before and after, he had some successes and some failures. Although he was surely becoming ever more experienced and ever more sophisticated in his dealings, the shadow of his father continued to hang over him. It sometimes appeared as if Emil was intentionally throwing his weight around so as to embarrass Walther and embitter even his better days. In the end the younger man could draw little satisfaction from it all and was almost forced to seek alternatives. These were always there, bringing him some, though never quite sufficient consolation. Rathenau was by then a frequent contributor to the *Die Zukunft,* and became intensely engaged in dialogue with like-minded people on various intellectual and artistic matters, publicly and privately. Only fragments of these numerous encounters can be retrieved today, but even the little we know confirms the impression that his circle of acquaintances was rapidly growing and that he had become entangled in the intellectual life of his time, even beyond the limits of Berlin.[3] Rathenau would send offprints of his essays to various people, often to other authors, and they almost invariably replied, sometimes further engaging him in diverse literary arguments. Since he was always eager for feedback and in need of encouragement, it was Rathenau that initiated such contacts. By then he knew, of course, that unveiling his views in public could be hurtful, too. Critics were sometimes congratulatory, but they could also be disparaging, even malicious.

In 1908 Rathenau published his second volume of collected essays, entitled *Reflexionen*. Though the book sold for the strikingly low price of three marks, it was printed in an unusually large format, on particularly heavy paper and with titles and subtitles in bright, elaborately designed red letters.[4] The thirteen reprinted pieces were divided into three sections, dealing with ethics, aesthetics, and economics, followed toward the end by a fourth section, entitled "Unwritten Writings," containing as many as 197 aphorisms varying in length between a single sentence and a few paragraphs. The longest section of the book, dealing with economic matters, reflected Rathenau's handling of issues that lay within his professional expertise. Interestingly, however, he was far more daring and original when he dealt with topics that were less familiar to him, allowing himself greater intellectual boldness and more unrestrained fantasy. Characteristically, the provocative piece of 1904, "On Weakness, Fear and Purpose," opened the book,[5] and the first section also included "A Tractate on Bad Conscience," a convoluted piece, originally written a year earlier, dealing—though indirectly—with a contemporary controversy on reform of the German criminal code. Rathenau treats this subject allegorically, weaving a story set in France of the Napoleonic era, at the center of which stands the universal issue of fratricide, presented in the form of a dream. The intricate approach suggests a deeper layer of meaning. In this piece, written shortly after the death of his brother Erich, Rathenau was trying to come to terms with his contradictory feelings towards him and with his barely suppressed sense of guilt. His pain is clearly apparent here but so is his firm resolve to overcome it and get a new hold on life.[6]

The section dealing with aesthetics contains a reworking of an essay that had appeared in his earlier volume, *Impressions*, under the title "The Physiology of Art Appreciation." It is interesting to observe how the more mature Rathenau changed the lighthearted tone of the older version to fit his new philo-

sophical ambitions, while retaining the main ideas virtually unchanged: "Aesthetic pleasure is engendered," Rathenau claimed,
"when a hidden general law is perceived." He then examined
other definitions of artistic appreciation, carefully constructing tools for the criticism of modern art, to be applied in the
following piece. Thus, in "On Modern Painting," Rathenau
left out the immediate controversial issue that had motivated
him three years earlier to express his views on this subject, but
maintained much of the text, appearing yet again under the
original subtitle: "Critique of Modernity." The earlier debate,
dealing with the tension between French Impressionism and
German "fantastic" art à la Arnold Böcklin, no longer seemed
relevant now. The basic claim, though, remained intact. Modern art, wrote Rathenau—Max Liebermann's nephew, member
of the Pan Club, patron of such artists as Edvard Munch—
tends to blend our sensitivity and stress the outward, visual
side of painting at the cost of its deeper meaning. As in the first
version of this article, Rathenau was calling for the revival of
what he considered a true German art, reasserting itself in
order to express the special and unique German soul, thus regaining its well-deserved glory.[7]

Only some of the ideas that appeared under the title "Unwritten Writings" at the end of *Reflections* were actually more
pretentious. It is also only here that both the paradoxical title
and the aphorismic form suggest a direct Nietzschean influence. The first edition of Nietzsche's collected works had appeared in 1906 and the first volume included his "Five Prefaces
to Five Unwritten Books," originally presented as a gift to
Cosima Wagner in 1872 and not generally known before. Nietzsche's aphorisms were, of course, quite famous by the time
Rathenau published his own. Although they could hardly be
compared in sophistication or originality, Rathenau's fragments were wide-ranging in subject matter, sometimes intrigu-
ing, occasionally even brilliant. Interestingly, most of them

dealt with issues that had been briefly formulated by Rathenau somewhat earlier, during a trip to Greece in the spring of 1906. At the time, he sketched his ideas under the heading "Breviarium Mysticum." It was found among Rathenau's papers after his death, and contained references to the central theme of his future writings: the meaning of the human soul and its overriding significance even in modern times, in the midst of a materialistic world, ruled by cold reason and practical calculations.

Doubtlessly, *Reflections* could be considered a pompous book, in form as well as in content. Kessler reported that it had been generally ignored and often treated "smilingly and with scorn."[8] But this has been shown to be hardly supported by the facts.[9] The book attracted considerable attention, though perhaps less for its ideas than for the identity of its author. It was reviewed rather widely in the German-speaking press and finally established Rathenau's fame as a writer. It also aroused the interest of Samuel Fischer, the up-and-coming publisher in Berlin of these days, bolstered by a team of outstanding professional editors, who then took Rathenau under his wing and fortified his independence as an author.

Most telling were the contradictory attitudes towards the book expressed by some of Rathenau's close associates at the time. Hugo von Hofmannsthal had been initially impressed by Rathenau and at first repeatedly sought his company. By 1908, he seemed to have changed his mind. On receiving a copy of *Reflections* he reacted with open condescension: "What a subtly unpleasant book!" he wrote in a letter to Kessler, "What a mixture of pedantry, pretension, snobbism . . ." He seemed to take particular offense at that "stale and crafty 'Deutschheit,'" which according to him was so often "reproduced" by Jews.[10] While his own Jewish ancestry and his repeated efforts not to be considered a "Jewish author" must have played a role in this reaction, it also reflected a more general attitude. Here was a wealthy industrialist, writing about the interests of the downtrodden; a businessman in the gown of a philosopher; a Jew amplifying the virtues of Germanness. The combination made people uneasy, sometimes outright suspicious, even hostile. Many seemed to discern here a sheer lack of authenticity, combining what they considered the worst features of both Jews and Prussians.

But not everyone shared this attitude. Among others, Stefan Zweig published an admiring review in the *Neue Freie Presse*, and Rudolf Borchardt saw in it the only book dealing with "living and lived politics" that had appeared in years. The author, according to him, was a writer of the first order, endowed with that rare quality, so neglected but so needed in the service of present-day Germany, a quality that he chose to call "universality."[11] Borchardt, however, preferred not to publish his views and conveyed them only to his friends. This may not have bolstered Rathenau's standing in public but it was the beginning of several years of a close relationship between the two.

In any case, *Reflections* put Rathenau on the map, so to speak, even if its success was by no means decisive. Clearly, an independent career in literature had not as yet brought him fame and prominence of the kind he was seeking. While at one point he wished to "buy himself a cottage and practice philosophy," Rathenau never managed to leave business behind and devote himself to intellectual matters alone.[12] He did, however, buy himself a "cottage," though it was more of a miniature palace. In September 1909, Rathenau paid over a quarter of a million Reichsmarks to the Prussian royal exchequer for a small *Schloss* (mansion) in the little town of Bad Freienwalde. The land had originally been the property of Friedrich Wilhelm II, a late eighteenth-century Prussian monarch, who had built upon it an intimate country house for his second wife, Frederike Luise, completed just before his death in 1797. David Gilly, one of Prussia's outstanding architects at the time, and Peter Joseph Lenné, a renowned garden planner, collaborated in building the little palace, decorating it in a mixture of late baroque and Prussian classicism. The queen's life there had never been quite as happy as she had hoped. Still, a whole mystique of feminine court life grew up around the building, giving it a unique flavor. Rathenau renovated the run-down two-story structure, added a balcony supported by Greek-style columns, and filled the rooms with period furniture, paintings, and precious objects. It was meant to be his refuge from the bustle of city life, but the entire project was also a kind of artistic adventure, giving him an opportunity to parade his wealth, his status, and especially his refined taste.

On Good Friday 1911, Harry Kessler—by then no longer an unqualified admirer of Rathenau—visited Freienwalde and was enchanted. In his diary he described the white and silver salon with its ornamentation of trees and foliage as a "jewel of decorative art," admiring the upholding of the gentle femininity that had characterized the building in its original arrangement, and complimenting Rathenau on his "tactful" renovation.[13] Others were not always so positively impressed. Harden abhorred the very idea of a Jewish industrialist occupying a Prussian country house, and visited there as rarely as he could. Carl Fürstenberg felt that the place lacked warmth and that Rathenau's restorative efforts gave it the aura of a museum. The owner himself, however, enjoyed the time he spent in his "cottage," and during the following years spent many weekends and summers there, driving by car, a distance of some fifty miles and almost one and a half hours at that time, in order to work on his books, catch up with his correspondence, paint, and take care of the lovely garden. He brought over relatives and friends, though the house was not really equipped for an overnight stay of more than a couple of guests, and his loyal servant, Hermann, could hardly provide the company with a cuisine fit for Berlin's uppermost crust. In addition, Freienwalde was near to some Prussian aristocratic residences, Bethmann Hollweg's country

Rathenau's country house in Freienwalde today, showing the added balcony.
Courtesy Dr. Reinhard Schmook.

house for instance, and these—though never prone to accept newcomers—added their prestige by mere proximity.

At the same time Rathenau was also busy designing and constructing his city residence in the Königsallee 65 in Grunewald, Berlin's most elegant western suburb. During his earlier days in Berlin he had made use of the family property in the Tiergarten quarter. But when he came back from his second African tour, in the fall of 1908, his father let him know that he had managed to acquire the neighboring plot and was planning to move from his modest bourgeois residence to a new "Palais," to be built for the aging couple in the familiar Victoria-Strasse. Walther must have been annoyed, but this did finally give an additional push to his building spree. In Berlin he operated not merely as a conservator cum renovator but also as his own architect, leaving only the final drafts to the professionals. "I seem to manage the finest work only in visual things," he wrote to Lili Deutsch, and one cannot help thinking of the fine paintings he was producing during these very years: landscape pastels and a self-portrait in 1909, an especially impressive portrait of his mother in 1910, and many pencil and charcoal sketches. This, as usual, brought him no real satisfaction: "it is too easy, without deep responsibility," he complained, "almost a woman's work."[14]

Having carefully watched over every detail, Rathenau moved into his new home on January 17, 1911. It was a villa in the Prussian classical style, an inward-looking, two-story building visually dominated by straight vertical and horizontal lines, with a narrow entrance, as if to fit only one person, and spacious rooms—spartan and ostentatious at the same time. Kessler, who found Freienwalde so lovely, thought the house in the Königsallee was a caricature. He detested what he considered its "antiquated interior," the lack of any "family context," especially the tastelessness and the snobbism it radiated. More

Walther Rathenau, St. George's Church, Bad Freienwalde, 1917.
Courtesy Walther Rathenau Gesellschaft.

Rathenau's portrait of his mother,
Mathilde Rathenau, 1910. Courtesy
Walther Rathenau Gesellschaft.

even: he sensed in it "dead *Bildung*, petty sentimentality, and stunted eroticism."[15] Years later, after Rathenau's assassination, the Viennese Jewish author Joseph Roth was impressed in a very different way: "He lived wonderfully," Roth wrote in his *Reports from Berlin 1920–33*, "among great books and rare objects, amid beautiful paintings and colors, with timeless, sublime, tiny, fragile, impressive, tenderness-eliciting, powerful, dreamy things; surrounded by evidence of the human past, of human wisdom, human beauty, human strength and human sufferings; by the breath of the eternally human."[16]

This, then, was now the center of Rathenau's social life. Being unmarried, he had to initiate and arrange for hospitality by himself, serving occasional breakfasts, lunches, or dinners in grand style, as required. Kessler reported "too many people" on one such occasion—a gathering where no real contact could be made. There were always too many Jews and too many intellectuals for his own particular taste.[17] Others had different complaints. This is how Franz Blei, an Austrian writer, critic, and translator, living in Berlin at the time, described an evening at Rathenau's villa: "Dinner, the one that was being served, was in quantity and quality so modest, that . . . after the first experience of fish, lamb cutlets, and dumplings—and there was never anything else—[everyone] pretended to eat while they in fact made sure to have eaten before. Finally, after a tiny glass of champagne, never refilled by the servant, appeared that bottomless pot of black coffee, intended to keep the guests awake till the early morning for conversation . . ."[18] And in such conversations, one hears repeatedly, Rathenau was the main if not the only speaker.

Walther Rathenau's villa in Berlin. Courtesy Amir Teicher.

This is probably a particularly malicious description, but evenings at Rathenau's could surely never hope to be like the carefully conceived occasions at the Fürstenbergs, at the Deutsches, or for that matter at Edith and Fritz Andreae's, Walther's sister and brother in law. Moreover, all these soirées in Rathenau's town villa and his country house could not cover up the fact that much of the conviviality characteristic of his earlier years in Berlin was now lost. Rathenau usually impressed new acquaintances by his deep voice, his thoughtfulness, the width of his interests, and his conversational brilliance. But with time, some of his best friends, men who had been enchanted by him, lost their patience. It is interesting to follow up Kessler's growing frustration with Rathenau, disclosed in his diaries. The two disagreed on substance, such as on the merits of modern art in general and on the work of individual artists in particular, but Kessler was finally exasperated by matters of style. Rathenau would speak "like a preacher or a rabbi, never less than quarter of an hour, a speech instead of an answer, little content, mostly dogma," he wrote, unable to hide the streak of antisemitism that cropped up occasionally in his diary.[19] And Kessler was not alone. Hofmannsthal was among those who were annoyed by Rathenau's patronizing habits, but his distaste for Rathenau went much further. In a diary entry from December 4, 1911, Kessler reported Hofmannsthal's statement that he had never known anyone in whose company he felt so completely void, anyone who so completely canceled him out, so fully dismissed his whole being. This, one ought to remember, from a man who was then at the peak of a splendid career. By the end of 1911 Hofmannsthal already had behind him two premieres of operas by Richard Strauss for which he had written the librettos—*Elektra* and *Rosenkavalier*. The reported conversation took place only a couple of days after the first performance of his *Jedermann* in Berlin, directed by Max Reinhardt, which was soon to prove his most popular play and

is to this day an obligatory part of Germany's theatrical reper-
toire. Moreover, his reaction to Rathenau, he insisted, was no
reflection upon himself. It was entirely due to the fact that Rathenau, as he saw it, was a creature of pure pose, to whom no
one could really relate and with whom no one could develop
true friendship. Others present at this conversation seemed to
concur, and one of them jokingly described Rathenau as "Jeho-
vah at the coffee table," an early version of the sobriquets that
would often be hurled at him during the postwar years: "Jesus
in a tailcoat," "the prophet in a tuxedo," or, to quote Kerr, "the
Diogenes of large-scale industry."[20]

Gerhart Hauptmann, yet another famous author of the
time, and since 1905 likewise a close friend of Rathenau, reacted more mildly to Rathenau's failings. The two seem to have
had much in common, at least during the first decade of their
friendship, and Rathenau's flights into the world of art and philosophy were often appreciated and even encouraged by Hauptmann. On February 26, 1911, while Rathenau was visiting the
Hauptmanns on the Italian Riviera, we read the following in
his diary: "Hauptmann seriously wishes I would abandon industry for literary work. Scruples not accepted."[21] Still, he too
did not always take Rathenau seriously. He addressed him
mockingly as "Sir Walther," and seems to have never forgotten
the fact that Rathenau was after all a wealthy businessman, even
when he himself was well over his proletarian phase, and had
become a property owner in his own right.

In the end, no one was more positively inclined toward Rathenau, and for so long, as Maximilian Harden. We have seen
him opening the pages of *Die Zukunft* to Rathenau and intro-
ducing him to the literary elite of Berlin. One can likewise follow their friendship through thick and thin in some fifteen
years of their correspondence. The exchange reveals a steady
flow of communication, overcoming temporary ruptures and
always remaining as affectionate as was possible between these

two proud and self-centered men. In the early years, there were occasional disputes of the kind that are unavoidable between author and publisher, as well as some disagreements over principles, none of which seriously disturbed their relationship. Later on, as we saw, Harden resented Rathenau's ventures into politics, while Rathenau on his part, came to dislike Harden's journalistic eccentricities. With time the two disagreed ever more frequently on matters related to artistic taste and literature, sometimes so much so that the atmosphere between them became less than cordial. Still, both cherished their relationship and managed, time and again, to heal sporadic frictions and regain intimacy. For Rathenau, who had no family of his own, Harden's friendship was of the utmost importance. But Harden too was ready for many concessions in order to uphold it. He wrote witty personal letters to Rathenau, often relying on their common Jewish background, and kept up their regular meetings, discussing matters till late at night, even when disagreements were strongest.

Harden's allegations against the Kaiser and his entourage in 1907 created the first serious rift between the two friends, as we have seen.[22] While Rathenau refused to line up publicly in Harden's defense, in private he apparently made every effort to explain and excuse his action. Kessler recounts a breakfast with Hofmannsthal and Rathenau at the Automobile Club in December 1906, in which the latter took a psychological approach —a Freudian approach, one is tempted to say, narrating the sad tale of Harden's early life and describing him as a mistreated child who always remained in a state of indignation; a complicated person but by no means an evil spirit. Even the cynical Kessler found this touching, if not entirely convincing.[23] But at that time, it was Harden that was unforgiving. Later on, when Rathenau's efforts to enter politics required public support precisely of the kind that Harden could elicit, the latter was less than forthcoming. And with time, the two saw less and less of each other. Through much of 1911 and early 1912, while they continued to send each other offprints and books, even gifts and flowers on special occasions, their correspondence often consisted of nothing but strings of excuses—for not meeting, for not taking time out for each other, for telling or not telling the whole truth, and so on.

The final break came unexpectedly. It was related to yet another problematic relationship within the web of interests and emotions that bound together the Berlin social elite. The rich and cultured in fin-de-siècle Berlin made up a human environment in which bourgeois conventions and virtues were proudly upheld for all to see while new social options and new kinds of license were experimented with repeatedly. Women in this environment were ostensibly kept in their traditional place at home. Since they usually had servants, even domestic chores did not really preoccupy them. They had much leisure and were often in a position to acquire a fair amount of *Bildung*, enough, sometimes, to make them not only desirable wives and impressive hostesses but also real partners in intellectual and cultural matters—usually to their husbands and occasionally to their lovers. Friendships between educated men and such able women were of course nothing new. Goethe's strings of talented women friends and his few but well-documented love affairs always served as a model, while many similar cases were recorded during the following century. Beginning sometime in 1905–6, Rathenau, himself unmarried, was deeply involved in such a relationship. The woman in question was Franziska Elizabeth Kahn, known as Lili, married since 1893 to Felix Deutsch, eleven years her elder and Emil Rathenau's second in command at AEG. Lili Deutsch held elegant soirées in her home and befriended many interesting men, among them both Maximilian Harden and Walther Rathenau. However, it was surely her relationship with Rathenau that was soon characterized by more than the usual, acceptable mix of confidence and intimacy. For the first time, probably for the only time in his life, Rathenau had an intensive, ongoing relationship with a woman, as open and as warm as he could or would allow himself to entertain.

We know relatively little about this liaison. The two corresponded, of course, as was so common at the time, even among people who lived nearby and met very often. In addition, both were frequently away from Berlin, Rathenau on his endless business trips and both on vacations and pleasure excursions. It seems that after Rathenau's murder, his mother—anxious to preserve a spotless image of her son—destroyed Lili's letters, while Walther's disappeared with the rest of Lili's possessions as she fled from Nazi Germany in 1939. She herself perished either in Belgium as the Germans marched in, or at sea on the way to America.[24] She did, however, show all or some of the letters to Harry Kessler, when he was writing his biography of Rathenau in the late 1920s, and allowed him to quote from them on condition that he did not mention her name. Indeed, all that was left in writing from this perplexing love affair were Kessler's extensive, but selective and cautious quotes. They do tell part of the story, but they leave much to our imagination.

From the very beginning, this was a troubled relationship. As early as July 1906, we find Rathenau less than contented: "What do you actually want from me?" he writes, "With nature, with my God, and with myself I am in good standing. You know that. You too like me well enough sometimes and spoil me from time to time. What else, then, should happen? What shall I do with people? Should I arrange for a window pane in my breast so that you could afterwards record the 'Excitement'?"[25] This was apparently a reply to accusations from Lili concerning his exaggerated self-importance, his coldness, or his lack of sensitivity. He then hit back at her, blaming her "egoism" and her wish to control him. "Thank God," he concluded, "now you can quarrel with me as [much as] you wish, since in any case I would rather be scolded by you than praised by others." Early in 1909, presumably again in reply to Lili's accusations of insensitivity and lack of warmth, he found himself on the defense again. First of all, he was at pains to establish that he could not "belong completely to anyone," and this not simply because he was his own master but because he was in the hands of powers that were leading him and deciding the course of his life, regardless of his own volition. He, in fact, wills nothing, moving like "a wanderer in the night," seeing only a few steps ahead; his life—an offering to the "powers"—brings neither hope nor any real reward. Moreover, he added, it was his "polyphonic nature" that made him incomprehensible to others. "Others" couldn't hear the melody in this blend of voices, but he could; he knew it was there. She did too, he claimed, concluding rather mildly with: "Do remain what you are, and be for me what you are for me."[26]

Obviously she wanted more. She expected him, so it seems, to carry their affair beyond verbal exchanges and felt disappointed, perhaps even insulted, that he never did. It is instructive to remember that Lili's sister Clara had a prolonged and finally unhappy love affair at about the same time. Her partner was Otto Brahm, the famous theater critic and director of some of the major theaters in Berlin. He was an associate of Max Reinhardt and Gerhart Hauptmann but also a friend of Clara Kahn's own husband, Paul Jonas. At one point the affair almost led to the breakup of her marriage, but then, despite everything, continued in one form or another till Brahm's death in 1912. Presumably, a full-fledged affair with Rathenau would have been an option for Lili too, but it never came to that. Some of Rathenau's biographers explained his reticence by his presumed homosexuality. After all, a close friendship with a woman, often in fact a married woman, was not an unknown tactic for hiding homosexuality. Such a friendship could have also provided that much-needed feminine intimacy that was sometimes sought out by homosexual men. But in Rathenau's case other obstacles were equally impassable. An open love affair with Lili Deutsch would have certainly led to a break with Felix, her husband, long Rathenau's rival in AEG, and would have necessarily brought about unbearable tension with Emil Rathenau, too. Walther was by then no longer intimidated by his father, to be sure, but he did feel responsible for him. Following Erich's death, Emil, then sixty-five years old, was never his robust self again. He needed both Deutsch's and Walther's assistance. Having tried all his life to gain his father's love and respect, Rathenau could not risk a conflict with him at this juncture. Clearly, moreover, Rathenau was not a passionate man, and as a man in his forties, neither was he any longer an excitable youth. He may have been a homosexual, but he was above all a calculating, ambitious man. He was by no means ready to jeopardize his hard-won achievements by taking a hasty amorous step. And he apparently never did.

Matters came to a head in April 1912. For a number of years by then, Lili had kept close contact with Harden too. Since Rathenau was unwilling to become her true love, nothing stopped her from having intimate relationships with other men too, if only as a way of pressuring Rathenau or of adding a heightened sense of adventure to their disappointing affair. "Did you really think I wouldn't tell you if Walther came to me?" she wrote Harden sometime in 1911. "Before you, who know more about me and see more clearly through [my] outer wrapping than anyone else," she confessed, "I show myself weak or strong, just as the case may be."[27] Finally, and for no apparent reason, she decided to show Harden a letter written by Rathenau in 1908, in the aftermath of Harden's critique of Germany's colonial policy, a bitter, unfriendly letter, as Rathenau would later characterize it himself in his diary.[28] The combination of political disagreement and private rivalry was apparently too much. At first, since Harden immediately told Rathenau of Lili's indiscretion, the two men set out to patch up their friendship. For both of them, this must have been more important than their links with Frau Deutsch. They met and discussed matters exhaustively, and on April 11, 1912, Rathenau's wrote an exemplary letter to Harden. He apologized for his fury at the time and explained that in rereading the old letter, he found some of his harsh expressions completely unwarranted. "I ask you from my heart," he concluded, "to forget this sad period of our friendship—it was fortunately short and stirred from the outside—just as I have forgotten it. I likewise forget the incomprehensible act of that woman who meant so much to me till recently and who has now so outrageously taken her leave." Rathenau assured Harden that his feelings towards him had never chilled and that his high appreciation of his person had never diminished. Let us never again allow "people, things or views," to endanger that wonderful camaraderie between us, he wrote. It is a rare gift and ought to be cherished.[29]

In fact, with time Rathenau managed to patch up relations with Lili Deutsch too. He at first resisted her approaches and avoided her for many months. Later on he allowed at least partial reconciliation. "I will never yield again," he wrote to her from a vacation in Rome in December 1913, "but neither will I ever leave you. I will always come when you call, but I will hold back in silence, as long as the time has not yet come."[30] But as in Harden's case, relations with Lili too were never the same. Meanwhile, however, Rathenau's full attention had been required elsewhere. By mid-1912, Emil Rathenau's health had deteriorated, causing general anxiety. Above all, the question of succession within AEG became increasingly urgent. Lili was naturally part of the intrigues, as the two heirs apparent happened to be her husband on the one hand and her now partly estranged almost-lover on the other.

Less self-evident was Harden's role in this later chapter of the affair. While writing friendly letters to Rathenau, he seems to have been actively intervening behind the scenes to strengthen Deutsch's position. And once again, it was Lili who made sure that Rathenau always knew of these intrigues. Finally, it became impossible to overcome the insults, the bitterness, and the mutual animosity. Rathenau, repeatedly displaying his vulnerability, continued to seek some form of reunion, but Harden was unrelenting. In the end Rathenau had to admit: "The wounding harshness of your words can mean nothing else but the desire to end our friendship. We were united for eighteen years, and I gladly think of that time with gratitude and affection. Farewell, Maxim," he wrote on December 29, 1912.[31] He did leave the door open for second thoughts even then, but matters between the two only grew uglier. Insults over the telephone, in letters, and in telegrams finally drew from Rathenau a challenge to a duel, while Harden, more modern but also more cynical, and less drawn to dramatic gestures, found it beneath his dignity even to reply. It was a pathetic ending to a prolonged lovers' quarrel.

Thus, at the beginning of 1913, Rathenau stood all alone. He remained on speaking terms with Harden and on outwardly friendly terms with Lili and Felix Deutsch, but the old warmth and intimacy—to the degree that Rathenau had been able to sustain them before—were gone. By then he may not have immediately felt the weight of his loss, because he was so exceedingly busy and worried. At the beginning of May 1912, Emil's diabetic condition caused a severe gangrene. He was swiftly operated upon and a foot had to be amputated. When Emil's condition got worse, Walther moved to the upper floor of his parents' residence to keep his mother company and be constantly available for both his parents. He was doubtlessly a very devoted son. At the same time, none of his other activities came to a halt. On the weekend of June 22 and 23, for instance, he spent some time in Freienwalde, then left on Tuesday for three days in Paris, and traveled from there to Cologne and Düsseldorf before coming back for the next weekend to his country house. On the next Monday he was again on the move, this time to Basel, and the next day to Frankfurt, managing a quick trip to Bad Homburg to arrange accommodation for his ailing father in one of the better resorts of that peaceful town, and so forth and so on. The few in-between days in Berlin included endless meetings—morning, afternoon and, evening—dealing with various business matters, partly taking on his father's engagements; then he was on the road again—to Zurich, Breslau, and Milan.

And all the while he was writing—continually, even obsessively. In fact, writing had become his refuge in times of personal crisis. Indirectly, of course, it also offered him an alternative kind of human contact. Rathenau's articles were read and discussed by friends and colleagues, sometimes before and often after publication. While intimate friendships became increasingly rare in his life, the circle of more casual acquaintances around him continued to grow. For a man like Rathenau this may have even been a relief.

At first, the new writing surge seemed to start in a low key, reminiscent of the earlier stages of his literary experimentations some fifteen years earlier. Still in his "Bitterfeld exile," Rathenau began with a few technical pieces, in line with his professional expertise. He then moved to handle the Jewish issue, which was apparently often on his mind, before he took on more general philosophical themes in ethics, aesthetics, and even metaphysics. After a prolonged pause following the publication of his *Reflections*, 1911 finally saw the appearance of a string of new essays: first a piece on mass transportation, written with Wilhelm Cauer, a railroad expert and professor at the Technical University of Berlin, and a *Neue Freie Presse* article, "The Next Generation of Businessmen," dealing with the difficulties of selecting Germany's future industrial leadership. Rathenau was using his professional experience to climb from local business affairs into the world of complex organized capitalism.[32]

What first drew public attention to Rathenau's rather hesitant publications at the time was a typically provocative sentence at the beginning of his article on the business community: "Three hundred men, who all know each other, hold in their hands the economic fortunes of the continent and seek their successors from their own milieu."[33] The antisemites, substituting "Jews" for "men," came back repeatedly to this quote, especially during the postwar years and in conjunction with the claims put forward in the *Protocols of the Elders of Zion*, the most effective, though entirely fraudulent antisemitic publication of the time. Rathenau never managed to distance himself from this unfortunate sentence or to assuage the suspicion it aroused. Moreover, the interesting mixture of the personal and the general in this essay, later to become Rathenau's literary trademark, was almost entirely lost because of the excessive attention given to that single quote. In fact, it was here that Rathenau formulated for the first time his main critique of Imperial Germany, arguing that in an industrial age an agricultural elite, namely the old Junker aristocracy, could no longer lead the country, and that a system hindering the development of young talents, disregarding the maxim of equitably selecting the best-qualified, and choking all idealism in favor of the simple pursuit of profit, would finally weaken both the nation and the state. And clearly Rathenau was not only thinking of the "big picture" but contemplating his own fate. He described the world of industry as it must have seemed to men in his branch: an international network, highly bureaucratized and mechanized, requiring vision, competence, and experience. While in his earlier writings, he had insisted that intuition was more important in business than rational thinking, he now argued, showing a new maturity, that "a great businessman is one who strives to realize his ideas, achieve power, and gain responsibility."[34] One could read in it his desire to take over the leadership of AEG from his father and the men of his father's generation, or one could more generally find here his overall frustration at being unable to realize his own plans, at failing to achieve true leadership and gain that greater degree of power and responsibility to which he so ardently aspired.

In the mid-1890s, when Rathenau had been thinking about his unfulfilled ambitions, he had almost instinctively turned to the "Jewish question," and this pattern was now repeated. An article published by the *Deutsche Montags-Zeitung,* making propaganda for conversion to Christianity as the only way to full Jewish assimilation, gave him the opportunity to clarify his position on this vexing subject yet again. Rathenau responded first with a lengthy essay in the form of a letter to the *Montags-Zeitung,* and then, within a few weeks, sent two additional pieces to another journal, *Der Tag.* All three were later reprinted under a single title, "The State and Judaism."[35] They provide an interesting perspective on Rathenau's mood and his changing attitudes at the time.

The first piece, originally entitled "Jewish Conversion?," argues along the lines suggested in Rathenau's early correspondence and then in his "Hear, O Israel!" Rathenau never saw conversion as "a solution," but while he had at first instinctively rejected this option, by now he was in a position to reformulate and refine his arguments. Facing closed doors first in the army and then in politics, he apparently needed to reexamine and then to reaffirm his decision to remain within the fold. Conversion, he felt obliged to reiterate, required of educated and enlightened Jews not only adherence to Christian moral tenets, which were universally acceptable, but also adoption of a "mythological dogma," as he put it. By choosing to do so, they could not hope to evade the accusation of opportunism. Neither could they ignore the fact that by doing so they were coming out in support of an outdated and patently unjust public policy. Living among many baptized Jews, such as Harden, Dernburg, and Fürstenberg, Rathenau was repeatedly faced with the pros and cons of conversion. Still, it was primarily a matter of principle as far as he was concerned. He would not pretend to believe in what seemed to him patently unbelievable; he would not pretend to make an act of faith in order to gain material advantages; and he would not be persuaded to support, even if indirectly, an unjust policy of discrimination. Surely, some of his best friends might well take offense at his arguments, but perhaps by now Rathenau did not care. After all, he was convinced that others, most emphatically his father, would fully endorse his standpoint.

The similarities between Rathenau's positions of 1897 and 1911 are obvious; but so are the differences. While in his piece of 1897 the main target was unassimilated and according to his criteria culturally inferior Jews, this time he turned against the Prussian state, its unfairness, the deep injustice it was perpetrating, and even worse, its counterproductive policies. To be sure, the hostile and condescending tone of the earlier essay had not entirely disappeared. Rathenau made it perfectly clear that the community he set out to defend included only the "cultivated Jews," whom he still urged to continue their self-improvement and compete with their Christian compatriots "in all virtues" while serving "their land" with "twice as much love."[36] But on the whole the tenor of "The State and Judaism" is very different from "Hear, O Israel!" Rathenau exposes the absurdity of state discrimination against the Jews by first ridiculing the inconsistency that allows baptized Jews to be exempt from restrictions placed upon the unbaptized, and then by stressing Jewish talent and contributions, especially in the economic sphere, as well as by insisting on their loyalty and patriotism. As in the earlier essay, he is trying to make a general point here, too. It goes well beyond the Jewish issue, he claims. It is the sorry state of Prussia that worries him, since not only Jews are blocked in their efforts to achieve leading positions. The entire bourgeoisie is systematically held back in Imperial Germany. Everywhere, the better man must retreat in the face of aristocratic supremacy and reactionary policies. Unmistakably, Rathenau is speaking of himself too. If the time of full equality for the Jews has not yet come, if one must as yet "wait for God to straighten things out," as he put it, then he himself ought to keep waiting also, confidently and patiently, meanwhile doing his best in such spheres that were open to him. "The State and Judaism" perfectly captures Rathenau's frame of mind at the time. On the one hand, he was no longer idealizing the Prussian state or venerating its nobility. Instead he felt it was lagging behind, held back by its feudal prejudices. On the other hand, he was not yet ready to give up all hope. Change was finally a matter of time, he believed. One must wait for improvements loyally and patiently, while intensifying one's efforts in one's own sphere. This for him was primarily the world of industry and finance, once again, but at the moment it also included his literary career. In any case, now that he had restated his position on the Jewish issue, the ground was cleared for his next writing venture.

Rathenau's *Critique of the Times*, powerfully promoted by his new publishing house, S. Fischer, was published on January 11, 1912.[37] A couple of days later, the first review designated it as "the book of the season."[38] It was reprinted seven times during the first year and by 1925 saw as many as twenty-eight editions. Almost overnight Rathenau became a literary celebrity, and with good reason. The book was brilliant. It was far more ambitious and far more interesting than anything Rathenau had written before. Many of the ideas in it had appeared in previous essays, but the scope and the thrust of this novella-size volume was incomparably more impressive. It contained an analysis of the origins of modernity, its effects on all spheres of life, especially in Germany, and a bold prognosis for the future. It was written in a concise and elegant style, sophisticated but eminently readable.

Apart from its ambitious scope and its appealing style, the book was a curious mixture of original insights into the issue of modernization together with a rehash of various ideas that were common currency at the time. It contained praise for the achievements of modernity together with sharp criticism of its implications and suggestions for ways to overcome them. Rathenau's description of the onset of modernity clearly relied on his industrial expertise and was therefore more concrete, even technical, than parallel descriptions given by less practical men. The central characteristic of modernity, noticeable according to Rathenau since the middle of the nineteenth century, was the process of "mechanization." This he saw as a response to the challenge of enormous population growth, which had produced an unprecedented increase in demand, leading in turn to numerous inventions, a far-reaching reorganization of production, and hence eventually to an entirely new kind of economy. Thereafter, mechanization, having succeeded in supplying the growing demand, had continued to offer further material benefits, had induced a true "hunger" for all kinds of luxury, and had thereby managed to sustain demand and encourage increased production in a never-ending cycle.

It is easy to see behind this description Rathenau's core experience in the electrical industry, above all his awareness of its success in creating rather than responding to public demand for a new form of energy supply and for the requisite technical innovations. The stress he placed in this book on the interplay of market forces, on efficient organization, on the bureaucratization of industry, and on the inevitable all-inclusive system approach to production reflected his own business practices and endowed his analysis with a coherence and concreteness rare in writings of this kind. Rathenau's stress on the role of the state in the process of modernization likewise grew from his personal experience. The various levels of government, he explained, took care of providing proper education for a population destined to live under modern conditions, supplied the necessary means of transport and communication, established a supportive judiciary, and finally endowed the whole system with a sense of stability, so crucial for ongoing prosperity. It was all happening within a society that was quickly becoming ever more homogeneous; a society within which all were required to excel in the same virtues and knew, ideally at least, only one distinction: between those who could and those who could not lead under the new circumstances. It was a very different society from the traditional, feudal one, in which a racially pure aristocracy had ruled over racially mixed lower orders, ran his argument. Echoes of his racialist distinctions between Men of Courage and Men of Fear, between the Brave and the Wise, were to be heard here. But Rathenau was convinced by now that the old elite did not possess the mental tools required for leadership in the modern world. These former "Germanic masters of the West" must now be replaced by men of another mettle: flexible, curious, rational, lacking any sense of the transcendental; like the Jews, to be sure, but not necessarily the Jews; like the Jews, but not only the Jews. It was the bourgeoisie, he explained, controlling the world of capitalism, that had proved capable of dealing with the challenge of modernity and that would eventually make the economically successful nations into the most powerful ones on earth: England first and foremost, America later, and finally Germany. If Napoleon had argued in his famous conversation with Goethe that in their day and age "politics was destiny," Rathenau was convinced that "economics was destiny" in his.[39]

Still, if forced to choose between Napoleon and Goethe, it was surely the latter that Rathenau would have preferred. The

bourgeoisie could succeed in "feeding the masses" and producing the necessary "mechanization," he wrote, but it could create neither political nor true cultural values by itself. It could
neither define nor put forward ultimate transcendental values.
These, manifested in religion, art, science, or even in politics,
were therefore sadly lacking in the modern age of mechanization. Furthermore, "mechanization" endangered "individuality" and blurred "collective identities," so that under the new
circumstances Prussia, for instance, could no longer show any
originality or vision. Even nationalism, he explained, could not
now inject society with the needed vitality. After all, it too had
grown as a reaction to the unequal division of the benefits of
mechanization. In the end, however, it could not respond to
the challenge of the capitalist age. Capitalism knew no political boundaries, just as it accepted no customs barriers. It was
cosmopolitan by definition. The tension between nationalism
and cosmopolitanism, then, was another unhealthy outcome of
the age of mechanization, forcing us to find a proper middle
way between the two, a way that would permit continuous economic growth without giving up established, age-old collective
identities.

Both the strengths and the weaknesses of Rathenau's future writings were already clear in *Critique of the Times*. But his
rush to highfalutin formulations, his vagueness, his insistence
on easy solutions to deep-seated dilemmas, and especially his
tendency to seek these solutions in higher spiritual, even mystical realms, became apparent only in his next magnum opus:
On the Mechanism of the Spirit, to which he later added the subtitle: *Concerning the Kingdom of the Soul*.[40] While *Critique of the
Times* was dedicated, fulsomely indeed, to Gerhart Hauptmann,
"as a sign of gratitude that I, as a German, owe the poet of our
era, and as a gift of friendship," the following book was rather
clumsily dedicated "to the young generation." In a letter to Lili
Deutsch four weeks after publication, Rathenau insisted that

only that generation would be capable of understanding him and acting upon his ideals. Under other circumstances, Walther implies, he would have dedicated the book to her. It *was* hers, he told her in a rare flash of self-perception, not only as a profession of faith, but also as a "sublimated experience."[41] Clearly, this book expressed his innermost convictions. He always claimed that it was his most important work. To his great disappointment, however, in contrast to the *Critique of the Times*, the second book, hastily published in the fall of 1913, had very little impact. It was first reprinted only in 1917, in conjunction with the appearance of Rathenau's third book, and was scantily and not very favorably reviewed. In fact, it remained an almost forgotten work.

The book was clearly a follow-up to the successful *Critique of the Times*. It set out to expand upon the final promise of that earlier work and to point out a way of truly overcoming the debilitating consequences of mechanization, so as to reach a new age of "pure spirituality." The major concept here was the "soul," which had first been used by Rathenau in his cryptic "Breviarium Mysticum" of 1906 and had since then constituted a major building block of his thought, central to his efforts to flee rationalism, and standing for the more refined, more sublime side of man's mental capacity. In his worldview, as we already saw, courage confronted fear and strength was pitched against wisdom. Now this dualism was expanded. The human mind, Rathenau explained, contained two basic elements, coexisting in permanent tension: the intellect—the source of calculated, goal-oriented behavior, and the soul—the home of everything that was intuitive, unspoken, authentic, and transcendental, ultimately emanating, as he believed, only from pure love. Rathenau's world was thus divided between men who possessed a soul and men who did not, between soulful and soulless civilizations, soulful and soulless nations and societies. The dividing line, however, was and remained fluid. He had always believed that "although some were born with a soul, all could attain one,"[42] and the attainment of a world populated by "soulful men" was no utopia for him, even though it still lay in the remote future.

In fact, Rathenau declared, the difference between the soulful and the soulless is best seen as a collective phenomenon, manifested in the history of various nations. While becoming soulful is a matter of evolution on all levels, it is more particularly meaningful in community life than in the life of individuals. It is on the communal level that we first encounter an emerging sense of belonging, become ready to offer the ultimate sacrifice and experience the truest love. Our soul then conquers the intellect, directing our action in the world, defining our ethical goals, and choosing for us, so to speak, the objects of our love. The capacity for such life of the soul, in any case, is not evenly distributed. It is most often and most completely found among the Germans, and then, in descending order, among the Indians, the Semites, the Greeks and Romans, and so on. As in the case of racism, Rathenau's "theory of the soul" helps distinguish among human groups and, even more importantly, helps place them top to bottom in an unchanging order. Such distinctions can be found in various spheres, he explains. Aesthetics too, for instance, can be soulful or soulless. To be sure, art cannot emerge on completely soulless ground. Once it is there, however, it will grow away from artisanry, "stepping into the heart of creation," lifting itself beyond mere stimulation of the senses onto the realm of the soul. Here, too, it is the Germanic world that ascends the uppermost heights; its "four evangelists," to use Rathenau's own language, are Shakespeare, Rembrandt, Bach, and Goethe.[43] Everywhere, artists are the pioneers of humanity en route to the Kingdom of the Soul, where men are motivated neither by their needs, nor by the will to amass property and power, nor by ambition in general. They are instead moved by the search for true joy of creation, satisfaction in labor, responsibility in social life, a sense of solidarity, and the need to serve mankind. Growing in the bosom of mechanization, such qualities will finally overcome its pervasive negative effects.[44] "Only an inner revival, a reforming of human will," according to Rathenau, can break "the magic spell of fear and craving." Neither institutions, he insisted, nor laws, nor the action of individuals will bring about a new way of life; only sentiments. Once these are transformed, the rest will follow. Finally, he concludes, Christ's main ideals will be realized. We will then stand at the gates of the "Kingdom of the Soul," that which hovers over this "poor and mundane book," as he puts it; that kingdom which is no less than heaven itself, "God's Kingdom."[45]

The most disconcerting aspect of the book revealed itself most completely, indeed in this final paragraph. Walther Rathenau, so often insisting on his Jewishness, was announcing the approach of Christ's kingdom. He, a man of vast worldly goods, known for his political and literary ambitions, was posing as an evangelist, prophesying the dawn of a new age of the soul, in which both property and honor would be discarded in favor of life in the service of others. It required a great leap of faith to take such preaching seriously. This explains, no doubt, the irritation that the book aroused. Some objected to the verbose representation of a heavenly sphere that in principle evaded the tools of analytical thinking, to the plethora of logical constructions employed in order to prove the poverty of reason. Some felt it was the work of an amateur and resented Rathenau's intrusion into spiritual matters, even while others admired him precisely for this and eulogized his ability to write "from life."

To be sure, the concepts of "mechanization" as well as the contrary "eternal soul" were not unknown themes at the time. Rathenau's book, however, failed to persuade even the true believers. In a world of open class struggle and deep social divisions, of radical political antagonisms and serious cultural rifts, his harmonizing vision struck a strange note. His efforts at dialectical thinking ended in concepts of evolution rather than revolution and in demanding change that would be carried out "within the system." According to him, the capitalist order of things, thriving on mechanization, was not to be destroyed by the approach of the "Kingdom of the Soul," but rather was kept alive in a reformed version. His was a "third way" that relied on what could be considered empty phrases and that left even his admirers less than convinced. The most crushing critique came from the pen of Robert Musil, the Austrian author, who would later capture the Rathenau of these years in his novel *A Man Without Qualities*. Now, Musil himself was a fierce critic of rationalism, and for him too the human soul was at the center of the attempt to escape its implications. But Rathenau's approach struck him as false, inauthentic, even absurd. The attack on rationalism here, he felt, was not a reflection of a mystical experience, but an all too elaborated construction, philosophically messy, a kind of "pseudo-systematics." "We do not have too much intellect and too little soul," he sarcastically announced, "but too little precision in matters of the soul."[46]

The cool reception of what he considered his most important literary-philosophical work must have added to Rathenau's dark mood at the time. Later on, he talked of a "deep contempt of my life-work," even about a crass rejection of his personality that emanated from Musil's critique.[47] As late as May 1917, while insisting that the book did "preoccupy and influence the new literature," he still found it necessary to comment that it had received the "academic honor of prophylactic disregard."[48] In the aftermath of the publication of this volume, Rathenau must have realized that his efforts to reach success by writing, in themselves—as he well knew—a sublimation of heartbreak and disappointment elsewhere, had succeeded only very partially, and in any event not nearly as much as he had wished and expected. His experience in the literary sphere reenacted prior episodes: it was only a relative success and it left him more lonely than ever before.

5

Hitting the Glass Ceiling

RATHENAU'S LAST PIECE written for *Die Zukunft* appeared at the end of October 1912. It was a patriotic cycle of poems, commemorating the so-called Prussian War of Liberation in 1813, in preparation for its approaching centenary. The cycle is divided into three sections, each opening with a biblical quote and ending with one from a Christian hymn. All in all it includes twelve rhymed verses, suffused with conventional pathos. It is more like occasional poetry, commonly written for family events, than like the antiwar poetry of Fritz von Unruh, for instance, whom Rathenau befriended during these years, or Rilke's "Duino Elegies," begun in that same year. While Rathenau was ostensibly eager to join the artistic discourse of his immediate intellectual milieu, these verses reflected poorly upon his artistic taste and indicated that he was influenced by political rather than aesthetic considerations.

Far more impressive were his directly political essays of

these years, all written in his customary elegant prose. Most were printed in the Viennese *Neue Freie Presse*, enabling Rathenau to express his views without rocking the Berlin boat too much, and all of them read like hesitant feelers of someone who was reaching into the circles of power; like memoranda sent to politicians, or like notes for future conversations with them.

In "England and Us," published in April 1912, Rathenau explored the international situation in the aftermath of the second Moroccan crisis. His perception of friends and foes was clear enough. France, "our pretty woman next door," was hoping to turn us into "a Central European second-rate power," he wrote, but she was too weak to accomplish this task on her own, hence the entente with England. That country, a "manly world empire," felt increasingly threatened by the German naval program. In a worst-case scenario it might start a preventive war against us, ran Rathenau's argument, but since it was on the whole a country that rejected "politics of the fantastic, of passion, adventure, or desperation," this was unlikely. England had, however, created an asymmetric situation by allying itself with France, and therefore it was its duty to work for relaxing the existing tension and to offer Germany "two hands in peace," or at least "a meaningful treaty of neutrality." After all, Rathenau believed, "Germany's entire political credit relies on its mission as a peaceful power." "Whoever denies that we are peace-loving and moderate, would at least not deny that we possess the wisdom of self-preservation," he wrote. The two peoples, the English and the Germans, had much in common and even admired each other, but he was convinced that at this particular moment it was England's turn to prove its friendship and show its faith in Germany.[1]

Soon afterwards, Rathenau proceeded to turn a digression in this foreign-policy treatise into a full-fledged article on what he saw as the sorry state of Prussian statesmanship. His critique appeared under the title "Political Selection" and was published this time too in faraway Vienna.[2] In a whole century, Rathenau claimed, Prussia had produced only one real statesman, and that too by sheer luck, namely Otto von Bismarck. At the same time, England had managed such a feat continuously, France intermittently, and even Austria often enough. This was not a question of "raw material," he asserted. After all, Prussia managed to produce first-rate leadership in industry and business, which differed from politics "in subject matter rather than in method." In that sphere "we have experienced true selection" based on talent, merit, and achievements, while in politics, Prussia was bound by sheer "aristocratism," to use his word, and by institutional traditionalism that made her no more than a respectable Central European power, far from what she could have been, considering her "military and cultural predominance."[3] The dangers facing Germany, according to Rathenau, did not stem from the working class, since socialism "lacked the power of positive ideas." Its "sluggishness" stemmed from the outdated prominence of the aristocracy, on the one hand, and the exclusion of the bourgeoisie, on the other. This theme preoccupied him obsessively now. It was reiterated in his "Offering to the Eumenides," published in March 1913 and a year later in his essay on parliamentarism. The situation of 1913, he now explained, was in no way like that of 1813. If Germany was to withstand the challenges of the future, it urgently needed a fundamental readjustment as a precondition for developing "a policy of strength" as clearly befitted it, and a "just constitution," as befitted any modern, life-affirming state.[4]

In sharp contrast with his books, where Rathenau was moving in spiritual, transcendental spheres, his essays of these years project the image of a practical man, sometimes using an inflated philosophical jargon to argue his case, but basically moving within the normal political discourse of his day; a man well versed in the details of Germany's foreign policy no less than in its domestic affairs. In addition, a piece Rathenau published on Christmas Eve 1913, under the title "Germany's Dangers and New Goals," gave vent to his premonitions of things to come. Here, too, the matter was down to earth and practical, namely the question of the systematic acquisition of raw materials as a top priority for Germany's future. In view of its insignificant share of overseas colonies, Rathenau explained, itself a result of a patently unjust distribution of the "world inheritance," Germany was sooner or later bound to reach an economic impasse. Since it necessarily depended on world commerce, nationalistic economic policies in general and protective tariffs in particular could only worsen the situation. Prussian feudalism (*sic!*), he insisted, dictated a tariff policy on agricultural goods, created unjust profits for aristocrats at the cost of everyone else, and continually exacerbated relations with potentially friendly countries. Assuming this situation could not be radically changed, there remained only one solution, Rathenau concluded: the creation of a customs union of Central European countries, later to be joined by the major Western powers too. Germany would thus manage to organize an economic unit of equal size and equal capacity to the American one, and contribute to the development of all, even the most backward regions "within our own sphere." "At the same time," he continued, "this would rob nationalist hatred among the nations of its sharpest sting."[5] What kept Europe from peaceful coexistence was no longer, according to him, the different "religions, languages, cultures, and constitutions," but problems of economic competition. "If Europe's economy melts into one common unity, and that is likely to happen sooner than we think," was Rathenau's prophecy, "so will its politics. This means neither world peace nor disarmament nor general lassitude, but mitigation of conflicts, conservation of power, and the solidarity of civilization."[6]

Once again, hints of such a European vision could be found

in Rathenau's writings earlier too, but it was now set out unambiguously. It was not an outgrowth of well-wishing idealism but a result of hard-nosed practical considerations. Rathenau sought for ways to respond to concrete economic challenges and for means to overcome the obviously approaching political crisis. At this stage his ability to think on a grand political scale, setting out a strategy for solving Germany's predicament, became apparent. The main pillars of his analysis were his respect for Great Britain, his disdain for France, and his envy of America. Upon these premises, he then evaluated the strength as well as the weakness of his beloved Germany, and became well aware of the need to stay watchful lest she would lose even her current, limited world status or plunge into a ruinous war. Placed under pressure, Rathenau realized, Germany might be forced to take ever more radical measures, but the consequences were far from predictable. In the worst case they might turn out to be catastrophic. Rathenau was aware of the risky combination of Germany's domestic and international policies, though he never wavered in his fundamental loyalty to, even trust in, the present constitution of the Reich. Despite his critique, he remained a royalist, basically affirming the system of both capitalism and imperialism, and his loyalty and trust would remain intact even in much more precarious situations in the years to come.

Meanwhile, the international atmosphere grew very tense. Years of imperial rivalry and a dense network of alliances and counteralliances threatened to bring to an end the fragile European peace. But by July of 1914, most people still did not expect war to break out. The bourgeoisie was enjoying its summer vacation. Rathenau's parents were convalescing in Switzerland. At the end of the month, weeks after the international crisis began following the Sarajevo assassination of the Austrian Archduke Francis Ferdinand and his wife, Rathenau himself was still confident that war could be averted. "Six powers fear and abhor war," he stated in a short piece, written towards the end of July and published by the daily *Berliner Tageblatt* on July 31.[7] Four of them had no real interest in the emerging crisis at all, since it was in fact no more than a local affair and ought to be resolved by a compromise. After all, "the issue of whether or not Austrian representatives would be able to participate in arbitrating Serbian internal affairs is no reason for a world war," was his sensible judgment.[8] But Rathenau knew that war was a real option, and under certain circumstances, he too would see in it a desirable option for Germany. He must have been well aware that deep and long-standing rivalries were motivating the European powers, beyond the immediate incident in Sarajevo. In fact, by the time his article appeared the die had been already cast.

War began with resounding cries of enthusiasm everywhere in Europe, most particularly in the Prussian capital of Berlin. Lower-class people, bourgeoisie, and aristocrats—all suddenly seemed to breathe a sigh of relief: the time of procrastination was over, decisions would have to be finally made, and the nation as a whole was expected to come together in an effort to achieve a resounding victory in what was considered by most men and women—in fact on both sides of the lines dividing Europe—an honorable and just war. Germany, with its main ally the Austro-Hungarian empire, flanked by Turkey and later on by an assortment of occupied smaller powers in the Balkans, faced a war on two fronts with the formidable Triple Entente of France, Great Britain, and Russia. These quickly marshaled the human and material resources of their vast imperial territories and were helped first by Japan in the Far East and later on by the forces of the United States. But in August 1914, the crowds gathering in the streets of Berlin enjoyed a rare moment of hope, solidarity, and a sense of brotherhood. Many volunteered for army service, including well-known personalities from all walks of life, and all expected a quick victory, say by Christmas of that same year. The Prussian-German army, led for the last time by the generals of the old regime, proudly marched into battle.

Rathenau, not quite forty-seven years old, was no longer a candidate for recruitment. On August 6 he sent a handwritten note to Bethmann Hollweg, asking to be employed in the service of his fatherland, mentioning his year in the army reserve, his knowledge of English, French, and some Italian, finally also his capacity to take on any administrative job, attained in many years of working as an industrial entrepreneur.[9] This was a strange letter, no doubt. After all, Bethmann knew him well enough and needed no such self-effacing résumé. Moreover, by the time the letter was sent, Rathenau was already active on two other fronts, so to speak, taking the initiative himself. To begin with, he now wished to adjust the idea of a European customs union to the new circumstances. In the prewar years, such a union had been intended to counteract British competition and ward off American supremacy. Now, in wartime, Rathenau was hoping for it to emerge from victory and bolster Germany's preeminence for all eternity, no less. It was to be first established with Austria-Hungary and then extended to include defeated France and Italy together with various other European states, large and small. To be sure, Rathenau was not the only one who argued in this vein. By September 1914 Bethmann Hollweg was discussing with a number of highly placed business magnates, and under the watchful eyes of his vigorous minister of internal affairs, Clemens von Delbrück, the possibility of a customs union operating under complete German domination. A memorandum to this effect, signed by the chancellor, was found in the late 1950s by historian Fritz Fischer in the Prussian Military Archive and served as proof of Germany's aggressive planning at the outset of World War I.[10] But in fact, such plans were neither new nor were they secret at the time. Rathenau's model was perhaps unique in that he was willing to give up at least some territorial annexations in order to achieve economic advantages. But he too at this point saw in the future customs union a tool for enhancing Germany's position as a world power, giving due weight to its technical and organizational aptitude as well as, of course, to its moral superiority. Some of his colleagues in heavy industry would not think of any future arrangement unless far-reaching border changes, ensuring their particular interests, were first attained. Rathenau's calculations of loss and gain were less self-serving, and both more realistic and more sophisticated.

In any case, none of these plans had a chance of materializing. They were at first no more than vague directives for later action, and everyone, Rathenau included, had plenty of time to reformulate, revise, and finally drop all of them with the changing fortunes of war. More immediate and practical were his interventions in discussion of ways of enhancing production and controlling the distribution of raw materials in wartime Germany. This too, interestingly enough, had figured in his prior strategic planning. Now, having tried to interest some highly placed government officials in this matter, a meeting between himself and General Erich von Falkenhayn, the Prussian war minister, was finally arranged and a few days later, Rathenau was asked to head a new Raw Materials Office (in German the KRA) to be established within the War Ministry.

Two facts stand out in this story: the lack of any prior German plans for handling this crucial aspect of war, and the speed and efficiency with which the matter was then dealt with. Rathenau had often complained of the incompetence of the old aristocratic elite, both before and during the war. But here, it seems, things could not have run more smoothly. He immediately drew up a plan for replacing imported raw materials and using existing stocks in the most efficient ways, and set out to implement it. The first step included the registration of all the available resources; then came the establishment of a system through which their usage was controlled by massive state intervention whenever and wherever necessary. By mid-September Rathenau mentioned "two dozen men" working in his new office, most of them on a voluntary basis. Early in 1915 the number had grown to a hundred, with many more indirectly employed outside the War Ministry, and finally by March, before leaving his post, he reported two hundred men plus "five times as many" working away from the central unit, mainly in the numerous so-called war companies established during his eight months in office.[11] By then it had become apparent that hopes for a short war were futile and that economic affairs would be as important in deciding it as military action. The significance of Rathenau's project could not be doubted. Still, his own subjective reaction to the situation remained mixed. Being called to fulfill such an important role in the heart of the Prussian bureaucratic establishment and having carried out this complex mission so quickly and efficiently could be considered a huge success. But even this success, once achieved, did not seem to lift his anxiety regarding Germany's fate, nor did it relieve his lingering personal gloom.

Rathenau was, in fact, deeply troubled throughout these months. In letters to family and friends he tells of long hours of work, sleepless nights, and the complete abandonment of all other activities. Though he must have felt a great deal of satisfaction, this hardly shows in his pronouncements at that time. He did allow himself occasional moments of exaltation, such as in a letter of August 24: "How inwardly necessary this war has been! How the old unbearable [existence] has turned into hope!"[12] But this was the exception rather than the rule. In the aftermath of the war, in fact, a quote from one of Rathenau's later publications, repeated almost verbatim in Bernhard von Bülow's memoirs, was used by General Ludendorff in his efforts to blame the defeatism of the home front for German capitulation. According to this view, Rathenau's verdict at the outbreak of hostilities had been that "[O]n the day that the Kaiser and his paladins on their white chargers ride victorious through the Brandenburg Gate, history will have lost all meaning."[13] Rathenau then fiercely objected to this "accusation" and claimed he had been quoted inaccurately and out of context. Elsewhere, however, he repeated this statement himself and admitted being critical of the war and the way it had been managed from the start. He does seem to have confronted it with a great deal of skepticism. On the whole, notwithstanding the occasional outburst of robust patriotism, he was apparently more worried and less enthusiastic in August 1914 than most men in his immediate milieu. He complained that the reasons for the war were obscure, that it could have been avoided, and that it was being conducted unprofessionally and irresponsibly.[14] "A wrong note is being sounded in this war," was his privately expressed verdict in a letter of December 1914. ". . . Necessary or not, higher power or not, the way in which it happened was not right. What would a prize for victory look like that could justify so much blood and tears?" he asked.[15] Still, war did open new opportunities for Germany, he had to admit. Like most of his contemporaries, Rathenau did not have any principled aversion to war as a tool of political struggle in general, or to this war in particular as a tool for repositioning Germany among the world powers. What most emphatically clouded his hopes was—once again—the failure of leadership on the German side. "I wish I hadn't been looking behind the scenes," he wrote as early as November 1914; "We are being ruled by a caste that is highly self-confident, but incapable of initiative," he added,[16] and in an even darker mood: "Our fate hangs by a thread, and who protects us? adventurers, fools and pedants." Finally here is how he summarized his position: "I believe in victory but I fear the end."[17]

His own contribution, to be sure, revealed nothing but competence and professionalism. Rathenau could compliment himself for creating in record time a situation in which Germany would be supplied with all critical raw materials for any length of time, enabling her to wage war as long as she wanted or had to. It could, in fact, be argued that only one other person contributed so much, single-handedly, to the war effort, namely Fritz Haber, the inventor of synthetic ammonia, crucial for both fertilizers and explosives, a renowned chemist, an ardent German patriot, and a converted Jew. But unlike Haber, Rathenau did not lack misgivings in performing his task. He was well aware that by succeeding in carrying it out he was also contributing to the prolongation of the war and thus to its potentially disastrous consequences. In a letter to one of his few close friends as early as August 1914, this is what he had to say regarding his work at the War Ministry: "If I listen to my innermost being, I know that in so doing I am turning myself into a tool of a process through which I am contributing to the overthrow of the gods to whom, before August 1914, the world prayed, a world to which I belong, and through which I became what I am: an individualist. That is what, together with the difficulty of the assignment, weighs me down at this late hour, my friend."[18] Thus, even in the midst of hectic activities, Rathenau's ambivalence was unmistakable. Already when he was given his wartime task, he had lost much of his confidence in both the civil and the military leadership of the Reich. Moreover, this particular task was bound to remove him ever further from his earlier friends and colleagues. The KRA aroused much opposition. Its interference in the production and distribution of so many different raw materials clashed with innumerable private interests. Rathenau was repeatedly accused of favoring AEG in the various bureaucratic arrangements he initiated, and the war companies under his supervision were blamed not only for the over-bureaucratization of the war economy but also for creating sheer chaos in some areas, such as transport, industrial financing, and the distribution of energy. While large-scale firms eventually cooperated more or less willingly with his emergency projects and found ways of profiting from them in practice even as they criticized them in principle, smaller enterprises felt left to their own fate in stormy waters and accused Rathenau of unfairness. Reichstag representatives were voicing these accusations, too. It was a lonely job for a lonely man.

Though Rathenau's business activities continued, as did his writing career, his previously boisterous social life practically came to a halt. Many of his older ties fizzled out now. Rathenau's correspondence at this juncture often seems to include nothing but professional notes and occasional letters in reply to comments regarding his books. At the same time, however, it contains evidence of some interesting new contacts, too.

During the immediate prewar period, the possibility of joining a new intellectual circle, eventually to be named the Fortekreis, preoccupied Rathenau quite intensively. This international group was originally made up of friends of the Dutch author, psychologist, and reformer Frederik van Eeden, and consisted at first, around 1910, of eight members, including the American writer Upton Sinclair, the Swedish psychoanalyst Paul Bjerre, the anarcho-socialist Gustav Landauer, the philosopher Martin Buber, the nationalist theologian Florence Christian Rang, and Erich Gutkind, a German-Jewish author from Berlin, serving as Eeden's main contact in the German capital. Among the many literary, ideological, and political circles at the time, this was a particularly heterogeneous group, committed to the mysticism of a chosen elite and a modernism that combined subjectivity and science, individualism and the principles of an altruistic community. By mid-1912 Rathenau was sought after by some members of this mixed group in their efforts to recruit additional members, perhaps also in their search for financial support. He must have been flattered by their approach and was initially positive in his reply. The fact that about a third of the group consisted of Jews disturbed some of the original members, especially Rang; it did not disturb Rathenau. But the enterprise was short-lived. With the outbreak of war, the members' conflicting attitudes towards it resulted in repeated clashes. Rathenau's overt German patriotism seemed like warmongering to van Eeden; Rang's militarism brought about Landauer's secession.[19] In any case, under the pressure of war, these men, mostly living outside of Berlin or even outside Germany, could not be expected to ease Rathenau's loneliness.

At the same time, his correspondence reveals two new addressees: Fanny Künstler, an unmarried teacher and author, Jewish by origin, and Wilhelm Schwaner, a journalist, active in the Germanic folk movement and the editor of one of its major periodical publications, the *Volkserzieher*. Both were most unlikely associates of Rathenau, completely outside his normal milieu: Künstler a single woman, Schwaner an outspoken antisemite. It reflected, perhaps, the measure of Rathenau's loneliness that he allowed such cursory contacts to linger on and eventually came to invest such emotional energy in them. Both approached Rathenau after reading his major oeuvres of 1912 and 1913. Both admired him fiercely. Both were not content with mere intellectual exchange with him, seeking to create some kind of inner bond. They seemed to offer what Rathenau had such a heartfelt need for at this point in his life, but for all his initial openness, he could not really respond to their call for intimacy.

The case of Schwaner is particularly interesting. By 1913, he was a veteran of various Germanic associations, both of the strictly Christian and of the mythology-oriented variant. The title page of his *Volkserzieher* had carried the swastika since 1907, and its rhetoric was fiercely antisemitic. A couple of years later, the energetic and volatile Schwaner moved to Berlin-Schlachtensee, dividing his time between the Prussian

Wilhelm Schwaner, 1900, portrait by Toni Schwaner. Courtesy Walther Rathenau Gesellschaft.

capital and his summer house in the Upland countryside of Hessen, near Rattlar. His first letter to Rathenau is dated December 3, 1913. While contemplating the "misery of my people" and blaming it most particularly on the Jews, he recalled, someone handed him Rathenau's *Critique of the Times.* As a result, "the 'dark' Jew has redeemed the blue-blond German." He wished to let Rathenau know that among such "blue-blond thick-headed men, some have warm, pure hearts," and offered to "shake his hand in newfound brotherhood."[20] Rathenau answered immediately. Apparently he was not put off by Schwaner's eccentric rhetoric. On the contrary, he seems to have been fascinated by it. He thanked Schwaner for his "good and manly letter" and sent him his *Mechanism of the Spirit* for further reading. A couple of days later, he was already trying to arrange a meeting, and the two soon met, late in March 1914, in Rathenau's Grunewald villa.[21] Schwaner was overwhelmed. This was a completely new experience for him. The warm welcome by one of Berlin's richest men and his willingness to engage in long, intensive, and apparently intimate conversation with him must have come as a complete surprise. He reacted enthusiastically, first by sending Rathenau his own *Germanen-Bibel*, a collection of texts intended to define a modern Christianity of "pure Germanic blood," adding a small volume each for Rathenau's valet and his driver—an extraordinary gesture, no doubt. Soon, Rathenau fell into Schwaner's extravagant style, quoted from the Romantic poet Eichendorff, and allowed the relationship to reach an unexpected level of closeness. On April 22 he received what could only be seen as a love letter from his new friend: "Do you love me?" writes Schwaner, "I love you! I love you very much!" He waxes lyrical, avowing that their friendship ought to be handled like the most tender violets, and their meetings best held in the dark of night. Even that does not make Rathenau uneasy. "I answer your questions with a full and happy yes," he writes back on the following day.[22] Needless to say, they are by then using the familiar "Du" and meet regularly, with and without Schwaner's wife, at the latter's home or in the Königsallee, even occasionally in Freienwalde. "Till long after midnight," Schwaner describes one such experience, "the two of us sat on the shore of the Oder and talked of school and our youth, of people and religion, of life and death, of heaven and earth. Even after one o'clock we could not rest, and lay with open eyes till the sun called upon us . . ."[23]

Of course, this meeting of souls may have never occurred precisely in this way. After its fervent beginning, the long correspondence between Schwaner and Rathenau, lasting till the latter's death, did not contain any more such openly homoerotic overtones. While Rathenau does try to respond in kind to Schwaner's rhapsodic outbursts, his tone remains cool and sober, always with a strong didactic accent. Rathenau seems

first to agree with Schwaner's ideas, but he then hastens to in-
terject his objections. Jesus after all, he reminds Schwaner, was
a Jew; he himself, though Jewish, is nothing but a German. Despite all the talk of blood and ancestry, faith, language, history,
and culture are much more important than "physiological matters," as he put it, and the heavenly soul is after all alive in every
human spirit—regardless of blood or nationality.[24] "Your work
is not my work," Rathenau decisively asserts as he distances
himself from Schwaner's Germanic propaganda. But he continues to seek his friendship, helps him repeatedly in financial
matters, and, most uncharacteristically, opens his heart to him.
"For too long I have been accustomed to inner loneliness" he
writes. Till recently he has still regretted having no household
and family. But the facts of life must be accepted. He has only
a few wishes left now: to complete his literary work and to continue his father's life project. "I have grown gray in this year of
war," he states in a letter to Schwaner on September 16, 1915,
"I feel this inwardly too."[25]

Rathenau's dark mood at the time is reflected most particularly in his letters to Fanny Künstler. The correspondence with
her began on an intellectual note, and like that with Schwaner,
centered on discussing aspects of Rathenau's books. However,
she soon moved from complaining over her writer's block and
asking for his help as an experienced author onto a more personal level, seeking his sympathy and eventually his friendship,
perhaps even his love. Rathenau was clearly not interested. He
usually answers her long-winded letters politely but rather
curtly, though not without some effort to open up to her. He
sent her confusing, contradictory messages. Rathenau's grumpy,
even depressed tone, common in his earlier letters to his
mother and then to Lili Deutsch, is here clearly repeated. In a
note from Freienwalde at the end of July 1914, he mixes, as was
his habit, a description of nature around him with sighs of personal despair: "Ah, the end is there," he writes, "the days fade

away; in every thought lies something of a leave-taking."[26] Later on, in mid-September, after the beginning of the war, his gloom is further intensified: "I often wake up at night with worries. The year has lost its colors and its seasons; I feel winter." It is "powerlessness and remoteness" that surround him, he tells her.[27] He is constantly tired, overworked, enjoying neither nature nor a good book, not even music. In any case, by the spring of 1915 Fanny's insistence and Walther's dark mood collide and the correspondence between them comes to an end.

Resigning his post at the War Ministry must have constituted a turning point in Rathenau's life. It required a reassessment of both his career options and his social choices. But soon, other distressing circumstances crowded out his self-searching and inner conflicts. Emil Rathenau died on June 20, 1915. At the family graveyard monument, Walther, "the only remaining son," as he felt he ought to explain, delivered the only eulogy.[28] This must have been an embarrassing scene. Though seeming to speak spontaneously, Rathenau had long labored over this speech. It opened with a claim to find solace in "Jesus' trust in the eternal spirit," and ended with words of the traditional Jewish burial ceremony. In between, despite his sincere efforts, Rathenau could not bring himself to show real passion. Nor could he pass over what he considered to be the deceased's weaker points or hide his resentment at the burden he always had to carry as his son. All this crept out from behind the verbiage of unbounded admiration and praise. The great man was a hidden genius, Walther contended. But then, counting the special gifts that made up this genius, he first came up with Emil's "simplicity," or what he decided to name his "childlike simplicity." Emil was in the habit of transforming even the most complex issues into straightforward, easily comprehensible ones, Walther explained, and it was to these simplified questions that he always found self-evident solutions. How different this was from the way his son operated, ran the obvious subtext, how incapable the dead man was of comprehending the complexities with which his son grappled. Then to "simplicity" Walther added "truthfulness," as the other aspect of the same quality. Whereas the first sounded initially like criticism and was then turned into a virtue, the second, clearly denoting a virtue, soon sounded more like criticism. Emil's third gift was his "vision," stated Walther—the vision of an industrial entrepreneur, to be sure, of a technical innovator. And finally came "love," first "love of things" and only later "love of people"; love "in general," his son assures us—not necessarily in particular, we must assume. It was genuine love, Walther was trying to convince his audience, but it was devoid of gentleness, he hastens to add, of devotion, of tenderness, laments the son. It could arouse love in others, in "thousands of others," he knew, but did it arouse love in Walther himself?

A letter to Schwaner, written a week after the funeral, seems to imply a positive answer to this question: "We discovered each other late, my father and I; first came respect, than friendship, finally love." Only in death, he added, did he find himself truly united with his father, "peaceful and confident in his presence."[29] This was more than what he had allowed himself to say publicly, but still reflected a tortuous relationship, in which love, presumably the first prerequisite of a father-son relationship, came last and was truly felt only at the final moment of separation. This was how the mature Walther Rathenau saw the link to his father: "Whatever I did," he wrote to another friend at about the same time, "related, at least partly, to him." Now, with Emil's death, he confessed that he had lost the last vestiges of his youth, "since as long as the father lives, a trace of childhood continues to hang over us."[30] Rathenau was forty-seven years old at the time. He finally felt an adult, finally a free man.

But not entirely. At first, following his father's death, Rathenau reentered the business world with great energy. "I feel

Emil Rathenau about 1905, portrait by Max Liebermann.
Courtesy Bildarchiv Preussischer Kulturbesitz.

committed to his work for as long as it endures without him,"
he announced.[31] Although AEG could clearly operate without
the Rathenaus at this stage, Walther insisted on holding on to
his father's legacy. The doubts that plagued him for years, in fact
as long as his father was alive, had now disappeared. Business
turned into a calling and combining business affairs with a

writer's career seemed entirely feasible, even desirable. Politics was for him, at least for the time being, no more than a sideline.

The reasons for this are unclear. To begin with, it is difficult to explain Rathenau's resignation from the War Ministry only seven to eight months after he had taken upon himself to be the head of the KRA, a post that clearly testified to his political ambitions. Of the various possible reasons, the most likely is that the post did not prove a springboard for more influential political positions, as he might have expected. In mid-1915, it was not Rathenau but Karl Helfferich, head of the Deutsche Bank in Berlin, who was appointed minister of finance. As an official of the War Ministry Rathenau felt, and was probably made to feel, a complete stranger, being both a civilian and a Jew. In replying to letters by one of his aristocratic female admirers, who had repeatedly urged him to seek another public office, he first explained that he was fully preoccupied elsewhere, but then added pointedly that this would in any case be impossible since he knew of no office that was "requiring [his] services."[32] A couple of years later, writing to the same addressee, he was more explicit: "Although I as well as my forefathers have served our country to the best of our abilities, nevertheless I am . . . as a Jew, a second-class citizen. I can neither become a political office holder, nor even a peacetime [army] lieutenant. I could have avoided such discrimination by converting, but in this way, according to my conviction, I would only deepen the breach of law committed by the ruling classes."[33] While this little digression may not fully explain his resignation at the time, it does reflect his own later interpretation of the event: his sense of repeatedly facing a blocked route in the realm of politics, of being held back in his climbing by a glass ceiling.

In any case, following the intermezzo in the state bureaucracy, Rathenau was ready, perhaps even eager, to return to the business world. He was by then a highly experienced and well-connected figure, with a strong base in AEG. Within a few months of Emil's death, the hierarchy of the firm was reshuffled, apparently to the satisfaction of all involved. What had caused so much bad blood in 1912 was now achieved relatively smoothly, if not completely without friction. Rathenau remained chairman of the supervisory board, but was also nominated as "President of AEG." In itself this was no more than an honorary title, but it did enable the son of the legendary *Generaldirektor* some influence within the board of directors, now headed by Felix Deutsch. In the remaining war years Rathenau concentrated on developing AEG's armament production, including the large-scale manufacture of airplanes and various types of ammunition, soon to constitute 45 percent of the firm's total turnover. Working in the spacious and elegant new offices of AEG along the Spree in Berlin, designed by the fashionable architect Peter Behrens, was for the rest of the war and into the early postwar years Rathenau's major occupation. It was certainly a full-time job and he gave it his best. In fact, following some initial difficulties at the beginning of the war, the firm thereafter continuously grew, making enormous profits. This occasionally produced some moments of embarrassment for Rathenau, especially as AEG actively participated in building and arming the German submarine fleet, to be employed in the war despite his own publicly expressed opposition. But, as he later liked to put it, he—like his father before him—was merely an employee of the firm, responsible to its shareholders. He must have drawn considerable satisfaction and many benefits from its success.[34]

Generally speaking, by the summer of 1915, Rathenau also seems to have regained some of his pleasure in life. Relations with Harden were reestablished, and even recovered some of their previous warmth. Rathenau was touched by Harden's eulogy of his father, published in *Die Zukunft* a week after Emil's death. In many ways this was a much less ambiva-

lent appreciation of the older man than Rathenau's own funeral speech and at least as complimentary. The two men now
met, as before, for long evening conversations, for strolls in
Grunewald's peaceful streets, sometimes alone and sometimes
with others. Harden's political reorientation, from an outspoken and extreme nationalism at the beginning of the war to an
increasingly moderate position both on the issue of war aims
and on the needed internal reforms, created a common platform for the two of them, at least in the short run. Other old
friends, such as Hauptmann and Wedekind, were also back in
Rathenau's life to some extent. He was once more entertaining in the accustomed venues: in his Grunewald villa, in
Freienwalde, or occasionally at the Automobile Club and the
Hotel Adlon. Even new friends and acquaintances were beginning to surface, especially as a result of Rathenau's membership in a number of new clubs and associations.

Having left the War Ministry, Rathenau was soon engaged
in efforts to organize the Deutsche Gesellschaft 1914, a club
for the German elite of that time. After almost a year of preparation, the club was established in the fall of 1915, bringing together a few hundred outstanding men from all walks of life.
Though presumably apolitical, the tone of its deliberations was
consistent with the mildly conservative mainstream in wartime
Germany—supportive of Bethmann Hollweg and endeavoring
to uphold the so-called spirit of 1914. In official meetings as
well as in informal discussions, members normally backed moderate war aims and supported limited constitutional and social
reforms. All this seemed to fit Rathenau's general political posture from before the war: parliamentarism—but only at the
right moment; integration of Social Democracy and the trade
unions—but without giving up the predominance of capitalism; finally, peace with minimal annexations as long as it was
based on a resounding German victory. Most members shared
these views: leading government officials, diplomats, journal-

ists, outstanding scholars, a few industrialists and bankers, some lawyers, physicians, and the like.

Rathenau made two speeches before the club members. The first was a report on his contribution to the war efforts during his time as head of the Office of Raw Materials.[35] This aroused much respect; even the press in enemy countries seemed impressed. The London *Times* published an article under the title "A Businessman at War," based on a report in the *Chicago Daily News,* praising Rathenau's achievements and calling for Britain to allow its own "Rathenaus" to work in similar ways and in similar capacities.[36] Considering the fact that his activities at the War Ministry was kept under some degree of censorship, the public echo the speech aroused was, no doubt, impressive. Some thought Rathenau flaunted his achievements too much, and later even the originality of his measures was doubted, as Wichard von Moellendorf, his colleague at AEG and his right hand at the KRA, claimed to have been the first to draft plans for these measures and to have then been manipulated by Rathenau into a secondary position.[37] This was patently untrue but it yet again helped strengthen Rathenau's sense of being insufficiently appreciated. It was after all an emotional pattern typical for him throughout his life, perhaps a residue of the time he was seeking his father's love and approval, for ever remaining unacknowledged for what he felt he was doing or had actually done; for ever having to see his successes ignored.

Past achievements in any case lost much of their glamour as Germany faced ever more critical problems, both at the front and at home. In war, modern weaponry grafted upon traditional strategies created a prolonged standstill on land, originally expected by no one, while maritime blockades and counterblockades achieved nothing but deadlock at sea. And as the war was prolonging itself, it was time to think of approaching postwar problems too. Rathenau was among the first to do so. In his second speech at the Deutsche Gesellschaft he dealt with the economic difficulties Germany was about to confront in peacetime, and in his customary didactic tone, he listed the challenges offered by his vision of the future. Eventually, he prophesied, Germany would depend upon a new kind of economy, in which luxury would first be limited and then replaced by "new sources of joy and pleasure"—"more noble pleasures," to be sure. In such an economy, all "healthy and strong men" would contribute to useful production and be "wasted" neither as "students of the history of art" nor as small retail shopkeepers, "selling beer and tobacco."[38] Reforms would have to include a significant reduction of futile legal procedures, of excessive capital exports, perhaps also of the private ownership of finance and manufacturing. And finally, under the expected pressure of postwar conditions and in order to provide the state with sufficient quantities of needed resources, an end would have to be put to both inherited wealth and inherited poverty, as he put it, and a number of large-scale monopolies, under the sole supervision of the state, would be established to serve as its solid foundation.[39] Rathenau hoped for a country less noisy and less colorful, characterized by labor that was ennobled through self-sacrifice, reaching for "the eternal, the absolute, the generally valid," seeking and achieving both "social justice and civil freedom."[40]

The lecture, given on December 18, 1916, must have caused considerable unease in the audience. The mixture of astute insight and sheer puritanism must have left them speechless. In contrast to the many reactions to the lecture on raw materials a year earlier, there were only sporadic comments on this one, whether in Rathenau's correspondence or in the press. Some time later he was made aware of Gustav Schmoller's unfavorable reaction to his lecture, first through the report of a third party and then by reading the unsparing comments of the famous economist himself.[41] Otherwise the lecture seems to have simply fallen flat. Immediately thereafter, at the beginning of the new year, Rathenau was indeed not only physically ill but also mentally depressed. In a letter to Lili Deutsch he allowed himself to complain of loneliness, and commented on the "greed and scorn of friends, not one of whom will ever, ever! come to our aid." "Smilingly they block the way on the path to the abyss," he wrote bitterly, "and some must actually be forced to make room for the tottering wagon, till they finally manage to break the spokes."[42] Although he makes every effort to assure his lady friend of his cheerfulness, the letter leaves a strong impression of despair.

These were, to be sure, very difficult days for Germany as a whole. The decision to begin unrestricted submarine warfare and thus practically force the United States into the fighting, was taken in January 1917. Rathenau, who was of two minds about this at first, soon came to oppose the move. In a letter of 26 February, he explained his opposition by sensibly arguing that it was an experiment that, like a jump over an abyss, would succeed only if it could fully succeed. Moreover, he did not think it would shorten the war. On the contrary, it was necessary to prepare for its "prolongation for an unpredictable period."[43] But despite his many connections, even with the highest military commanders, Rathenau had little if any influence on decisions of this kind. He could do nothing to alleviate the situation. Hence, as in the past when Rathenau was feeling despondent and unappreciated, the Jewish theme resurfaced.

The trigger was a renewed public discussion regarding Jewish life in Germany. The beginning of the war and the Kaiser's promise to uphold "domestic peace" in order to lead the country to victory had presented the Jews with an opportunity to display their patriotism and enjoy a sense of solidarity with other Germans both at the front and at home. Jews of all walks of life, members of the liberal "Central Association of German Citizens of the Jewish Faith" (CV), as well as Zionists, Orthodox, Reform Jews, and those who claimed to be entirely secular or unattached, were now eager to become brothers in arms.

Indicative of this mood was the CV's decision to institute a moratorium on the fight against antisemitism. Any action of this sort, it was now felt, could be interpreted as contrary to the declared "domestic peace" and arouse undue resentment even among fair-minded observers and decent officials. Despite the fact that reports from the front noted cases of bigotry and discrimination, while complaints about Jewish war profiteering and draft dodging were heard up and down the country, Jews held to their passivity, determined to prove themselves worthy. In 1916, the worst battles of the First World War on the Western Front, at Verdun and on the Somme, produced no tangible results despite the use of enormous amounts of ammunition, especially artillery shells, and hundreds of thousands of casualties. The German forces also had to resist a renewed Russian advance on the Eastern Front, directed against a collapsing Austrian defense; and their inadequacy in fighting a war on two fronts became apparent. The price had proved boundless and the probability of defeat could no longer be denied.

This had many consequences for the home front too, one of which was an increasingly aggressive anti-Jewish public campaign. Rathenau felt the force of this campaign too. His position at the head of the KRA had been often misrepresented and now he was repeatedly denounced, sometimes together with other wealthy Jews, for personally benefiting from the war. By mid-July 1917 Rathenau found it necessary to reply to a veiled attack against him by Houston Stewart Chamberlain, a rabid antisemite. Listing his loyal services to the Fatherland, Rathenau demanded a disclaimer. But even when Chamberlain apologized and the matter was set aside, he found it difficult to return to his previous routine. In an earlier letter, addressed to Schwaner on August 4, 1916, he stressed that he had no intention of trying to dissuade the antisemites from their hatred. This would surely be a futile task, he explained, and cause only more relentless attacks. In fact, "the more Jews were to fall in this war, the more insistently their opponents would argue that they were all sitting behind the front, waiting to profiteer from it. The hatred would be doubled and tripled, and not only this hatred," he added, "but every hatred and every dispute that is at all likely in our land."[44] Nevertheless, by the beginning of 1917, he was visibly shaken by the anti-Jewish atmosphere around him and seemed ready to act publicly against it.

Rathenau never participated in the struggle against anti-semitism. When the controversy over the so-called "Jewish census" erupted in October 1916, he made sure to keep clear of it. By then the antisemitic agitation had intensified and the War Ministry decided to begin gathering statistical informa-tion on Jewish participation in the war effort, rejecting the al-ternative suggestion made by the Catholic Center Party leader Matthias Erzberger to launch an investigation into all confes-sions. The "Jewish census" was finally carried out and, as could be expected, only proved Jewish patriotism. A population of just over half a million sent some hundred thousand soldiers to the war, of whom about four-fifths served at the front and at least twelve thousand fell in battle. Still, regardless of the re-sults, the whole affair was conceived by the Jews as a direct af-front. They considered the census a discriminatory procedure, contrary to the principle of civil equality that had been made law of the land over forty years earlier, and felt deeply insulted, indeed outraged. For some this proved a turning point in their lives. Ernst Simon, for instance, by then serving at the front and later to become a well-known thinker and educator, re-counted in his memoirs that it was the "Jewish census" that finally shook him out of the "dream of community" between Germans and Jews, and served as the last proof "that we were foreigners, standing at the side, [people who] must be sepa-rately categorized and counted, listed and administered."[45]

Rathenau was spared the front line experience of discrimi-nation, and like many Jews in leading positions, he must have thought it better to disregard the entire affair. There were clear limits to his display of Jewish solidarity. When he was approached by representatives of the CV with an offer to join their organization, he politely refused, using as a reason their links with Orthodoxy, from which he consistently wished to stay aloof. Zionism too was not an option for him. "The majority of German Jews," he wrote when asked to join a new Zionist group in November 1918, ". . . have only one national sense: the German. Like our ancestors, we want to live and die in Germany and for Germany. Others may establish a 'Reich' in Palestine—nothing draws *us* to Asia."[46] In the spring of 1921, in another private letter, he did show more interest in the Zionist project in Palestine, expressing the wish to visit it in order to judge the situation for himself as soon as his "obligations allow[ed]," but he never changed his mind on the main issue.[47] To Richard Lichtheim, by then president of the German Zionist Union, he explained that the Jews were not a nation but a community of individuals with a particular mind set and "some incorrigible characteristics." "This man, otherwise so intelligent," commented Lichtheim resignedly, "could see the Jewish people only one-sidedly and therefore so mistakenly."[48]

Be that as it may, Rathenau did have his own conception of Judaism, to which he now seemed to return as he had often done before, especially in times of crisis. Soon he was also given the opportunity to define and explain his views in public. This came about following the publication of a pamphlet by one Curt von Trützschler-Falkenstein from Darmstadt, entitled *The Solution of the Jewish Question in Germany*. Rathenau first entered into correspondence with the author and shortly afterwards, in June 1917, made his reply public by printing it under the title *A Polemic About Faith*.[49] Here he tried to describe what Judaism principally meant to him: a religion without church and dogma, without canonical books, without any supervising human agency, encompassing the purest belief in the "oneness of God." A rough comparison with both Catholicism and Protestantism provided him the background necessary for stressing the fundamental difference between church and faith. Thus, Rathenau argued that while he himself generally relied on the gospel, he remained free to go "his own way" in matters of morality, like most of his Christian friends. Under the special circumstances in Germany, ran the argument, joining one particular Christian community through conversion meant not only losing this kind of freedom but also taking a political side. A Christian state, he concluded, ought not to mean a state with an official church, but one that was inspired by Christian ideals and therefore characterized by true spiritual freedom, an earthly reflection of "the Kingdom of the Soul, the Kingdom of God." He could easily identify with such a state as a Jew, and conversion, demanded yet again by Trützschler-Falkenstein, would then be simply superfluous.

In contrast to his previous comments on the immorality of conversion and its unethical political implications, Rathenau was now stressing his high regard for the Jewish faith, arguing its perfect suitability to modernity in cultural as well as in political terms. Since the publication of "Hear, O Israel!" two decades earlier, he had moved slowly but surely into the mainstream of Jewish self-definition in contemporary Germany. Staying aloof from Jewish organizations had more to do now with his individualism, perhaps also with his political ambitions, than with any principled opposition or hidden hostility to Jews or Judaism. Neither his appeal to the high moral standards of the Christian gospel nor the claim that it was in fundamental agreement with the tenets of Jewish ethics were by then new arguments. They were sounded by various Jewish authors in and around that time, and finally seemed to suit Rathenau's more conciliatory position vis-à-vis his co-religionists.[50] Being a German-Jew was apparently no longer a source of such agonizing inner conflict for him as it had been before.

The race issue, too, seemed to have lost its poignancy. In a letter of October 10, 1917, we read: "I consider all race theories as a waste of time und acknowledge only one thing that turns peoples into nations, nations into states: the community of soil, experience, and spirit."[51] By now, any mention of his earlier books, both his *Impressions*, containing the article "Hear, O Israel!," and *Reflections*, in which his views on race and racial theories were set out in print, seemed to embarrass him. The tone of "Hear, O Israel!" was wrong, he once explained; it was not only unkind but truly cruel, and since "no one can be changed through cruelty," it was also futile.[52] In a later letter to Schwaner, written in March 1919, Rathenau tried yet again to dissuade his friend from positions he had once held himself. Class differences, he now argued, were much more important than physical matters of body and blood. "Germanic [men] of Tacitus's breed are the greatest rarity," he stated, and in fact "the relatively purer Germanic [men] are more different from average Germans than these are from average Jews." Particularly objectionable to him now were claims of superiority based on the color of "eyes, skin, and hair"; he went on to assert that "at its peak the human spirit is everywhere the same."[53]

Shortly after the publication of *A Polemic About Faith*, we find Rathenau explaining the situation of German Jewry in a private letter addressed to Gottlieb von Jagow, state secretary at the Prussian Foreign Office.[54] In it Rathenau divided the Jews of Germany, a little over half a million, that is about 1 percent of the population, into three groups, in perfect parallel to their class position. The first third, he argued, included the assimilated Jews, or the "regenerated," as he chose to call them, using the common idiom of the time. These were men like himself, carrying no outward sign of their Jewishness, all of them honest and useful citizens, contributing well over their share to the splendid edifice of German culture. The second group included the Jewish middle class. Though these were normally somewhat better situated than their German counterparts, they did "occasionally get on our nerves," he admitted, "because their unpleasant characteristics are visible while their good ones are latent." Nevertheless, they too "cannot be considered to harm the state" and in many ways they were irreplaceable, injecting a much-needed "industrial intelligence" into the German economy. The last third consisted of the Jewish proletariat, still manifesting "medieval qualities," he thought, clinging together while leading the life of ritual Orthodoxy. Even they, Rathenau claimed, were normally far from being "antinational" like the Danes, the Poles, or the Alsatian minority. "Like you, I am of the opinion," he wrote to Jagow, "that amalgamation ought not to proceed too quickly." But apparently unlike Jagow, Rathenau believed a proper "solution" to their predicament would only be achieved through the properly balanced behavior of others, namely with complete disregard of origin and confession by state and society alike, "just as in England and America." A certain measure of "social antisemitism," he admitted, directed only at "those who provoke it," would be "more useful than harmful." But antisemitism directed at those "who do not provoke it" was anathema to him now.

In October 1918, as the German forces on the Western Front were collapsing and he was completely preoccupied with the dangers ahead, Rathenau still found time to explain, in responding to an invitation to join the German Freemasons, why this was not an option for him. He believed it would be wrong on his part "to join an association whose members take a principled stand against the original descent and confession to which [he] belonged."[55] Once again, insistence on his identity as a Jew is unequivocal, underlined as always by a strong sense of defiance. It was still a matter of honor for him to remain Jewish, and despite everything else he might have said, it was and remained a matter of basic loyalty. At the time, yet another stage of his life was coming to an end, and in dark days, as before, Rathenau was reexamining his Jewishness, finding ways of reasserting it, and perhaps even seeking some solace in it.

6

Politician Manqué, Prophet with a Vengeance

ALTHOUGH BEING JEWISH and German at the same time no longer pained the mature Rathenau as it had before, this duality continued to constitute a formative element in his life. He knew, of course, that it played at least some role in restricting his career, particularly in the field of politics. And since no public office was going to be offered to him at this point but political issues continued to preoccupy him on a daily basis, he once more chose to rely upon networking as a substitute.

For some time now Rathenau had been cultivating his relationships with the politicians within his circle of acquaintances, adding a number of new ones to his list during the war years. Having left his post at the War Ministry, he remained in touch with his former boss and later chief of the General Staff General Erich von Falkenhayn, as well as with a number of other top military men, such as General Helmuth von Moltke, Falkenhayn's predecessor, and General Hans von Seeckt. From the end of August 1915 he corresponded with no less a figure than General Erich Ludendorff. Finally, visiting the Eastern Staff headquarters at Kovno in November 1915, Rathenau was even introduced to Field Marshal Paul von Hindenburg, the hero of the battle of Tannenberg, the most renowned military figure of the day. Naturally, lower officers also became part of Rathenau's group of informants and correspondents, instructing him in strategic and tactical issues, of which he had originally known very little, and soon becoming addressees of his advice and targets of his pressure. By now it was typical of Rathenau to be always extremely well informed and then to quickly develop very precise opinions on all controversial matters. Some of his views were insightful, even prophetic; others were short-sighted, even wrong; still others were repeatedly revised by him in the course of time. In all cases, however, he was prone to defend his position in long drawn-out conversations and in detailed letters and memoranda to various policymakers. At the same time he made it his habit to lecture to friends and colleagues on political and military matters on every occasion, often late into the night.

From the outset Rathenau saw Britain as Germany's main enemy. The British, Rathenau believed, accustomed to be in the lead worldwide, were determined to weaken Germany and exclude her as a competitor. In a memorandum sent to Bethmann Hollweg and Ludendorff as early as August 30, 1915, he explained that "our purpose" ought to be first and foremost the breakup of the Entente, and that this must be done by forcing Russia to its knees. After all, "Russia had loved all its conquerors, just as the Russian peasant woman clamors for a beating," was his considered opinion.[1] It would eventually love us, if we conquered large parts of the country for long enough and offered the Russians a "bearable peace," as he put it. Rathenau's claim to know a thing or two about Russia depended probably upon the prolonged experience of AEG in that country. Although Russia was within Felix Deutsch's sphere of responsibility rather than his sphere, Rathenau was aware of the economic potential of the eastern giant and thought that taking care of its financial and industrial needs, not without decisive and continuous military pressure to be sure, would sooner or later do the trick. Annexation in the east, then, should be kept at a minimum, he argued, so as not to alienate the local population and leave the door open to negotiation. While he knew such a policy could mean a severe blow to Austria-Hungary, this seemed secondary to him. And in the end, he concluded, all that could anyway happen only after "we finish off France."[2]

Typically, Bethmann dismissed Rathenau's memo as "hazy," while Ludendorff replied immediately and at great length. It may have been Rathenau's blunt style that attracted the general, but clearly, the advances of the wealthy, powerful industrialist appealed to him. In the end the link with Rathenau did prove useful to him, especially when later on public pressure had to be applied to Germany's decisionmakers in order to convince them to hand over increasing powers to the rising general. Rathenau and Ludendorff remained in more or less intensive communication at least until mid-1917. They were strange bedfellows, no doubt. In his diary entries reporting on his Kovno trip, we read that Rathenau was unimpressed by Hindenburg, whose comments, he found, had "little color," but was full of praise for Ludendorff.[3] For a long time he refused to see how dangerous this man was: a willful dictator, guided by boundless personal ambition, who would lead Germany to fatal defeat and finally, almost inevitably, would turn into one of Rathenau's most hateful personal enemies. At the time, however, the latter admired what he considered Ludendorff's willpower, his energetic initiative, his practical turn of mind, and his unfailing courage. Rathenau made repeated use of their familiarity in order to offer Ludendorff advice on a variety of issues, to report to him on various meetings, often informal ones, with officials, diplomats, or men of letters, and to brief him concerning the general mood of the country, all the while avoiding any open conflict with the self-assured, domineering general, even in the few cases where he disagreed with him. A major case in point was the controversy over the pros and cons of a sustained blockade of the British Isles by means of unrestricted submarine warfare. As mentioned above, Rathenau vacillated for a long time on these issues. At first he insisted upon postponing his final decision as long as the relevant data were incomplete or inaccurate. Later, when he finally made up his mind, he never argued in principle against this strategy, nor was he ever unduly impressed by the fear of substantial civilian casualties that would necessarily be its result. Still, he did eventually take the less popular side and come out against the submarines warfare. In a detailed letter to General von Seeckt in November 1916, treating all the outstanding issues of the war one by one, Rathenau explained his position as being motivated by the wish not only to prevent America from joining Germany's enemies, in itself surely a very important goal, but also, and especially, to avoid an atmosphere of rage and hatred in enemy countries—a situation in which "the whole world would be against us." He would support "this instrument of last resort," he assured Seeckt, but only when and if it were to lead "with a measure of certainty" to England's decision to seek an end to hostilities.[4]

As a matter of fact, Rathenau was also ready to support the use of other "instruments of last resort" at this stage of the war, and again regardless of their human cost and moral implications. The forced transport of Belgian workers to Germany is the most striking example. By the summer and fall of 1916 it had become clear that victory, if it were to be achieved at all, required total mobilization. Late in August and in view of the difficult situation, Hindenburg and Ludendorff were called back from the east, the former to become chief of the Army

Supreme Command and the latter as his chief of staff. In practice, it was Ludendorff who now had the last word on all military matters at the front and on all political matters at home. The so-called Hindenburg Program, instituted at that time, meant a dramatic increase in the production of munitions, to be organized and controlled by the military. It brought about an overhaul of the entire economic system of the Reich, including the full exploitation of resources in the occupied parts of Europe, east and west. It also meant much pressure to expand the overall workforce and maximize its output. All this fitted Rathenau's notion of a centrally controlled war economy. and in a series of letters to Ludendorff he encouraged him to carry out the program in full. Historians of this stage of the war seem to agree today that the Hindenburg Program represented a triumph "not of imagination but of fantasy," and that it eventually "undermined the strength of the army, promoted economic instability, created administrative chaos, and set loose an orgy of interest politics."[5] Rathenau's criticism at the time, to the extent that he made any, was limited to details. To be sure, he had been neither the initiator of the plan, nor responsible for its execution, as was later insinuated, but he clearly supported it, in principle as well as in practice. When a shortage of labor for reaching production quotas became apparent, Rathenau, with other financial and industrial magnates, such as Carl Duisberg, Krupp, and Stinnes, backed the War Ministry's plan of forcibly transporting unemployed Belgian workers to Germany. Although this was clearly against international law and despite the fact that earlier in the war he himself had urged the German governor general of that country to "administer Belgium for the Belgians," Rathenau now supported the plan and thought it ought to be carried out "regardless of questions of international prestige," even if this threatened to sabotage the American aid program to the civilian population of that country. In fact, Rathenau espoused a measure that belonged to the "darkest memories" of the First World War.[6] The particular interests of AEG might have played some role here, but more important was his eagerness to achieve German victory at all costs. His moral priorities at that time could not have been better manifested. In private letters he was repeatedly critical of many aspects of the conduct of the war—not only of unrestricted submarine warfare, but also, for instance of the failing food program, which led to virtual famine in the winter of 1917. Gradually, he also came out against any demand for vast territorial annexation as a legitimate war aim under the circumstances. But in public, his patriotism and the need to parade it, as well as his personal loyalty to some of the leading figures in the political and military hierarchies, and perhaps also his lingering hope to be given a more official responsibility again, gave his criticism an ambivalent tinge. It led him to a closer agreement with the establishment than he would later care to admit.

This fundamental ambivalence was not unique to Rathenau. Some industrialists in his milieu harbored more militant, even pan-German political views, often quite openly seeking to serve their own interests. At the same time, others, especially intellectuals from among his friends, came to voice more critical views about the declared war aims and the generally irresponsible government of the Reich. Quite a few, in both camps, shared Rathenau's vacillation. Max Weber, for instance, every bit as much as Rathenau a burning patriot and enthusiastic imperialist at the outset of war, later also became an opponent of unrestricted submarine warfare, a supporter of internal reforms in the direction of parliamentarism, and a critic of Germany's civilian and military leadership. Despite many differences in principle and in details, both—increasingly worried about Germany's future—tried to influence the course of events, without, however, ever completely losing faith in the old regime.[7] Even by the spring and summer of 1917, Rathenau was still on friendly terms with many of the leading figures of this regime. In April, he sent a detailed memorandum to the chancellor, stressing the need for moderation in internal affairs as well as the urgency of restructuring the German economy to match the rising social and material pressures.[8] Early in May, he reported in his diary on a long private dinner with Bethmann, discussing matters of state first in the company of a number of ministers and then tête-à-tête. The next day, in yet another long private letter, Rathenau—as he had used to do in the past—expounded upon his views concerning aspects of the situation that had apparently not been discussed the previous evening, primarily regarding the need to neutralize Russia on the Eastern Front.[9] But by July 14, Bethmann was forced to resign. Rathenau hastened to send him a note of encouragement, visited him at his country house, and reported to anyone who cared to listen on the ex-chancellor's depressed mood and sense of betrayal. Soon, however, he set out to make sure that his other channels of communication were open, that he remained well informed as before, and that he could continue to voice his views and give his advice to Germany's leadership.

At about the same time, Ludendorff invited Rathenau to his headquarters again. The two discussed various issues, including the question of war guilt, submarine warfare once more, and plans for the future economic order in Germany. It is possible, though there is no hint of this in the documents, that the general was at this point weighing the possibility of offering Rathenau a political post. The long conversation, however, must have convinced him that Rathenau was not his man. According to the latter, Ludendorff still saw eye to eye with him on most issues. They openly disagreed only on the effectiveness of submarine warfare, not a minor issue to be sure but admittedly somewhat limited. Rathenau tried to minimize these disagreements.[10] In fact, he never lost confidence in Ludendorff until the very end of the war, though he must have noticed that the gap between them was widening rapidly. Their correspondence dwindled. For a couple of months Rathenau was still trying to make his influence felt by writing to other officers at army headquarters, but finally, this channel too was cut off.

Rathenau had many reasons for the growing anxiety he now felt. Prophecies of doom recur in his writings, reflecting his ever darker mood. At this point in the war, even partial victories turned into a source of concern. Every success, and these were becoming few and far between, caused "the discrepancy between military and political events to disappear," he felt, so that one could now hear of peace terms that would in fact be impossible to achieve "without occupying both London and Paris at the same time."[11] The electoral success of the new right-wing Party of the Fatherland, formed in opposition to the parliamentary resolution in favor of peace "without annexations," caused him much distress, too. So did the official entry of the United States into the war on April 6, 1917. He looked with apprehension to postwar times, writing: "I see the beginning of the worst internal strife at the moment when the external strife would come to an end."[12] And during the summer months, spending some quiet days at Freienwalde, this was how he described his life to Gerhard Hauptmann's wife, Margarete: "I live between the Spree and the Oder [i.e. Berlin and Freienwalde], between pressure and nature, work and leisure, and cannot really cope with either. The future makes me ache all over, and that is the most devilishly effective means of disturbing and scaring off any relaxation in the present."[13]

He still kept up an occasional public appearance that communicated confidence and hope. In an interview given to a Swiss newspaper on October 6, 1917, Rathenau presented Germany as capable of a resounding victory, predicting that France would never regain Alsace and Lorraine, and forecasting the future weakening of both England and France as world powers.[14] According to a letter from a contact at Ludendorff's headquarters, this interview was much appreciated there.[15] It did not, however, bring about a rapprochement between Rathenau and the military leadership; nor did his trusting attitude to plans for a new offensive in the West early in 1918. Finally his skepticism gained the upper hand. Driven to the margin of the decisionmaking power elite, he could do little more now than lecture his friends on the situation, impress them with his detailed knowledge of the events, and exasperate them with his oratory.

Frustrated in his hopes of taking a more active part in what had become a life-and-death struggle for his beloved fatherland, Rathenau turned back to writing, as he had done before when unable to set in motion a political career. His book *In Days to Come*, begun before the war and slowly completed after his resignation from the War Ministry, was published in March 1917. It offered a view of an alternative future of a communally oriented national life, without falling into what Rathenau considered a socialist, materialist trap. Socialism, he explained, was based on "complaints and accusations" and included no "luminous goals."[16] Together with capitalism, it too must be transcended, and that could only be done by "men standing on firm ground," men whose life was "based upon a genuine participation *in* the world and genuine responsibility *to* the world," but whose eyes were nevertheless "turned to the sky." It could only be done, apparently, by men like Rathenau.

Once again, Rathenau began by reformulating and then reaffirming the closing ideas of his previous book. He opened by explaining the meaning and function of modern "mechanization," insisting as he had done before, that there was no way "back to nature and to unmechanized life," and that "our aim" was nevertheless to transcend present reality and reach for the "Kingdom of the Soul." In fact, in this more practice-oriented and less pathos-filled book Rathenau simply called his final goal human freedom. Having sketched his familiar spiritual road map, he was now ready to suggest practical means of moving along it. The book was divided into three parts, entitled "The Way of Economics," "The Way of Morals," and "The Way of the Will." In fact, the part on morals dealt with social issues, and the one on the will dealt with politics. Rathenau envisioned a collective economic order with strong centralized control, a society that eschewed material values, luxury, and an "empty life of amusement," seeking spiritual integrity—as he had argued before—through solidarity combined with a deep sense of responsibility. The state that hovered above such a society was to take care of the well-being of its citizens; it should be a true "people's state," an "organocracy," as he called it, stable and dynamic at the same time, incorporating "absolute and ethical ideals," and finally "dethroning mechanization" and "elucidating the divine elements in the human spirit."

Unexpectedly, considering the pressure of war at the time, the book turned out to be a great commercial success. Its marketing included advance publication of some provocative passages in the daily press, and in a new publicity stunt, the Fischer publishing house displayed it alone in the otherwise empty windows of Berlin's bookshops. It sold about sixty-five thousand copies up to the end of the war and was reviewed by some of the most outstanding intellectuals of the day, such as the theologian Ernst Troeltsch, the aging economist Gustav Schmoller, the sociologist Ferdinand Tönnies, the philosopher Max Scheler, and the novelists Stefan Zweig and Hermann Hesse. The author himself was, as usual, ambivalent towards this apparent public stir and, as usual again, chose to concentrate on the few critical and negative reactions. He soon felt criticized from all sides in a "hateful" manner and, as was his habit before, tried to defend himself whenever and wherever he could, in private letters and public appearances.

Despite his state of mind, most reviewers praised Rathenau as an author of great talent and *Bildung*, capable of dealing with metaphysics, ethics, and the philosophy of history, and at the same time an astute social critic and political theorist, "addressing the whole German nation and aiming at a radical restructuring of the German social and political situation."[17] However, all of them did seem to find faults in the new book, each, of course, in the area of his particular expertise. Rathenau's intentions were noble, argued Schmoller, but he was not sufficiently familiar with the economic resources of the Prussian state, so that his reform plans were unfit for the task, adding up in the end to no more than a utopia. His trust in human nature was admirable, wrote Tönnies, but it was unsupported by scientific observation. His faith in the "Kingdom of the Soul" was most welcome, stated Hermann Hesse, but though it came from the heart, it was not written "with the heart." It was an intellectual construct, Hesse claimed, pieced together by using the "tools of yesterday."[18]

Repeatedly, moreover, commentators stressed the tension between Rathenau's actions as a second-generation big industrialist and his critique of hereditary wealth, crude materialism, and luxury consumption. His willingness to compromise with the existing system, declaring himself a monarchist despite all the system's failings, seemed disingenuous. His plans for parliamentary reform, to be implemented only at the "right time" and only in order to achieve limited goals, without losing in the process that much-appreciated "German uniqueness," made his entire critical construct suspect. His hopeful reliance, here as in previous books, on a vague spiritual revival rather than some form of practical institutional reform—all this may have seemed too much for his conservative colleagues and far too little for more outspoken liberals, not to mention the Socialists. Later on, in some of his essays, Rathenau did take further steps and demanded more radical changes, but in the midst of war, he felt compelled to limit his criticism and avoid a too pessimistic attitude. It was only when the system finally collapsed and under the pressure of a violent revolution that he allowed himself to become a radical. As a result, he was often considered an opportunist. Everything he wrote could be interpreted, and often was interpreted, as a means for bolstering either the position of AEG or his own political career. But if ambition was the motivation, the outcome did not justify the effort. Rathenau's public pronouncements first made him unfit for office under the old regime, his personal contact with its top echelons notwithstanding. It later made him—temporarily at least—unfit for office in the new republic too. As a manipulative tool his writings were simply counterproductive. Rathenau wrote what he thought. Presumably, he could not help it. "I have never written down even one line of thought in my life that I didn't feel I must write," he confided to Lili Deutsch in a letter of this period.[19] But it was precisely such writings that drove him, yet again, into political isolation and made him hopelessly sterile.

Rathenau was now approaching his fiftieth birthday, and he was ready for further self-searching and summing up. For the occasion, his former colleagues in the War Ministry arranged a dinner in his honor and then he was invited to celebrate with his old friends. The speech he gave on this second occasion is once again one of those revealing Rathenau documents.[20] For a man who found it so difficult to open up and share his feelings or his worries in the intimacy of personal relationships, he was sometimes breathtakingly open in public. In his speech on his birthday, Rathenau began by admitting the fundamental inner rift within his personality. Since his youth, he confessed, he had been aware of being handed by nature two contradictory talents: that of observing and that of acting, and it was this double-sidedness that made him so enigmatic to others and that so often led to their hostility. Even more, it was this that made his life so difficult and cost him so much energy and effort. Still, he was proud of having never repudiated his own self and of having thus fulfilled—to the best of his abilities—his innermost destiny. Rathenau then thanked his friends for standing by him. They were all dear to him, but more importantly, they represented the true essence of Germany, that spiritual Germany that he so loved and admired. "What really decides our future," he reassured his listeners, "will spring up and grow from our hearts, rising as a spiritual, atmospheric, and ethereal Being."[21] Thus, having opened himself up, exposed some of his inner self, Rathenau slid back into his own familiar diction: patriotism mixed with transcendental pathos.

Meanwhile, the war situation was deteriorating by the day. Domestically too, things were getting worse. Following the difficult winter of 1917 not much was left of the patriotic solidarity that had gripped so many Germans when war broke out in 1914. The population was cold and hungry and the rationing system did little to alleviate the suffering or to spread it more evenly. Censorship was gradually collapsing in the face of growing opposition, and massive strikes mobilized the labor force and politicized its members. Demands for higher wages and shorter hours were now coupled with calls for internal reforms and an end to the war. Then, in the aftermath of the Russian Revolution, German workers too tried their hand at the establishment of workers' councils, in order to coordinate their strikes and reformulate their goals. And just as the working class, its trade union leadership, and its political spokesmen combined their class interests with the call for peace *without* annexations, so their counterparts, the big industrialists, the agrarian elite, the right-wing political parties, the upper bureaucracy, and above all the military leadership, continued to urge peace *with* annexations, at the same time making every effort to preserve the old order and their own power positions. The nation was bitterly divided.

Rathenau's own solution, as defined in the closing sentences of *In Days to Come*, was soon overtaken by events. A mildly critical approach to government policies and the army leadership must have seemed entirely irrelevant by the end of 1917 and the beginning of 1918. Doubts and wavering concerning the usefulness of unrestricted submarine warfare were by then irrelevant, and willingness to give up annexations in order to achieve a positive atmosphere on the way to peace negotiations was less than the minimum required by the opposition of the day, not to mention the Allies on the other side of the front lines. Rathenau found himself estranged from his industrial colleagues, who in any case mistrusted him as a "state socialist." He could neither join the left-wing drive for a quick peace and a political reconstitution of the Reich, nor continue to hide behind vague formulations concerning spiritual revival or the "Kingdom of the Soul." Despite the apparent popularity of his writings, he was hopelessly isolated. Hectically trying to explain himself, he entered a whirlpool of writing and rewriting, publishing and republishing, so much so that Harden half-jokingly commented: "Walther, you too actually publish a journal of your own, like me; every month an issue!"[22] Rathenau was indeed busily adapting his views to the changing situation, clearing up this or that position of his, and in the process, confusing and sometimes alienating even his most well-wishing readers.

The New Economy, published in January 1918, contained a fundamental revision of some of the chapters of *In Days to Come*. Its basic theme appeared on the first page: "The economy is no longer a private matter but a communal one," Rathenau wrote.[23] Unlike the previous book of only a year earlier, however, in which the experience of war had played only a minor role, *The New Economy* was as much about the war as it was about a "new economy"—in war or in peace. Inevitable developments, Rathenau argued, had only been hastened by the war. This turned out to be nothing less than a world revolution and a judgment day combined into one; an event that would finally bring about "a changed humanity." Causing immense loss and suffering, the war was in fact destined to bring about true salvation, "in the name of justice and freedom, as an atonement for mankind and in honor of God."[24]

Rathenau's prophetic tone was by then familiar enough and could have been ignored, as it had been so often in the past. What could not be ignored were his practical solutions and his concrete plans of action. After all, the war was a grand political and social event in his eyes, not just a military affair. It had first brought about what would later be known as "the lost generation," the millions of young men killed in battle; then it had destroyed the country's various means of production, devalued middle-class property, and finally it had hidden all this behind the façade of an unprecedented upward turn of the economy— a fake one, to be sure, one that was entirely dependent on the continuous growth of government demand in time of crisis. In the coming "transitional period," Rathenau prophesied, Germany was bound to feel the scarcity of all major natural resources, as well as capital and labor. It would be impossible to overcome the resulting destitution if one refused to accept the simple fact that the old "mechanized paradise of an uncontrolled economy" had no chance of being recovered.[25] Neither communism nor socialism could save the day. They had been appropriate perhaps in an earlier stage but had by now been simply overtaken by events. The only solution was a new kind of "organized economy," a system combining the benefits of a free market and a planned "scientific" order, fit for the present stage of "mechanization" and for the needs of a postwar world. Only by instituting such a system could Germany achieve the required rise in productivity; only thus could the standard of living of its workers be kept at a civilized level; only in this way would it be possible to reach the correct measure of centralization, the correct size of the most efficient factory, and the most effective level of government supervision and interference. Only thus could the losses caused by a disproportionately large sector of trade and transportation, by the squandering of resources on luxury consumption and by excessive and "immoral leisure" be cut to the minimum. On the basis of the war experience, Rathenau further explained, the postwar system ought to be organized not simply from above, by the iron hand of the state, but through a network of sectoral and professional associations organized from below.[26] This corporate structure, a sort of modern guild structure, would turn a cold and efficient system into an organic body, joined by one will, sharing a single set of values, moving forward without undue bureaucratization, enjoying both self-determination and self-management. Free competition ought to be restricted, Rathenau preached, while initiative and innovation would flourish under the new circumstances. A competent bureaucracy would be no hindrance to growth since all would join forces to serve the interests of a single, united community. This new system, relying upon an ethics of cooperation, solidarity, and responsibility, was bound to come about in any case. It had only to be helped along in order to be established as quickly, as painlessly, and as smoothly as possible.

Rathenau must have known that this little booklet would provoke much opposition; he must have known that his colleagues in industry would be furious. Nevertheless, their actual reaction took him by surprise. *The New Economy* became a bestseller immediately upon publication. By the end of February 1918 it had already sold some forty thousand copies. And immediately afterwards, he found himself at the center of a minor public scandal. Many articles in the press praised him profusely while antisemites up and down the country got busy defaming him. The right wing–oriented Central Association of German Industrialists asked its members for donations in order to finance a campaign against "Rathenau's state socialism," and even its competitor, the liberal Hansabund, came out fiercely against the "Rathenau system." Representatives of the lower middle class, artisans and small shopkeepers, were also provoked by Rathenau's proposals. In the panic-stricken atmosphere of these weeks, a time of violent strikes, preparations for a new offensive, and expectations of an end to the war, Rathenau's cool-headed pessimism aroused unease all round. His was not the only voice calling for deep changes in postwar Germany, but it was he who at this point took the heat.

This, however, did not deter him. Unable to acquire real political influence, Rathenau was determined to say what was on his mind. In the manner of biblical prophets, he saw himself as a vessel for proclaiming new ideas, guided by a higher power. It was almost a decade earlier, in a letter to Lili Deutsch, that Rathenau had tried to explain this mental state: "I am in the hands of powers that control my life, regardless whether they lead me into Good or into Evil, whether they rule me playfully or seriously. It seems to me as if I can do nothing at will, as if I am being led, gently when I submit, roughly when I resist."[27] This was a feeling that accompanied him through much of his life. It may explain his bouts of what seem like uncontrolled actions or words, and his determination, for all his calculating and ambitious nature, to take his own path regardless of the consequences. For someone whose friends jokingly remarked that he was constantly waiting to be asked to take up the highest post, and whose vacillations often seemed like cautious maneuvering in the face of higher authorities, this proud obstinacy now appeared uncharacteristic, even confusing. In fact, such doggedness was as much an integral part of his personality as were his bending before the will of his father, his exaggerated admiration of the Prussian aristocracy, or his somewhat timid caution in treating men like Wilhelm Schwaner or General Ludendorff. Perhaps his boldness in taking exceptional views, almost as if he wanted to set himself apart, was a compensation for prior subservience and too much self-control.

After all, Rathenau dreaded isolation and badly needed human contact. His correspondence is the strongest evidence of that. The man was writing hundreds of letters each year. After about 1912, most of them were addressed to half-strangers who had reacted to his publications, including to the many offprints he sent out; and sometimes the recipients were men he had met by chance on various private and public occasions. Rathenau answered everyone, often extensively and always respectfully, with open friendliness, even a measure of warmth. These, however, were passing contacts. New friendships were rare. Ernst Norlind, a Swedish painter and writer, was one of them. The two corresponded, though not very intensively, from 1915 on, addressing each other with the familiar *Du* from the beginning. In September 1919 Rathenau felt the need to confess to Norlind that "Since my father and brother died—they are not dead for me—there has been no one of whom I could say in the highest sense that he was my friend—except you." "This is something I had to say to you," he added.[28] Shortly before, in 1918, he began a friendship with Lore Karrenbrock, living in Essen, who had read his *On the Mechanism of the Spirit* with great enthusiasm and managed to draw him into an intensive correspondence, lasting until his death. But such distant friends could not relieve Rathenau's loneliness. "More and more I am alienated from people," he wrote to Lili Deutsch in December 1917, even before the storm broke out over his *New Economy*, though meanwhile he was "holding the bridge" as long as possible.[29]

In fact, while the war dragged on and though Rathenau did occasionally try to swim against the tide, he mainly continued to vacillate on all the concrete, immediate issues. In the spring, in view of the intense preparation for a new offensive in the West that elicited waves of patriotic enthusiasm, he would not be drawn out of his skepticism. While he naturally hoped for victory, he did not believe that it could bring about an end to the war. Neither France nor Britain would be forced to surrender, and in any case war would continue at sea even if it were to come to a halt on land. The fierce trade war was likely to last much longer, even for years, he thought. If Rathenau had earlier felt, especially after his discussion with Ludendorff in July 1917, that German military decisions were all too often taken on the basis of intuition rather than of hard data or logical analysis, he now worried that senseless optimism was turning into a major feature of Prussian politics.[30] Nevertheless, while battles were still being fought, he did not find it in himself to come out more emphatically against the government. As late as the spring of 1918, struggling to keep an open channel to Ludendorff, he expressed the opinion that at least "our war leadership [was] in good hands."[31] Even in August he was supporting the transfer of political power to "one of the top military commanders," clearly meaning Ludendorff, although it had by then become obvious that the various battles on the Western Front were being lost one by one and that the military situation was deteriorating daily. Despite his efforts to keep a realistic view of the war situation, he was more often than not at one with both the Pan-German extremists and the spokesmen of heavy industry. Naturally, this did not suffice to make him a desirable ally to either of them. The former rejected him because of his stand on unrestricted submarine warfare; the latter because of his economic plans for postwar Germany. Rathenau was continuously torn between his patriotism on the one hand and his critical posture and realism on the other hand; between his calculated need to remain cautious and his urge to openly express his views. In the end his torturous indecision did not turn him into a man of the middle but into a man on the margin.

The most extravagant expression of Rathenau's isolation, his hectic search for answers, and his frustration at being repeatedly ignored was a longish essay he wrote in July 1918 and then published as a separate brochure sometime during the fall of that year, entitled "To Germany's Youth."[32] This was Rathenau's last attempt, a desperate one indeed, to restate his overall vision, while rephrasing his prior warnings and admonitions. In fact, little is new here, but the tone is significant. Explaining his turn to "the youth," Rathenau described his literary career to date as follows: "Many have read my writings," he states at the beginning, "the scholars to smile at them, the practical to mock them, and the interested parties to grow indignant and rejoice in their own virtue."[33] He was now making a final call directed at the younger generation, almost despite himself and since he must: "I am a German of Jewish stock," he repeats his standard formula. "My people is the German people, my home is the German land, my faith is the German faith, standing above confessions." And it is precisely these "two sorts of blood" that boil within him and force him to speak up though he knows full well that "every word would bring me new struggles, stirred by those who hate and pursue me." Rathenau begins by reiterating his trust in the absolute centrality of that "Kingdom of the Soul," to the description of which he had dedicated his magnum opus of 1913. He then completes his critique of prewar Germany, its various social classes, its political system, and above all, again, its failing leadership, before he turns to the analysis of the present war. Beyond its actual horrors, he explains, this war is a manifestation of a deep spiritual crisis, a turning point on humanity's road towards a higher realm; a grand human drama that can be brought to an end only through complete and equitable cooperation—political, economic, and most importantly moral—among all the warring parties. In the end, the Germans carry the greater burden of responsibility in this process, according to him, not because they have a greater share of guilt for the outbreak of war but because of their special mission as a nation in the service of higher transcendence, pure truth, and perfect justice. Despite their lack of spiritual independence and their long-standing and deep-seated preference for subordination, they still possess the mental attributes required for reaching towards a new world.

Surely, few people managed to read Rathenau's emotional and rather confused appeal during those days. Publishing a sermon of this kind at this particular point in time must have only strengthened his isolation. The pathos, even the hysteria that emerged from these pages clearly underlined the irrelevance of his preaching, the limitations of his reform proposals, and the gap between his soaring pretensions and what he could really achieve. Interestingly, however, once he had got his prophesies off his chest, Rathenau seemed capable of quickly recovering his shrewd self. Such alternations of mood and style had been always typical of him and were particularly apparent at times of crisis. As the war was coming to a catastrophic end as far as Germany was concerned, he oscillated between losing balance and flying into fantasy or rage on the one hand, and regaining his cool-headed power of observation and sure sense of reality on the other. Having allowed himself a fit of prophesying in a resounding, flamboyant style that was excessive even for him, Rathenau was now ready to come back down to earth, in order to appreciate the situation as concretely and objectively as possible.

Under the impression of repeated defeats, Rathenau was now ready to launch another wave of newspaper articles, informing the unsuspecting public of the seriousness of the situation and offering his views on what ought to be done. In the Germany of those days, he felt, the problem was psychological as well as strictly military. Perhaps even he was not fully aware of how bad things were. After the Allied breakthrough on the Western Front in August 1918, Rathenau still thought that Germany could avoid a complete collapse and believed that under the circumstances neither side was in a position to decide the war. In early September, the Balkan front collapsed too and at the same time American troops further tipped the balance in the West, threatening to bring about "a breakthrough on an unprecedented scale," to use Ludendorff's words—and with it, as in Russia, revolution. Facing such a scenario, it was later reported, some officers in a staff meeting at the Supreme Command broke down in tears.[34] The situation was desperate.

On October 2, the *Berliner Tageblatt* published Rathenau's call for steadfastness. Contrary to the assessment of the military, he was apparently still convinced that holding on for a few more weeks was feasible, and that it was essential if Germany was to be saved years of deprivation and misery.[35] The country was intact, the army still functioning, he argued, and the spirit of the nation was unbroken. Ludendorff's request for a complete and immediate ceasefire came immediately afterwards, and Rathenau, like almost everyone else around him, was overwhelmed. His reaction, however, was unique and, even by his own standards, unusually dramatic. His trust in Ludendorff was shattered at a blow: "Those who lost their nerve must be replaced," he wrote in an additional article entitled "A Dark Day," published in the *Vossische Zeitung* a few days later.[36] The general's call for a ceasefire was premature and mistaken, he fumed. Negotiations should not begin at such a low point. Even in defeat one should first strive to achieve a stable front line, clarify the details of the peace offer submitted by the other side, and in all events prepare a full-scale *levée en masse* in order to reverse the situation. "We do not want war but peace," he exclaimed, "but not a peace of subjugation."

Rathenau's outburst caused much consternation at the time. Historians and biographers find it difficult to explain. "Everything seems upside down with Rathenau's appeal for an 'insurrection of the people,'" summarizes one historian: "The high priest of corporate management calling for an insurrectionary people's war? A German-Jewish civilian firing up a *furor teutonicus?* A revolutionary French call to arms to defend an imperial monarchy? All this sounds surreal."[37] But as the same historian adds, this must all be set in context. Rathenau's was, indeed, the most outspoken public appeal for a "people's war" in the wake of the collapse of Ludendorff's strategy, but it was by no means the only voice of opposition. In some military circles, the panic-stricken call for ceasefire was likewise seen as premature. Outspoken opposition, though never made public, came even from officers in the field army. In fact, Rathenau's critique of Ludendorff was repeated in precisely the same terms: "A general who has the fate of 70 million people in his hand must have nerve," it was said. "If he loses his nerve, he must go."[38] And at the end of September, it was none other than the Prussian foreign minister, the retired admiral Paul von Hintze, who called for a *levée en masse* as a way of controlling the transition from war to peace and avoiding "a revolution from below." Others too considered the idea of a last-ditch national effort at this point. Some form of national resistance as a response to the ever more insistent demand for parliamentary reform was on the list of Prince Max von Baden's options as he took over the chancellorship on October 3, 1918, and members of his coalition likewise felt that "only the recognition of the insurmountable obstacle of popular resistance will bring the enemy to negotiations and secure for us the benefits of a negotiated peace."[39] The left-liberal Reichstag member Conrad Haussmann may have expressed an extreme position within his party, but he too suggested a continuation of the war if the purpose was more acceptable peace terms. "Germany is on its way to becoming the freest nation of the world," he wrote in an unpublished memorandum on October 19th. "Onward German people, defend yourself and your young freedom. . . . A free people that fights for its life is invincible."[40] And in a lead article in the Social Democratic *Vorwärts*, Philipp Scheidemann, one of the more sober politicians of the day, demanded the organization of nationwide defense if a just and equitable peace was not to be had.[41]

Considering this background, it is a tribute to Rathenau's

linguistic and rhetorical skills that it was his printed piece that finally created a public storm. His plea for a last-ditch fight to save the nation against enemies both within and without, combining an open attack on Ludendorff and a call for a volunteer insurrection, attracted a great deal of attention. Such a vision of "civil war, military coup, and food strike" all at once, was intended to appeal to all—the left, the right, and the center.[42] Soon, it was taken up by no other than Ludendorff himself. While the defeated general rejected the option of opening a "people's war" at the beginning of October, by the middle of the month the War Ministry was suggesting new draft regulations to supply the army with fresh recruits and the Supreme Command was entertaining new plans for a "final battle." In fact, a move of this kind from this quarter surprised no one. That Germany's irresponsible elite would further entertain wild notions was to be expected. That a man like Rathenau would come up with such reckless plans elicited surprise as well as widespread rejection. On the one hand it was a proof of his inner affinity with that elite, and on the other it was a measure of his desperation, even his panic at the prospect of Germany's collapse.

Once again, Maximilian Harden's political acumen proved superior to Rathenau's. Harden demanded an immediate stop to hostilities and eventually his sketch of a "policy of fulfillment" designed to reduce the Allies' spirit of revenge provided a much more realistic response to the situation.[43] In the end Rathenau too would adopt this line. Meanwhile, however, seemingly in a state of shock, he continued to express the most extreme views. He considered the ultimate peace terms the Allies were believed to be contemplating a *Diktat*, aimed at nothing less than the total annihilation of Germany. In an article entitled "To All Who Are Not Bound by Hate," which was published simultaneously in the press both at home and abroad, Rathenau argued that these represented an act of senseless revenge, aimed to extinguish "a living people . . . with its [living] and its still unborn children."[44] Discussing the matter in the various political clubs of which he was a member, he reiterated such views and reportedly delivered a string of "wild speeches."[45] He still thought, for instance, that if the German delegation to Versailles could not achieve better terms it ought to hand over the sovereignty over the country to the conquering powers. In this way the responsibility would be theirs, he insisted, while Germany would save its honor and preserve its conscience.[46]

Typically, however, he hastened to prepare himself for other eventualities, too. Having expressed his frustration and helplessness, he was quickly back with practical and concrete advice. Only a couple of days after the publication of "A Dark Day," and then again on October 15, Rathenau sent letters unfolding a detailed plan for the mobilization of the Prussian army to the new war minister, General Heinrich Scheuch. It was supposed to help save the economy and prevent a revolution.[47] On the twenty-sixth of that month, he sent a similar plan to Mathias Erzberger of the Catholic Center Party. Rathenau was by then engaged in various practical political matters, apparently on the assumption that his call for a "People's War" would come to naught. Was he offering his services in the hope of being finally appointed to a major post under the new government? This was certainly on his mind. In fact it could be shown that Rathenau's spells of energetic public interventions, whether through private or public channels, were often enough synchronized with available openings either in government or in the diplomatic service. And although he suffered repeated disappointments, Rathenau never completely gave up. It was no secret at this point that Prince Max von Baden was seeking an experienced businessman to add to his cabinet. Although he had been deeply impressed by Rathenau's call to arms, it is doubtful whether he even considered him seriously for the post. Instead it was Max Warburg, a Jewish banker from Hamburg, whom he asked to serve as minister of finance and who then declined, astutely commenting that being both Jewish and a capitalist made him "an impossible candidate."[48]

Rathenau's radical public posture, criticizing every move and giving advice on all matters, estranged friends and foes alike. While many wrote in support of his various suggestions, voices of censure were not lacking. Following his call to arms in early October, for instance, he was approached by one Dr. Heinrich Zellner, director of the Public Chemical Laboratories in Berlin, who wrote to him, expressing the feelings of many, no doubt: "You wish to be a mentor of the German people, you preach morality, ethics, and self-denial to us in numerous writings and articles. How does that fit with the fact that you own and possess millions upon millions, sit on so many supervisory boards, effortlessly and without any special achievement pocketing profit upon profit? . . . You can imagine with what feelings we read your books and articles, which you now shower upon us in various newspapers and journals."[49] And later on, repeating his previous accusations, Zellner added: "If you want to make an impression on us, give up the greater part of your property! Only then would I be able to concede to you the right to improve our people, myself included."[50] This attack, not free of antisemitic overtones, reflected the irritation aroused by Rathenau's behavior. If his hectic public appearances and publications were intended to gain him political influence, they had again badly misfired. By the end of October 1918, he bitterly wrote to one of his correspondents that the "violent agitation" against him had done its work: "No government can and will be engaged with me [now], nor any civilian political party. . . . Though my thoughts would not be obliterated by this wave of hostility, it has devoured me as a person . . ." "Almost no one stands by me while all the powers of the land are against me," he concluded. It was a case of gross ungratefulness, which he did not deserve.[51] "I am in the midst of battle," he wrote to Lore Karrenbrock in these days, "people don't like me . . ." and then in an even darker mood: "Our fate is awful. I saw it coming."[52]

7

Fulfillment and Catastrophe

THE WAR ENDED in revolution. During October 1918, hoping for better terms from the Allies, especially from President Wilson, Germany first turned from a constitutional monarchy into a parliamentary one. The conservatives who were still ruling the Reich considered this step far reaching enough as a show of good will vis-à-vis both the victorious countries and the domestic opposition. But by the end of the month, as the government seemed impotent and peace was not yet agreed upon, it was clearly no longer sufficient. Although demands for the Kaiser's abdication grew louder and the removal of the bankrupt High Command became clearly inevitable, the moderate government in Berlin remained paralyzed. The insurrection began in the port city of Kiel, when sailors refused orders to prepare for a new sea offensive. Following the imprisonment of a few hundred of them, refusal to obey orders spread everywhere, in the army as well as in the navy, followed by a wave of huge demonstrations in cities up and down the country. On November 9, when the uprising reached Berlin, the chancellor Prince Max von Baden was forced to announce the Kaiser's abdication, and on the next day a new government, composed of the two Social Democratic parties, the so-called Majority Socialists and the "Independents," took over. Its first task was to prevent complete chaos while it was arranging for a National Assembly that would establish a new regime. At the same time, a network of Soldiers' and Workers' Soviets was set up that operated as a parallel government, pushing the Social Democratic leadership to more radical constitutional and legislative measures, while itself also attempting to control the most extreme left wing of the revolution and to preserve some measure of order in the streets.

Three conciliatory agreements emerged out of this period of inner strife. As early as November 10, Friedrich Ebert, the Social Democratic majority leader, who had now become chancellor, reached an accord with General Wilhelm Groener, Ludendorff's successor, ensuring the loyalty of the army to the new regime in exchange for the latter's help in upholding discipline and restraining the revolution. Five days later, a Central Working Community (ZAG) between representatives of industry and labor, known as the Stinnes-Legien Agreement, was signed.[1] Accordingly, the employers recognized the Socialist trade unions, allowed for collective bargaining, and agreed to the introduction of the eight-hour day without reduction of wages. In return, the most widely acknowledged leadership of the working class promised to hold back radicals on the shop floor and ensure the calm necessary for the economy to continue running. The union leadership also agreed to postpone all plans for socialization or nationalization to a later, undecided date. Meanwhile, the Majority Socialists, supported by the liberal bourgeois parties, the trade unions, and even some of the Independent Socialists, managed to call for general elections in order to establish a National Assembly that would decide all outstanding constitutional matters and build up the First German Republic. Eventually, due to the continuing clashes in the streets of Berlin, this assembly met in Weimar, a small Thuringian town, renowned as a cultural center in the days of Goethe and Schiller, that now gave its name both to the new constitution that was confirmed there and to the republic that was thereby established.

Simultaneously with the elections to the National Assembly in mid-January 1919, negotiations for a peace agreement among all the participants in the First World War were launched in Versailles. It soon became apparent that the terms to be imposed upon Germany would be far more draconic than even pessimists like Rathenau had imagined. In his case, though, this was no cause for despair. Hopeless situations tended to spur him to action. Pen in hand, he continued to wage war. Already in December 1918 he had published two open letters: one, "To All Who Are Not Bound by Hate," was intended for publication in the press of the neutral countries; the other, addressed to President Wilson's personal adviser and special envoy to Europe, Colonel Edward House was a call directed at the Allied leadership from the midst of defeated Germany. In both Rathenau pleaded for his country's future. "The German spirit, which sang and thought for the world, will turn into a thing of the past," he warned, "and a people still young and strong today, created by God for life, will exist in a state of living death." The threat from the outside, he now believed, meant nothing less than the total annihilation of "German life now and for ever." As so often in the past, Rathenau now too was carried away by his own pathos: "*Herr Colonel*," he publicly confessed to House, "my own work is done and for myself I have nothing more to hope for or fear; my country has no further need of me, and I do not suppose I shall long outlive its downfall."[2]

Meanwhile, he was still there, begging for attention from the new power wielders. The pendulum of his changing moods swung between cool-headed realism and passionate sentimentality. For a number of weeks Rathenau was reporting to friends, in confidence as he was apt to say, that his letter had apparently had great influence on Colonel House, who had immediately sent it to the American president. The final offer in Versailles, however, proved him wrong. It shattered all hopes. Then, pulling himself together, he continued his public activity, trying to be as practical as possible.

The initiative for the Central Working Community, so crucial for the domestic affairs of the new republic during these days, came, in fact, from the Central Association of the Electrical Industry, an organization to which he was close. Although it was Stinnes who led the negotiations, Rathenau soon joined in and took an active part in them. Acceptance of the eight-hour day, for instance, was apparently a result of pressure by him, which finally convinced the other industrialists to concede to this "ideal of organized labor, for which it has yearly demonstrated on May First and repeatedly fought for thirty years."[3] The other side of this agreement, however, meant an indefinite postponement of any fundamental reform of the economy, so that by being involved in it, Rathenau badly compromised his principled position on the need for reshaping postwar Germany. In the midst of revolution, he too had to admit that preventing a complete economic collapse was a more urgent task than the implementation of long-term plans for restructuring the system. One had to prevent "liquidation," as he put it at the time, not merely "bankruptcy."[4]

Still, this did not suffice to set aside Rathenau's fundamental disagreements with his industrial colleagues. These had been deepening throughout the war. That by the beginning of October 1918, Rathenau found himself together with at least some of them in demanding continuation of the war resulted from his own contradictory lines of reasoning at that time and even more from his emotional, often hysterical, but in any case temporary state of mind. Later on, when party political allegiances had to be decided upon, only Carl Friedrich von Siemens and Robert Bosch, among the more moderate industrialists, were willing to be members of the Democratic Popular Union, established at Rathenau's initiative by the end of November 1918. The union was meant to provide a public platform for influential personalities acting outside the party political scene. Some of his acquaintances in the cultural world, who shared at least some of his views, were willing to give him a hand too. Among them were Gerhart Hauptmann, Friedrich Naumann, Ernst Troeltsch, and even Albert Einstein. But various personal disagreements soon led to a general atmosphere of ill will. Rathenau's plans for fundamental social changes and a reconstitution of the entire economic order alienated the few industrialists who did join the group, while his deficient social skills repeatedly made things ever more difficult for everyone. The union was soon disbanded and Rathenau, with others, joined the newly constituted German Democratic Party (DDP). It seems that for the first time he was now ready, even if only by default, to act no longer "from outside" but finally to exert his influence through conventional political channels.

Initially, however, this too came to naught. From the very onset of the revolution, disappointment upon disappointment followed in quick succession. In parallel to the Workers' and Soldiers' Soviets, a "Soviet of Intellectual Workers" had been organized in Berlin. Rathenau was not invited to join and was deeply hurt. After all, he believed, his writings had not only predicted the revolution but had even helped bring it about. The fact that "German youth has passed me by without thanks and greetings," as he put it, was a case of grave ingratitude.[5] He refused to acknowledge that as president of AEG, the epitome of bourgeois elitism, he would be a strange bedfellow of the otherwise revolutionary members of the Soviet, that his vehement call for continued resistance only a couple of weeks earlier had alienated vast numbers of people, and that his repeated expressions of opposition to socialism had been clearly registered by his "intellectual colleagues" in the working-class movement. Understandably Rathenau, being swept aside by the radicalism of the revolution, came to take a deeply pessimistic attitude concerning its fate. In fact, he never hid his abhorrence of "implementing Bolshevism" in Germany. Having always declined conversion to Christianity, he wrote to a friend in January 1919, he had no intention of converting now "to Karl Marx's faith."[6] In an interview with a French journalist later the same month, he explicitly reiterated that the greatest danger of the day was Bolshevism, "coming from the north," though this did not prevent him from considering action in support of the new Bavarian Soviet Republic less than a month later, nor from showing a great deal of interest in communist Russia, even expressing admiration for its achievements. He was vacillating but unfortunately did so in full public view. Seeing the logic of socialism, he continued to abhor its consequences. While he realized the affinity between his vision of the future and the socialist utopia, he also recognized how different the latter's motivation was from his own. In matters of both foreign and domestic policy, Rathenau ended by giving an impression of hectic confusion. It is not difficult to imagine why the new rulers of Germany wanted nothing to do with him.

This became evident when he was silently passed over in setting up the so-called First Socialization Committee on November 17, 1918, which despite prior decisions to avoid radical reforms was given the task of planning and organizing the nationalization of the major German industries. Rathenau was devastated. Soon he could no longer repress his feeling of having been insulted and wrote to Friedrich Ebert himself, demanding an explanation, "not only for [him]self but for the wider public too," as to why he had been left out of deliberations on a matter that stood in the center of his "life work."[7] "The representatives of the capitalist order consider me one of their most decided opponents, and I therefore never expected to be seen as an opponent by the revolution," he wrote to another Social Democrat.[8] But then, adding insult to injury, the new Social Democratic minister of economic affairs chose as his undersecretary none other than Wichard von Moellendorf, Rathenau's collaborator during the days of the KRA and his subordinate in AEG. Even he was apparently a more agreeable partner for the revolutionary government than Rathenau. The latter's unique vision of capitalism cum socialism, no matter how democratic and pro–working class its latest version now sounded, was plainly unpalatable to the ruling parties of the day.[9]

The leadership of the new DDP also had no intention of pushing him forward and failed to nominate him as a candidate for the National Assembly. Some saw in Rathenau's plans for strict economic centralization an attack against the middle class, the very stratum that the party sought to represent, and others simply feared he was too unpopular. By then, the entire liberal press was coming out against him, sarcastically naming him "the modern Francis of Assisi," or "the most paradoxical living creature of old Germany."[10] The unease concerning his efforts on behalf of AEG throughout the war reemerged as well. Finally, while fabricating the "stab in the back" plot as explanation of the fiasco on the front, Ludendorff and his right-wing circles initiated a campaign of slander against Rathenau, accusing him more or less explicitly of sabotaging the war effort. The attacks came from the left, the center, and the right, and it was only the final affront, when the assembly in Weimar burst into laughter at the mere suggestion that Rathenau be chosen President of the Republic.

In a private letter of December 21, 1918, written to a woman acquaintance and thus, as was his habit, more unguarded than usual, Rathenau summarized his situation: "I must now give up any public influence, since the satiated bourgeoisie pursues me as before with hate due to my presumed disruption of business and the revolution mistrusts me as a supposed capitalist and an industrialist. People who have confidence in me are few and far between."[11] In another letter written three days later, this time to his Dutch friend from before the war Frederik van Eeden, Rathenau, defending Germany and the Germans, mentioned his own efforts "to enlighten the Folk" and enumerated the reasons for his present helplessness. Towards the end he added that other reason, the one he only rarely mentioned but which was apparently always on his mind: "You know I am a Jew," ran his familiar declaration, "and in our country, where the government always relies on antisemitism to divert public attention, I—like many other able Germans—have suffered the worst persecutions and affronts."[12] Despite all this, he assured his confidant, he had never wavered in his loyalty to Germany, nor had he ever felt less than totally attached to its people. It was a loyalty that had never been fully appreciated, ran the subtext, and it was this unrequited love, he must have felt, that now cost him his good name.

In fact, his name was being smeared not only at home but even abroad. A newspaper article in Belgium demanded Rathenau's extradition as a war criminal, guilty of intentionally ruining Belgian industry and exploiting its workforce. Other newspapers, in France as well as in Switzerland, repeated and expanded upon these accusations. And as official Germany did not bother to support him, Rathenau felt compelled to defend himself. He did it as usual with great energy, but once again not very effectively. While the attacks against him were, no doubt, massively exaggerated, assuming a nonexistent "Rathenau Plan" that involved illegal and inhuman measures, his awkward attempts to deny any involvement whatever in these matters did not improve his situation.[13] Nor were his comments on the strictness of the German censors, who had presumably suppressed his calls for humanity and moderation, taken seriously abroad or at home.[14] While he was eventually left out of the Allied list of wanted persons, Rathenau remained persona non grata at least until late in 1920. Possibly, his insistence on putting himself forward only made things worse. A period of silence, away from the public eye, might have allowed him to gradually reestablish his reputation. Instead, he sharpened his pen and entered a new phase of ceaseless publications in both the daily and the periodical press, in Germany and abroad. Giving up hope of ever taking active part in politics, Rathenau was thrown upon his literary talent and in desperation made full, excessive use of it.

A few longer and more substantial pieces stand out among the flood of his writings at this time, especially his booklet *The Kaiser*, published in March 1919.[15] Typically, Rathenau follows neither the common liberal critique of Wilhelm II, nor the romantic view of the Kaiser that clothed him in a tragic robe. Instead, trying his hand at sketching a psychological profile of Germany's last monarch, Rathenau chose to stress his "goodness—pure and true," his friendliness, his deep interest in people, even his general "intellectual approach" and "spirituality." The arrows of his critique were not really directed against the Kaiser but, again so typically, against those who surrounded him; not even the Kaiser's closest circle, but in fact the members of Rathenau's own milieu. The burden of guilt lay, according to him, at the door of the upper bourgeoisie, the industrialists as well as the educated elite—all who had basked in the false glory of the monarchy, rubbing shoulders with Wilhelm's entourage, admiring the aristocracy, parading their familiarity with the court, and above all, enjoying the prosperity generated by its government: "Riches welled under the earth, cities were growing, earth and sea came to life. . . . Even mistakes turned to profit, every move seemed to succeed. . . . Could all this be wrong?" Political passivity, even subservience, combined with enjoyment of the pleasures of "the age of mechanization," was the root of all evil, Rathenau now claimed. The war too had been inevitable under these circumstances. It had operated as a "world revolution" and would not be truly over before completing its historic task, namely "moving people from below upward" and, just as in the Russian case, slowly but surely reconstituting state and society in the most fundamental way. As during the French Revolution, humanity was again in Clio's hands, according to Rathenau, carrying us from the worst chaos to a sunlit age of "freedom and responsibility."

There was everything in that small booklet: personal memories, philosophical contemplations on ethics and the nature of history, the shifting of responsibility from the institutional to the spiritual sphere, and a long-term perspective that evaded any practical solutions for pressing, immediate needs. Moreover, Rathenau's fierce attack on his own milieu smacked of that old familiar self-hatred, again making sure to exclude the author in a feat of amazing lack of self-consciousness. It was Rathenau in his familiar old style and it aroused the same mixture of unease and mistrust among his readers. In a biting review, Kurt Tucholsky, the sharpest pen of the republic, expressed his disdain of the author and everything he presumably stood for: whatever insights Rathenau brought forth, he argued, had been expressed more forcefully before, as for instance in Heinrich Mann's novel of 1916, *Der Untertan* (The Loyal Subject), in which the subservient nature of German bourgeois society was described in all its infamy. Of the rest, much was simply untrue. Rathenau's critique of the upper bourgeoisie was nothing but a reflection of his own behavior— before, during, and after the war. Tucholsky was merciless: "It is as such not shameful to have made mistakes during the war and to have supported Pan-Germanism, even when it was proven criminal. Not that. But it is shameful and shows lack of character afterwards, when such views are no longer valid . . . to join in singing a new tune." Tucholsky would neither forget nor forgive. He listed Rathenau's changing views, his share of the responsibility for Germany's collapse, and what he considered his lack of "manly backbone."[16] Finally the piece repeats that fatal Rathenau quote from August 1914, denying even the possibility of a victorious Kaiser riding through the Brandenburg Gate. This same Kaiser, Tucholsky reminded his readers, representative of a world doomed to extinction, was now suddenly praised and grandly forgiven, in what seemed from this reviewer's point of view a pathetic, senseless gesture. Rathenau was under fierce fire. It was perhaps the lowest point in his public career.

By the summer, he could no longer hold back and came out with an extensive "Apology." Appearing rather inconspicuously as an appendix to his booklet on the November Revolution, these thirty-five passionate pages attempted to give his side of the story, a final reply to all his detractors. Rathenau begins by first describing his youth, his studies, his years of training—"not in need but in worries."[17] Then comes his business career, above all his efforts to make a fortune on his own, uncontrolled and uninstructed by his father. Thirdly, a protracted defense against the accusation of being an amateur in philosophy and metaphysics, insisting on the value of *Bildung* over and beyond narrow professionalism and on the superiority of character to knowledge. "The German question," he even writes, "is a question of character."[18] Finally comes the claim that his lifestyle was nothing but modest and sensible, his many services to the fatherland are listed one by one, and his Jewishness is mentioned as a source of "permanent hindrance."[19] But of course, opponents never bothered to read the "Apology," and one-time friends—like Harden or Hauptmann—found too many half-truths in it. Rathenau's insistence on describing himself as a hard-working man, alien to any "concept of pleasure" and far

from any extravagant life style, could not but strike his acquaintances as misleading. Thomas Mann, who did not know Rathenau personally, disclosed only to his diary the impression he
now had of this "strange saint—half true, half false, half pure,
half turbid," though he then graciously added that Rathenau
was at least "struggling honestly," despite being "better off
than anyone else."[20] It was perhaps only Harry Kessler, who
finally concluded that "those alone are entitled to look down
upon him who have striven for the same object and who, with
an equally complex nature and without denying its complexity,
have achieved the unity that was denied Rathenau."[21]

In any event, no censure or criticism could stop Rathenau
now. His flow of publications continued unabated. During the
rest of 1919 he was repeatedly finding new platforms from
which to expand his ideas about the new economy, the new
state, and finally the new society—a booklet under this last title
appearing by mid-November.[22] Once again, Rathenau's critique of Germany's past centered on the deficiencies of its aristocratic leadership and the "childish passivity," meekness, and
submissiveness of the German people. Throughout this
longish essay, Rathenau lashes out at Germany and the Germans. One is reminded of his attack on the Jews some twenty
years earlier. These, to be sure, are profusely praised now:
"The fact that in spite of their small number they have produced more world-moving genius than all other nations put together, and that from them has proceeded the whole transcendental ethics of the Western world, has not prevented their
being pronounced wholly incapable of creative endowment,"
he bitterly comments.[23] Instead, the Germans come under fire
now. They constitute no nation at all, Rathenau exclaims: "The
system *looked* like a nation; in reality it was an autocratic association of economic interests bristling with arms." For character and will they substitute discipline, and instead of thought
and spirit one finds "a brutal, stupid community of interested

persons, greedy for power, presenting themselves as that Germany whose very opposite they are."[24]

"It is not we who liberated ourselves," Rathenau finally argued, "it was the enemy; it was our destruction that set us free."[25] He had already given vent to his critique of the "German Revolution" in an extended publication several months earlier, accusing it of simple-mindedly dealing with the wrong issues and above all of not rising up to become that "Revolution of Responsibility," which he so ardently awaited. From that point onward, according to him, only a long and difficult road could lead Germany to the "promised land." In letters of that time, he repeated the metaphor of a descent into a deep valley followed by an ascent to the peak. And such rising to the peak, ran his familiar argument, could not be achieved by material and institutional changes but only by spiritual means. Germany must finally mature, he preached, or it would never again get the chance of doing so. It must reach for a new kind of self-determination to give its life meaning and direction, and these would arise neither from national genius nor from superiority of race. The notion of the "superior blonde blue-eyed race" he now simply calls "rubbish." But "[t]he Faust-soul of Germany is not dead yet," according to him. "Of all the peoples on earth," Rathenau writes, "we alone have never ceased to struggle with ourselves. . . . Things of the spirit are taken seriously with us," and therefore not all hope is lost. We will still be able "to constitute a new people, united and cultured throughout . . . Class for class, man for man: this is how a people is redeemed. Yet in each case there must be readiness and in each there must be good-will."[26]

The New Society is a piece written from the heart. It reads like a rough draft—unorganized, repetitious, inconsistent, a true "stream of consciousness" presentation. Though it is as such a much weaker work than some of Rathenau's earlier writings, it is biographically very revealing. Rathenau has gone a long way. While many notions in this book are old Rathenau standbys, others have been completely rejected. As before, spirit and the soul are predominant, but the experience of war has brought Rathenau closer to the questions of the day. He is now compelled to struggle with the very real challenge of socialism and to suggest concrete economic, social, even institutional reforms. Only towards the very end is one thrown back upon Rathenau's familiar pathos, and the book concludes with a call for reliance on the will, better still on *good* will or on human solidarity that emanates from one's soul and expresses one's true spirit.

This is also an impatient piece. Rathenau, attacked from all sides, may have lost some of his self-control. He knew that his loyal publisher would print anything he wrote and even sell it. In any event, he considered this piece his "last work," and finally seems to have lost interest in writing altogether. He was seeking—yet again—other channels for expressing himself and other means of exerting political influence. Unexpectedly, considering the public atmosphere around him, we find Rathenau giving flamboyant speeches and gaining large audiences, even a growing number of admirers. The DDP had made it impossible for him to become a Reichstag orator, but he became a frequently invited guest speaker on its behalf. In many ways, Rathenau's spoken utterances at this point were better structured and more persuasive than his written ones.[27] His speech at the Democratic Club in the summer of 1920, for instance, was nothing less than brilliant. Here he challenged his audience to think beyond the confines of formal democracy. Like imperialism, democracy had come to Germany too late, he claimed. In the aftermath of the war, it had been finally accepted without debate. But by that time, according to him, it had become obsolete. The task of the future was to build up an entirely new social order, an order that would reach beyond individual needs toward collective ones, beyond human rights to social rights, beyond capitalism to an organic and communal economy.[28] True, these were Rathenau's old themes, but now, in time of crisis, facing a live audience, his arguments became much more compelling. His liberal party colleagues, while still objecting to the details of his vision, could not deny his talent and effectiveness as an orator. His speeches were interesting, passionate, even charismatic. In these speeches his political genius was finally revealed.

But the fact remained: Rathenau was "excluded from the run of things," as he put it.[29] It was his work in AEG that took most of his time, while his leisure was filled by preparing his speeches, keeping up his correspondence, and, last but not least, allowing his social life to flourish again. As was usual for him, even in difficult times, Rathenau was deeply entangled with the men of his immediate environment, establishing new friendships and striving to strengthen old ones. Some previous ties were by now badly fraying. The correspondence with Lore Karrenbrock, for instance, became increasingly awkward, as she wanted their relationship to be more intimate, referring to herself as "his child," while he made sure to keep her at a distance. In a letter of mid-May 1919, trying to encourage her at a time of need, he gently explained that she had created an inflated picture of himself, one that he could not possibly match "even from afar." At the same time he reassured her that he deeply cared for her "life and feelings," sending her contradictory, even confusing messages and thus, no doubt, contributing to the final breakup between them.[30] At the same time, his intensive correspondence with the philosopher Constantin Brunner, begun in January 1919, likewise dwindled to a trickle. Brunner, born Leo Wertheimer, offspring of an orthodox Jewish family from Altona, developed a unique personal religion, centering on the figure of Christ but staying aloof from both Judaism and Christianity. He lived a life of solitude in Potsdam, near Berlin, and in 1918 published a book on *Jew-Hatred and the Jews.*[31] Rathenau was impressed. He thought he had found in Brunner a soul mate, and their passing acquaintance quickly turned into yet another short-term "love affair" of the kind that occasionally reappeared in Rathenau's life. Interestingly, in this case too the passionate tone was first sounded from the other side. Referring to Jesus' message of love, Brunner was soon writing to Rathenau in very intimate terms: "I am reading and will be reading you, and that means that I love and will be loving you."[32] He found Rathenau's writings inspiring, at least initially, though later he objected to his new friend's "exaggerated respect for 'Germanness'" and even judged Rathenau's overall philosophical construct as "worthless." Nevertheless, he did continue to reassure Rathenau of his love: "You are lovable like a girl, you man, and indefatigable in giving."[33] In response, Rathenau attempted to open his heart. He did so in the manner in which he so often approached his female friends, namely by complaining and discussing his troubles. "I feel gray and ghastly," he writes to Brunner in mid-1919, and then, recalling Goethe's language and the atmosphere of Faust's dying scene, he adds: "thick earthly remains glue me down to the quaking soil . . ."[34] Knowing Brunner was there, however, he no longer felt alone, Rathenau had reassured his friend in a previous letter: "It comforts me that you are there," he writes: "It is as if no one else is there (as in a dream, when everyone has gone). The times are once more, I feel, worth living in."[35]

In addition to these tantalizing personal exchanges, Rathenau upheld the more regular part of his correspondence, and continued to enjoy his many-sided social life. Unique for this period were his frequent meetings with diplomats and business representatives of various foreign countries in Berlin. As a prominent member of Germany's business elite, fluent in French, English, and Italian, who was known for his conversational skills, Rathenau was a desired guest. To be sure, he himself felt that things were no longer as they had been before the war. It was with that special look, he confessed to Kessler, that his international peers were now receiving him—the look with which Christians always looked at prominent Jews, he explains, who were "tolerated, but pitied for their unpleasant relatives." He knew well enough these "polite, disparaging turns," and it was therefore doubly hard for him to bear them now, this time as a German. Still, it had to be born, for the sake of one's country, he typically asserted, even if one could easily use some comfortable ways out.[36]

Clearly, Rathenau did not seek a way out but a way in, and surprisingly, the opportunity did present itself. The first violent attempt to overthrow the republic occurred between March 13 and 16, 1919, when the forces of General Walther Freiherr von Lüttwitz marched into Berlin, trying to set up a new government headed by a relatively unknown former Prussian civil servant, one Wolfgang Kapp. The so-called Kapp Putsch collapsed under pressure of the unusually effective action taken by the working-class movement and its leadership, but for a short while the antirepublican forces did manage to present an effective united front. Rathenau, called for consultation with the new putschist government at the State Chancellery on March 16, presumably in order to mediate between the opposing powers, for once unequivocally took the side of the republic. Although by then the actual arrangements to end the putsch had already been made by others Rathenau's behavior during this incident inspired a new confidence in him. Soon afterward, when the newly established republican government appointed a Second Socialization Committee, he was asked to join it as one among twenty-two members, including a number of prominent socialist and trade union leaders, some well-known professors of economics, and a few big industrialists. In this company, Rathenau belonged to the moderate, pragmatic group, arguing for gradual change, a mild reform of capitalism, and by no means, of course, a full transition to socialism. Eventually, even these rather minimal reforms were never implemented, as Germany was facing the more urgent problem of war reparations, and the government, no longer in the hands of the socialists alone, was in no position to suggest, let alone enforce, any meaningful change.

By the beginning of July 1920, Rathenau arrived in the Belgian city of Spa as adviser to the German delegation, negotiating with representatives of the Allies on questions of disarmament and the large-scale German delivery of coal, as part of the overall reparation agreement. In fact, Rathenau had been busy thinking about the problem of reparations and making his own plans and calculations weeks earlier. He had his own way of evaluating the damage done by the war, especially to the French and the Belgian economies, and thought that reparations beyond the sum of fifteen to twenty billion francs would be excessive, bringing the German economy, in fact even the German people, to complete ruin.[37] The final amount decided upon by the special Inter-Allied Commission after the signing of the Versailles Treaty, however, was many times higher, and it took everyone in Germany by surprise, including Rathenau. From that point onward, he was continually preoccupied with this issue. His knowledge of the various European economies was invaluable, as were his negotiating skills. But in Spa he was only one of a group of industrialists called to give advice on these matters, though apparently second only to Hugo Stinnes. The two were there to defend the national interest, of course, but they found themselves arguing incessantly over matters related to their own, private economic interests. For the rest of the year, in fact, Rathenau was trying to defend the electrical industry against what one historian called "the onslaught of the steel industry in general and Hugo Stinnes in particular."[38]

Among Rathenau's enemies at the time, no one was more ruthless and dangerous than the shrewd Ruhr industrialist—"a man of purpose," as Rathenau himself once called him. Stinnes and Rathenau rarely saw eye to eye on any issue. An outspoken supporter of maximum annexations on the Pan-German model and always mindful of his firm's best interests, Stinnes allied himself with the liberal right in the Weimar Republic and entered the new Reichstag as member of the Deutsche Volkspartei. In the aftermath of the war, he had exercised all his influence to prevent the nationalization of the coal industry, clearly an option under the new socialist regime, while Rathenau, though having no real influence over the matter, was known to support such a step at least in theory. Their mutual mistrust ran very deep. "If he [Stinnes] had swallowed the whole of the German economy into his stomach and bowels," Rathenau once said, he would "still have himself celebrated as the savior of the Fatherland."[39] Stinnes, on his part, had reasons enough to oppose Rathenau. Although his biographer claimed he was no racist, he did state on one occasion that Rathenau's soul was "the soul of an alien race," and seems to have detested him as a Jew, above and beyond their concrete disagreements.[40]

In Spa, the differences between the two immediately came to the surface. The one wished to reduce the size of the coal deliveries at all costs, while the other was more concerned to gain the trust of the French through a policy that prefigured the later "fulfillment."[41] Eventually, the controversy within the German delegation brought the negotiations to a halt, but meanwhile it became apparent that Joseph Wirth, a Center Party politician and at the time Germany's finance minister, was systematically siding with Rathenau. Back in Berlin, Rathenau was asked to speak before the Reich Economic Council and was thus able to carry his struggle with Stinnes into the domestic arena. At first this was not very successful. When his onetime friend and present rival, Maximilian Harden, took the floor, he expressed full support of Stinnes and in his rhapsodic style elevated him into "a new Bismarck."[42] Still, it was Rathenau who was consid-

ered more useful to the government at this juncture. Despite
Stinnes's manipulations and the continuing public expressions
of hostility towards Rathenau, the latter was gradually becoming privy to all important economic matters of the day. Cru-
cially, moreover, he now had an influential political mentor, the
same Joseph Wirth, who would become Germany's chancellor
in May 1921.

This was a turning point in Rathenau's life, a trajectory
that took him away from the cyclical pattern of the past. No
more repetition of short periods of limited success and partial
satisfaction followed by longer periods of setback and isolation.
No more these depressive moods, overcome by writing bouts
that were unfulfilling in the end despite the high degree of public visibility that usually accompanied them. Rathenau was now
on the verge of a major political breakthrough. Repeatedly rejecting the alternative of being a party man, managing to irri-
tate even those who appreciated him, being all too often socially
inadequate and politically inconsistent, his chances of fulfilling
his ambitions of leadership had always been slim. Now, finally,
things were taking a new course.

What did after all help overcome Rathenau's disadvantages
was neither his fame as a writer nor his many social contacts,
nor his ongoing small-scale forays into politics, but his position
as an industrialist and a proficient business negotiator. For years
he had been publishing philosophical essays, meddling in transcendental speculations. Then he had written numerous political essays, analyzing Germany's present position and prophesying its future. But in the end he became a reliable expert
only in matters of large-scale economic system-building. A
touch of diplomatic sense added another qualification. And at
the time, it was these particular skills that were in great demand.

Germany was facing crisis after crisis. By mid-1921 it had
to deal with the so called London Ultimatum, issued on May 5
and containing the Allies' final demand for war reparations in

the amount of 20 billion gold marks, payable by May 11, as well as further sums, pegged at a total of 132 billion, to be paid in yearly installments for the foreseeable future. The cabinet immediately resigned and the new government needed all the help it could get. The situation was critical both domestically and internationally. The existing party system made complex coalition agreements necessary, thereby producing weak and ever-changing governments dependent on flimsy parliamentary majorities. Many thought the country could no longer be governed. At this juncture Rathenau appeared as a man capable of dealing with a variety of pending issues with the necessary discretion and expertise. Moreover, Rathenau, who had always seen the links between the economy on the one hand and social and political matters, on the other, had original ideas for handling such interrelated matters. He was capable of putting his plans on paper and explaining them publicly and within the overall political landscape of Weimar Germany, he suddenly emerged as a politician of a different kind. Sebastian Haffner, then still in his teens and later to become one of West Germany's most outstanding journalists, described the impression Rathenau left on his audience, particularly on the "fantasy" of his younger listeners, who realized, or so Haffner felt, that they were finally in the presence of "a great man."[43] Apparently, despite the agitation against him, not everyone objected to Rathenau. On the contrary, his intelligence and passion were undeniable and he now seemed to exude a special personal magnetism, too. This was effective at home and would soon prove effective abroad in explaining the German case to the French, the British, and the Americans. Most significantly, Rathenau now seemed indispensable for Wirth, who was desperately trying to alleviate Germany's many difficulties—short- and long-term, economic and political, domestic and diplomatic.

At first, Rathenau too thought the London Ultimatum should be rejected. He then grasped the seriousness of the situation as the French threatened to occupy the entire Ruhr region, in addition to the three cities on the right bank of the Rhine that they had already invaded in March 1921. Unusual times required unusual decisions, no doubt, and by the end of the month, following a few days of self-searching, Rathenau finally made "the most difficult decision of [his] life" and accepted the post of minister of reconstruction in Wirth's cabinet.[44] He was finally a cabinet minister, taking part in deciding Germany's future. This could not have been anticipated even a few weeks earlier. It was an undisputed achievement that finally put Rathenau into an altogether different league. In its dire need Weimar Germany had accepted a man of Jewish descent, previously considered unfit for office, to serve in the highest echelon. It was now up to Rathenau to show his mettle.

He found himself immediately *in medias res*. In private letters he claimed his task could not possibly be achieved by one person and that he considered himself merely the first among many destined to handle it: "One after another should jump into the pit, till it can be surmounted. In any case, it will never *be* surmounted if no one begins."[45] It was a leap into the unknown. Since his mother was on vacation in Carlsbad, Walther described to her in detail his new daily routine, consisting now of endless discussions till the early morning hours—official, semiofficial, and unofficial. In addition to cabinet meetings, Reichstag obligations, and a huge correspondence, he now met with men from industry, ambassadors and special envoys, other government ministers and officials, and socially too with the *grandes hommes* and *grandes dames* of Berlin—as usual.[46] And he did seem to be up to the task. Already in his first speech to the Reichstag, delivered on June 2, 1921, Rathenau formulated a new political approach, a "policy of fulfillment," intended above all to bring Germany back into the international community and establish her, against all odds, as a partner in rebuilding Europe.[47]

On July 12, following a few weeks of secret negotiations, Rathenau met his French counterpart, Louis Loucheur, himself a big industrialist, in Wiesbaden, not far from Frankfurt am Main. His show of good will created a new basis for negotiations, and though these were prolonged and complicated, they seemed to bear fruit. The Wiesbaden Agreement, signed at the end of August 1921, did not represent a dramatic breakthrough, but it was surely a starting point for bilateral negotiations between France and Germany. It considerably improved the overall atmosphere between the two countries. As expected, it also aroused vocal opposition from the right at home, like everything else Rathenau or in fact the Wirth cabinet as a whole was by then trying to do. At about the same time, the League of Nations decided on a partition of Upper Silesia; this step was linked, unjustly one should add, to the Rathenau-Loucheur negotiations, and the opposition believed its suspicions had been doubly vindicated. In fact, Wirth and Rathenau did hope that the Wiesbaden Agreement would influence the French to take a less militant stand on the Upper Silesian issue, but they finally had to admit defeat. Rathenau did not object to the consequent resignation of the government. He saw it as an act of protest and considered it a matter of honor, as did many of his colleagues in the DDP. When Wirth later agreed to form a second cabinet, the DDP refused to join in and Rathenau bowed to their decision. In fact, not being a member of the Democratic Reichstag delegation, he could technically have accepted a cabinet post again and it is not entirely clear why he did not do so. Perhaps because it had been made clear to him that he could continue to negotiate on all pending issues, probably even with greater freedom, as an unofficial envoy.[48] Or perhaps because he hoped to calm down the personal attacks on him by stepping down from constant public view, at least temporarily.

This may look untypical for Rathenau. However, the circumstances were different now. During the early years following its establishment, the republic was a scene of bitter civil war, moving in waves of increasing and receding violence. Deadly clashes came in clusters and were spread up and down the country. The first took place in December 1918 and January 1919; the second in March and April 1919, especially in Munich; then in March 1920, beginning with working-class demonstrations in Berlin and the strike in response to the right-wing Kapp putsch; finally, somewhat later, in the Ruhr area, where fifty thousand armed miners, the so-called Red Ruhr Army, faced organized military units in the city of Münster. Each of these clashes ended with hundreds of casualties, often as many as over a thousand. Strikingly, Rathenau's writings and correspondence contain no reference to these events. As an industrialist, he was occasionally concerned with the economic implications of the workers' action. The impression made by the complete chaos in Germany on foreign observers may have caused him some alarm, too. But this was never at the center of his attention. In fact, other bourgeois memoirs from that time leave the same impression. Apparently, while fighting raged in the poorer sections of Berlin, Munich, and Hamburg, life went on more or less normally in the bourgeois neighborhoods of these towns. Between the Spartacus uprising in January and the March strikes in 1919, Frau Betty Scholem, for instance, clearly shocked by the events of the revolution, nevertheless found time to shop for a new rug to replace the old one that "looked like a sweeping-cloth" in her dining room.[49] Sebastian Haffner, to take another example, remembered that during much of that time one could hear shots in the distance but "couldn't figure out their meaning."[50] In Rathenau's neighborhood one could probably not even *hear* the shots. But he, unlike the young Haffner, was surely in a position to figure out their meaning.

Another aspect of the ongoing unrest may have caused him more anxiety. During its first three and a half years, the republic saw a great many political murders and attempted murders. Most of the victims, to be sure, were on the far left wing of the political spectrum and only a few were prominent public figures. Still, the danger was real and present. Matthias Erzberger, the veteran head of the Catholic Center Party, was murdered on August 26, 1921, during Rathenau's term of office at the Ministry of Reconstruction. Erzberger, who had been a member of the German delegation sent to sign the Treaty of Versailles, had been targeted before, too. Now, no longer in office, though planning his political return while vacationing in a peaceful Schwarzwald village, he was located by his assassins and gunned down. This caused a serious public stir, of course, and the police, though not able to catch the murderers, did uncover the right-wing terrorist network that had been responsible for it. Theirs was clearly not a one-time business. "Organization Consul" was making a concerted effort to undermine the republic by well-chosen political assassinations. Rathenau was an obvious target. During the summer months of 1921 he received numerous threats and his friends were repeatedly warning him. Wilhelm Schwaner, always quick to inform Rathenau of the worst vilifications against him, was now sending more than his usual warnings of danger. He commented upon the "flood of mud" hurled at Rathenau and quoted in full a five-stanza verse, calling for Rathenau, "the Jew-swine," to be "bumped off," sung on a train by uniformed youth adorned with large swastikas.[51] Kerr too warned Rathenau, specifically about the political attacks directed at him from the Deutsche Volkspartei, Stinnes's political home.[52] While Rathenau was by then quite experienced in dealing with Stinnes and his colleagues, he could not remain indifferent to the insults hurled at him by the even more radical parliamentary right wing party, the Deutschnationale Volkspartei, led in the Reichstag by his old wartime rival, Karl Helfferich.

Helfferich's aggressive style was by then notorious. It was

his treatment of Erzberger that finally caused the latter's resignation from the government and pushed him to sue his detrac-
tor for libel, thus preparing the ground for his assassination.
Now, the more influential Rathenau became, the more frequently and fiercely Helfferich chose to attack him. By the end
of 1921, expressions of hostility toward Rathenau became ever
more threatening. In a letter to an old woman friend, Rathenau
in fact connected his recent resignation from the cabinet with
the "excessive agitation of circles oriented to the right" against
his policies. They had made it impossible for him, he wrote, to
continue his work.[53] But if resigning from the government was
intended to dampen the agitation, this proved to be a failed tactic. Rathenau, after all, stayed at the center of the international
political scene even after his resignation and by the end of January 1922 took office again, becoming Germany's minister of
foreign affairs, taking upon himself, this time even more directly, the task of repairing his country's international standing.

It may have been too late. Soon after the Wiesbaden Agreement, relations between Germany and France became tense
again. The French government refused to consider any change
in the form or tempo of the reparation payments, insisting that
the Germans ought to be able to settle their two major problems on their own, namely their lack of sufficient cash, as the
due date for the next reparation-payment drew nearer, and the
wildly galloping inflation. Both were the result of economic
manipulations on the part of Germany, it was widely believed
in France, and both had to be handled by the Germans before
any plan for a moratorium on reparations could even be considered. In contrast, the British realized the futility of trying to
extract payments from a bankrupt German economy and tried
a more conciliatory and, according to their view, more realistic
approach. It therefore became more practical to negotiate with
them at this point and Rathenau soon took off for London. On
November 28, 1921, he finally entered into intensive, though

still informal negotiations with British officials, including the prime minister, David Lloyd George, trying to ease off the financial burden set upon Germany. Once again, Rathenau was not the only industrialist negotiating with the British at the time. Hugo Stinnes had already been in London, seeking support for his own plans to revive the German economy. Rathenau, though, speaking for the Wirth government in Berlin, seems to have established better rapport with the British side. In a meeting with Lloyd George, the two went into the details of the economic entanglement but also discussed "the world situation as a whole," matters related to Soviet Russia, even French politics and politicians.[54] At the outset the two agreed that Germany, "having saved the West from Bolshevism," deserved better treatment and that "[i]t would be a disaster for Europe if [it] were to be *broken up*," as the prime minister apparently put it.[55]

Rathenau met the entire British political elite during his days in London, including Churchill and Stanley Baldwin. He impressed some of them while exasperated others. Lord Beaverbrook, the newspaper publisher, saw in him nothing but "one of those pedagogically inclined Jewish philosophers without a clear overview of the situation and without a precise plan for the solution of the problems."[56] Still, Rathenau managed to convince his hosts to bring first Loucheur and later even the shrewd and experienced Aristide Briand, by then once more the French prime minister, for further negotiations in London, and a second journey to London, on December 18, strengthened the chances of some compromise on the reparation issue. By the end of the month Rathenau was dispatched to Paris, where it was finally agreed to convene, this time officially, in Cannes, in order to settle all outstanding matters.

Rathenau headed the German delegation, arriving in Cannes on January 11, 1922. A day later, before any progress could be achieved, Briand was forced to resign, due to the overwhelming opposition to his policies in the French parliament, joined by a few dissenting voices within his own cabinet. In any case, a set of temporary arrangements for the immediate reparation payments have already been agreed upon, reducing the burden on Germany, and a short-term moratorium on all payments between March 21 and May 31 was achieved. A more comprehensive settlement would then be negotiated, it was decided, in an even more prestigious international conference, set for late May in Genoa.

All in all, Rathenau was quite successful. In German government circles at the time, even partial and temporary lightening of the burden of reparations was highly appreciated. His appointment as minister for foreign affairs followed as a result. It was, as usual, immediately registered in his correspondence. Rathenau first wrote to his Norwegian friend Ernst Norlind and then to his two women confidants at the time: Lore Karrenbrock and Lili Deutsch. He was writing to the latter on the last day of January towards midnight: "I stand before this task with deep and serious doubts," were his words, "what can a single man do against this petrified world, with enemies at his back and in consciousness of his limitations and weaknesses?" And he added: "I will set about it with all my best intentions, and should it not suffice, *you* will not forsake me with the others."[57] During the coming months—his last months—the ties with Lili Deutsch were strengthened again. His success may have given him that self-confidence he so badly needed in trying to approach her. She was still the only person whose approval he always needed, whom despite everything he completely trusted, and with whom he could be more open than was his habit. For the outside world he was now "at the peak of life" no doubt, but for her he remained the suffering, deeply split man she had known so well for so long.[58]

However, he had little time for matters of the heart now. Whether these months at the Foreign Ministry did in fact rep-

resent the peak of Rathenau's life is, of course, a matter of perspective, but one thing is clear: in his new post he had definitely
reached a new maturity. He was moving with great assurance,
working day and night, meeting foreign politicians and envoys,
sitting on committees, answering a wave of diplomatic notes,
giving speeches, and so forth and so on. Everything he did was
well calculated and thoroughly thought out. Rathenau had
finally come into his own.

Take, for instance, his speech before the Main Standing
Committee of the Reichstag on March 7, 1922. Rathenau first
explained the policy alternatives available to Germany at the
time. He then argued the benefits of "fulfillment" and stressed
that its limits too must always be observed, defined by what he
considered an ethical question, namely "how much can one
press the [German] people." This line of argument clarifies his
support of the Wirth government's rejection of a huge increase
in taxation, demanded by the Reparation Commission earlier
that same month. It gave credit to Rathenau's analysis: fulfillment was the only way, but it must have its clear limits. Germany must take on the rebuilding of all destroyed areas in the
previously occupied territories, especially in the west, but it
cannot be asked to provide cash payments in quantities that go
beyond what he considered "reasonable valuation." After all, a
solution of the reparation problem was interwoven with the
overall worldwide debt situation across the world financial
market as a whole, he lectured the Reichstag members, and a
complete subjugation of one country would only result in the
ruin of that entire market. Germany's adversaries, the European
nations as well as the Americans, must and would recognize all
this, he believed. Meanwhile, he warned against placing too
much hope in the approaching international conference in
Genoa. It was hard to imagine that representatives of forty nations could solve the numerous outstanding problems. They
could, however, work for a better atmosphere, for more trust

and respect among the participants, and finally, such a joint meeting could prove a "milestone in the general development toward world peace."[59]

This was a hopeful speech, despite its cool realism; a speech by a man with a wide and long-term perspective on events, unfolding his logical and moderate plans and displaying a great deal of energy, harnessed to implement his vision. But within days it became very difficult to hold on to this positive posture. Pressure from the Reparation Commission continued unabated and at home inflation was beginning to take its final mad course. In a speech on March 29, Rathenau was already less buoyant. Repeatedly referring to the previous speaker, Gustav Stresemann, who represented the opposition, he in fact found himself strengthening the latter's arguments one by one. "We want fulfillment," he said, "as long as it is in the range of the possible; not as an end in itself but as a way to peace." It was impossible to expect, however, "that a collapsing world will be rebuilt by the efforts of only one nation, regardless of how willing this nation is to cooperate in that rebuilding."[60] By April 1922, the policy of fulfillment carried out under Wirth's and Rathenau's leadership seemed to have brought little results. Rathenau was leaving for Genoa under less than hopeful circumstances. America decided not to participate, a fact that drastically reduced the possibility of any financial settlement being reached there. Raymond Poincaré, who replaced Briand as prime minister of France, was taking a consistent hard line against Germany, and Lloyd George, so willing to cooperate only a few months earlier, was now trying to live up to his ally's intransigence. Months of negotiations, endless arguments, and reams of statistical data left the leadership of the Western powers unconvinced.

Rathenau's trust in fulfillment became weaker by the day. From the outset it had threatened to violate his sense of honor, and now it also appeared to be futile. His personal mood, too, turned sour. Immediately after arriving in Genoa, overwhelmed by press conferences and elegant social events, he sent out one of his tormented letters to Lili Deutsch. "This time . . . there's nothing but leave taking," he wrote, as usual late at night, tired and unhappy, adding: "I know it means the breakup of one's life, what I must perform here, whether I want it or not. For whoever bends his back under this burden, even for one moment, will be crushed."[61]

Germany, like the Soviet Union, was invited to the conference, to be sure, but—again like the Soviet Union–was not really treated as an equal. The Soviet delegation was housed thirty kilometers away from Genoa, in the picturesque port town of Rapallo, and negotiations between the Russians and the Germans were intensive from the start. In fact, the Soviet delegation had stopped over in Berlin on its way to Genoa. The Russians opposed plans by the Western powers, with which Rathenau was a willing collaborator, to establish an international financial and economic consortium for rebuilding the postwar Russian economy. They hoped to be able to break up what they saw as a capitalist front against them and tried to reach a separate agreement with Germany, a link between the two outcast nations, working together to improve their economic position and parade their political independence. While Rathenau totally rejected the Russian overtures, Chancellor Wirth was more willing to consider them, and the head of the East European Division at the Foreign Ministry, Ago von Maltzan, supported them enthusiastically. Even so, the Soviets left Berlin empty-handed. On arriving for the Genoa conference, however, they were surprised to find France and Britain quite willing to negotiate with them, while Rathenau, who had hoped to be able to mediate between East and West, seemed to be left out in the cold. He expected an invitation from Lloyd George to join the preliminary discussions on the eve of the conference but none came. The possibility that Russia, sup-

ported by the Western powers, would present its own demands
for war reparations was a true nightmare, and at the same time,
his own reparation policy vis-à-vis the West threatened to end
in disappointment. It could all turn out to be a complete disaster. Rathenau felt compelled to act. Finally, he hastily called in
Maltzan to try and complete what had been interrupted in
Berlin, namely a separate accord between Russia and Germany.
Feeling manipulated by Lloyd George on the one hand and by
Soviet Foreign Minister Chicherin on the other, pressured by
his own expert advisers and even by his trusting chancellor, he
caved in and decided for what he had always considered the less
desirable option. At the last moment the long-awaited invitation to tea with the British delegation did arrive, reviving Rathenau's hesitations, but by then he felt there was no way back.
The Rapallo Accord between Soviet Russia and Germany was
signed on April 16, 1922, officially putting an end to any demands for reparations between the two countries, establishing
full diplomatic relations between them, and intensifying their
economic cooperation on the most-favored-nation principle.

Historians still argue about the long-term effects of the
Rapallo Accord. Apparently, and despite the drama associated
with its signing, it did not mean an end to efforts to improve
relationships between Germany and the Western powers, nor
did it settle all outstanding issues in the bilateral ties between
Germany and the Soviet Union. In the short run, however, it
created a sensation. The Genoa Conference continued its deliberations, but its purpose of creating a new atmosphere of
peaceful cooperation in Europe could no longer be achieved.
Poincaré, who had stayed in Paris, skeptical of the whole project, commented to an American journalist: "Fortunately, we
can always rely on Germany to do the heedless thing and isolate
itself." And Rathenau, who only weeks earlier had been es-
teemed by the British press for "his realistic approach, his wisdom, his acumen in financial matters," was now "a Pan-German

imperialist," destroying "the solidarity of the civilized nations . . . by signing an accord with the barbaric Soviets." The
Americans reacted just as negatively, and for a while it seemed
that the former Allies were reunited in their opposition to
Germany.[62]

Rathenau himself remained ambivalent about Rapallo. As
Germany's foreign minister he should have been in a position
to steer its policies in accordance with his vision. As it turned
out, he found himself acting against his own judgment. This
could paradoxically have improved his position at home, since
finally it was Rathenau himself who had come so close to putting an end to the policy of fulfillment. But it did not. To the
accusations of handling German interests in an "unmanly manner" in dealing with the West, there was now added the accusation of collaborating with the despicable Bolsheviks in the
East. Meanwhile, the failure to reduce the burden of reparations was considered by all as the major source of the galloping
inflation and with it the demise of the middle class. Since Rathenau too thought that reparations were the main reason for
the rapid devaluation of the mark, he could not very well respond to attacks of this kind directed at him by friends and foes
alike. Most particularly, he found it taxing to handle Karl Helfferich. It was apparently easier to come to terms with Hugo
Stinnes. In fact, on the night before he was murdered, Rathenau spent long hours in conversation with Stinnes, whose
views he now sought and with whom, he felt, further political
steps ought to be discussed. After a few weeks of hesitation, Rathenau was clearly contemplating a change of policy. He was
moving closer to his opponents. But by now it was—one final
time—too late.[63]

During the days just before and just after Genoa, the anti-
semitic tone of the attacks against Rathenau became increasingly shrill. In conversation Rathenau asked a friendly party
colleague: "Tell me, why do these people hate me so awfully?"

And the answer was: "Simply because you are a Jew and successfully manage Germany's foreign policy. You are a living contradiction of the antisemitic theories on the harmful effect of Judaism on Germany. That's why they want you killed."[64] Others too felt danger was looming. In early April, Kurt Blumenfeld, head of the German Zionist Organization, in the company of Albert Einstein visited Rathenau in his Grunewald villa. Their conversation with the busy minister lasted from eight in the evening till one in the morning. In arguing about Zionism, Blumenfeld recalled in his memoirs, Rathenau repeatedly shifted his ground, justifying his opposition each time from a different perspective, and thereby exasperating even these two sincerely well-wishing visitors. Finally, the two found a way of telling him that they thought he, as a Jew, "had no right to lead the German people as their Foreign Minister." Expectedly, Rathenau objected. He was the right man for the task, merely fulfilling his obligations vis-à-vis "this people" by serving it to the best of his abilities, he argued. And then comparing himself with Disraeli, and, in what his guests interpreted as a moment of weakness, he suddenly added: "Naturally, I would have rather be sitting in Downing Street than in the Wilhelmstrasse."[65] Be that as it may, Rathenau was well aware of his vulnerability and, though often obstinate and overbearing in controversy, he knew he was dangerously exposed now; helplessly exposed, in fact.

Helpless but amazingly calm and fatalistic. As a government minister he was entitled to be guarded by the police, but friends later described how he used to send them home, or demand, sometimes angrily, that they be removed.[66] "I know that my life is constantly in danger," he said to another worried friend during these days, "but what do you want, one can't protect oneself against it unless one becomes a prisoner, shuts oneself in, or lets oneself be constantly watched over by the police."[67] Reports of plans for his assassination reached even

Chancellor Wirth himself. A priest from Bavaria had made the trip to Berlin in order to inform the Catholic Center politician of what had been disclosed to him in confession. Wirth later remembered that when he told Rathenau of the threats, the latter was "pale and still" for a while, but then "his face and his eyes took on endless kindness and mildness. With an inner peacefulness that I have never seen in him . . . he approached me, put both his hands on my shoulders and said: 'Dear friend, it's nothing. Who would want to harm me?'"[68] To all who expressed concern, and many did, he invariably gave self-confident and poised responses. With a characteristic pathos he commented, for instance, that "[i]f my dead body were to be a stone in the bridge leading to understanding with France, then my life would not have been lived in vain, and my work as foreign minister would have been a success."[69] Or more emphatically still: "What will be will be. I have a task to carry on—perhaps not to complete. When my hour strikes—and not before—I will be taken. Then, if I left this country a little nearer to peace . . . I would feel that I did not depart too soon."[70]

Meanwhile, preparations for his assassination were rapidly advancing. Organization Consul, an off-shoot of the Ehrhardt Brigade of the Free Corps, was a nationwide terrorist organization with cells up and down the country and a determined leadership. Political assassinations, intended to weaken the republic and bring about its collapse, were their chosen tactic. The police search for Erzberger's murderers, and material collected following an early June assassination attempt on the veteran SPD leader Philipp Scheidemann, did bring to light many details concerning the organization's activities, but despite all prior warnings, the attempt on Rathenau's life could not be stopped. The two assassins and their driver completed their murderous mission exactly as planned. They made sure their victim had been hit and then took off and disappeared. Acting fast and with unusual determination, the police force of Berlin soon apprehended the twenty-year-old driver, Ernst-Werner Techow, and then, in response to various leads coming in quick succession first from nearby Brandenburg and then from more distant Saxony, the murderers were found and surrounded, hiding in an old Thuringian castle. On July 17, during the ensuing shoot-out with the police, the twenty-three-year-old student Erwin Kern from Kiel met his death, and Hermann Fischer, his twenty-six-year-old accomplice from Chemnitz, shot himself.[71]

The news of Rathenau's murder quickly spread and an immediate call for a special session of the Reichstag on the afternoon of the same day produced a stormy confrontation. The right in general and Karl Helfferich in particular were attacked not only by the left, but most emphatically by Chancellor Wirth. Using a well-known Social Democratic formula, Wirth pointed to the right and exclaimed: "Here is where the enemy lies—and there is no doubt about it: this enemy is on the right!" Helfferich's biting and poisonous speech on the previous day, attacking Rathenau in the harshest language, was now seen as license for murder. The pro- and antirepublican forces stood against each other as they had never done before. The fronts were drawn more sharply then ever. In death Rathenau turned out to be a symbol of the republic for both sides, in stark contradiction to the conciliatory, in-between character of his policies. This explains the massive participation in the demonstration organized by the trade union movement the next day. Some half a million came to mourn Rathenau, conveying at the same time their republican loyalty. Further public gatherings took place in many other German cities, in Hamburg, Munich, Breslau, Chemnitz, and Essen. Messages of condolence came from all over the world.

Rathenau's murder was intended by his assassins to be yet another step in undermining the hated republic, creating chaos that would lead to a bloody elimination of its unworthy supporters. Killing him, while at the height of his career and in

Official ceremony in the Reichstag following Rathenau's murder, June 27, 1922.
Courtesy Bundesarchiv, Bild 183-Z1117-502, photographer: o. Ang.

Berlin, the center of the republic's political life, meant an "up-grading" of their prior terrorist activities. And as a Jew, he was a particularly appropriate target for the perpetrators and their sympathizers. He was certainly a convenient target: indifferent to danger, unprotected, constantly on the move. But even the assassins could not have imagined the extent of the reaction to their deed. Rathenau became a martyr of the republic. His death seemed to clarify the political scene, to force people to take sides, and in the end it gave the Weimar democracy a chance to defend itself. It did seem at first that the republic would be more vigilant now, alert in identifying its enemies and resolute in fighting them. This, however, was only the short-term effect. In the long run the assassination only fostered a deeper rift within Germany's body politic and did not weaken the opposition. The unexpected resistance of the republican forces may have forced the other side to choose less violent tactics, but the strategy was left unchanged and the final goal became ever more pressing. In the end, Rathenau's death did not change the course of events.

It was his life, many-sided, dramatic, full of inner conflicts, unusually productive and creative in so many different ways, not his tragic death, that made a difference: The life of a German and a Jew, struggling with this double identity, insisting on the compatibility of its components, and thereby exposing again and again his deep, tender humanity.

NOTES

Introduction

1. Alfred Kerr, *Erinnerungen eines Freundes*, Amsterdam 1935, 60.

2. Ibid., 151.

Chapter 1. A German Jew in the Making

1. There is a great deal of literature on Rathenau, most of it in German, including numerous biographies. The very first was Etta Federn-Kohlhaas, *Walther Rathenau: Leben und Wirken*, Dresden 1927, but among early works the most outstanding, and still gripping, is Harry Graf Kessler, *Walther Rathenau: Sein Leben und sein Werk*, Berlin 1928. It was soon translated into English (with slight modifications) by W. D. Robson-Scott and Lawrence Hyde as *Walther Rathenau: His Life and Work*, London 1929; reprint ed. New York 1975. All citations here are to this translation (hereafter Kessler, *Walther Rathenau*). Also in English see the three bio-

graphical essays: James Joll, "Walther Rathenau: A Prophet without Cause," in his *Intellectuals in Politics: Three Biographical Essays*, London 1960, 59-129; Hartmut Pogge von Strandmann, "Walther Rathenau: A Biographical Sketch," in his edition of Rathenau's notes and diaries, 1907–22, *Walther Rathenau: Industrialist, Banker, Intellectual, and Politician*, Oxford 1985, 1–26; and Fritz Stern, "Walther Rathenau and the Vision of Modernity," in his *Einstein's German World*, Princeton, N.J., 2001, 165–90, which despite its title contains, like Pogge von Strandmann's piece, a full sketch of our protagonist's life and work. In German, Ernst Schulin's slim volume, *Walther Rathenau: Repräsentant, Kritiker und Opfer seiner Zeit*, Göttingen 1979, was the first to make use of the systematically collected material for a new edition of Rathenau's works and correspondence. A decade later, following the collapse of the Soviet Union, Rathenau's long-lost *Nachlass* was discovered in Moscow, so that now historians can use both the originals and the printed, though as yet unfinished *Walther Rathenau-Gesamtausgabe*, edited for the Walther-Rathenau-Gesellschaft by Ernst Schulin, Hans Dieter Hellige, Alexander Jaser, et al. Of the various biographies of Rathenau in German, the most recent full-scale one is Christian Schölzel's *Walther Rathenau: Eine Biographie*, Paderborn 2006; see also Lothar Gall, *Walther Rathenau: Portrait einer Epoche*, Munich 2009.

2. On the development of Berlin at the time, see especially David Clay Large, *Berlin*, London 2001.

3. The best complete history of German Jewry is now Michael A. Meyer, ed., *German-Jewish History in Modern Times*, 4 vols., New York 1998. For my own perspective, see Shulamit Volkov, *Germans, Jews, and Antisemites: Trials in Emancipation*, New York 2006.

4. The phrase is Mack Walker's, in his *German Home Towns: Community, State and General Estate 1648-1871*, 1971; reprint ed., Ithaca, N.Y. 1998, 111–12.

5. On Emil Rathenau's life see Felix Pinner, *Emil Rathenau und das elektrische Zeitalter*, Leipzig 1918; Ursula Mader, *Emil und Walther Rathenau in der elektrochemischen Industrie, 1880–1907*,

Berlin 2001; and Ernst Schulin's essay, "Die Rathenaus—Zwei Generationen jüdischen Anteils an der industriellen Entwicklung Deutschlands," in *Juden im Wilhelminischen Deutschland 1890–1914*, edited by Werner Mosse, Tübingen 1976, 115–42.

6. Pinner, *Emil Rathenau*, 2.

7. This is Schulin's paraphrase of Maximilian Harden's obituary of Emil Rathenau, published in *Die Zukunft*, 1915, 397. See Schulin, "Die Rathenaus," 115.

8. I have made intensive use of *Walther Rathenau—Gesamtausgabe*, vol. V: *Briefe*, pts. 1: *1871–1913*, and 2: *1914–1922*, edited by Alexander Jaser, Clemens Picht, and Ernst Schulin, Düsseldorf 2006, throughout this biography. It is an extraordinarily detailed and meticulous edition of Rathenau's correspondence (hereafter *GA* V1, V2).

9. *GA* V1, 76.

10. Ibid., 97, and in all the following letters to his mother during this period.

11. Informative on Jews in German industrialization is Werner E. Mosse, *Jews in the German Economy: The German-Jewish Economic Elite 1820–1935*, Oxford 1987. See also Avraham Barkai, "The German Jews at the Start of Industrialization—Structural Change and Mobility 1935–1860," in *Revolution and Evolution: 1848 in German-Jewish History*, edited by Werner Mosse et al., Tübingen 1981, 123–49.

12. Pinner, *Emil Rathenau*, 142.

13. From a letter of March 8, 1883. See Conrad Matschoß, *Werner Siemens: Ein kurzgefaßtes Lebensbild nebst einer Auswahl seiner Briefe. Aus Anlaß der 100. Wiederkehr seines Geburtstages*, 2 vols., Berlin 1916, vol. 2, 771.

14. May 16, 1886, *GA* V1, 173–74.

15. The quotes in this paragraph are from letters dated July 5, 1896; January 23, 1897; and November 11, 1987; all ibid., 197–98, 216–17, 238, 259.

16. On this episode see *Walther Rathenau Gesamtausgabe*, vol. II: *Hauptwerke und Gespräche*, edited by Ernst Schulin, Heidelberg 1977 (hereafter *GA* II), 624–25.

17. See Jechiel Yaakov Weinberg, *Li-frakim*, Jerusalem 2004, 604.

18. January 23, 1887, *GA* V1, 217.

19. August 7, 1891, ibid., 365.

20. "Staat und Judentum: Eine Polemik" (1911), in Walther Rathenau, *Gesammelte Schriften*, 5 vols., Berlin 1918; vol. 6, Berlin 1922 (hereafter *GS*), vol. 1, 188–89.

Chapter 2. A Man of Many Talents

1. See Stefan Pucks, "'Eine weichliche, leidende, dem Beruf nicht genügende Natur'? Walther Rathenau im Spiegel der Kunst," in *Walther Rathenau 1867–1922: Die Extreme berühren sich*, edited by Hans Wilderotter, Berlin 1994, 88.

2. December 21, 1889, *GA* V1, 316.

3. November 24, 1893, ibid., 458.

4. *GA* II, 620.

5. Walther Rathenau, *Zur Mechanik des Geistes oder vom Reich der Seele* (1913), ibid., 264.

6. January 16, 1888, *GA* V1, 269.

7. Alfred Kerr, *Erinnerungen eines Freundes*, Amsterdam 1935, 63.

8. See Dolores Augustine, *Patricians and Parvenus: Wealth and High Society in Wilhelmine Germany*, Oxford 1994, 88.

9. See Gerald D. Feldman, *Hugo Stinnes: Biographie eines Industriellen 1870–1924*, Munich 1998.

10. For Weber's personal life see Joachim Radkau, *Max Weber: Die Leidenschaft des Denkens*, Vienna 2005.

11. Kerr, *Erinnerungen*, 59.

12. September 19, 1919, *GA* V1, 2256.

13. See *Walther Rathenau: Industrialist, Banker, Intellectual, and Politician: Notes and Diaries 1907–1922*, edited by Hartmut Pogge von Strandmann, Oxford 1985 (hereafter Rathenau, *Diaries*), 108 n. 81. See also Ernst Schulin, "Walther Rathenaus Diotima: Lili Deutsch, ihre Familie und der Kreis um Gerhart Hauptmann," in Wilderotter, *Die Extreme berühren sich*, 64, and his more recent comments in *GA* V2, 2256–57.

14. September 23, 1914, *GA* V2, 1371–72.

15. *GA* II, 620.

16. See, for example, Rathenau's correspondence with Wilhelm Schwaner, discussed below, pp. 127–30.

17. See Kessler, *Walther Rathenau*, 65.

18. The affair is analyzed in Hans Dieter Hellige's extensive introduction to the Rathenau-Harden correspondence in *Walther Rathenau Gesamtausgabe*, vol. VI: *Walther Rathenau–Maximilian Harden, Briefwechsel 1897–1920*, Munich 1983 (hereafter *GA* VI), esp. 160–68.

19. See, for instance, Kerr, *Erinnerungen*, 22–24.

20. Hugo von Hofmannsthal, *Gesammelte Werke, Lustspiele II*, Berlin 1977, 95–143. For details and analysis see Dieter Heimböckel, *Walther Rathenau und die Literatur seiner Zeit: Studien zur Werk und Wirkung*, Würzburg 1996, 161–66 and passim.

21. Robert Musil, *Der Mann ohne Eigenschaften*, 2 vols., Reibeck 1981, and see Heimböckel, *Walther Rathenau und die Literatur seiner Zeit*, 27–35 and passim.

22. September 29, 1892, *GA* V1, 414–15.

23. December 25, 1891, ibid., 372.

24. April 22, 1892, ibid., 396.

25. December 30, 1892, ibid., 432–33.

26. January 1, 1893, ibid., 433–35.

27. Ibid.

28. January 15, 1893, ibid., 438–40.

29. Credit for the discovery belongs to Alexander Jaser, whose edition of Rathenau's collected essays is due to appear as vol. I of the *GA* in the near future. I wish to thank him for showing me the material and sharing with me his immense knowledge of Rathenau and his writings.

30. The essay appeared in the *Freie Bühne für den Entwicklungskampf der Zeit*, vol. 4, no. 8 (1893), 940–44.

31. December 31, 1894, and March 9, 1895, *GA* V1, 485, 486–87.

32. For Harden and his relations with Rathenau I have used with great benefit the edition of the Rathenau-Harden correspondence and especially the extensive introductory essay by Hans Dieter Hellige in *GA* VI.

33. The essay was later reprinted in Walther Rathenau, *Impressionen*, Leipzig 1902, 1–20, but never included in his *GS*. I have used Thomas Dunlap's translation at http://germanhistorydocs .ghi-dc.org/.

34. See his letter to Wilhelm Schwaner of January 23, 1916, in *GA* V2, 1503. See also the discussion in Ernst Schulin, "Walther Rathenau und sein Integrationsversuch als 'Deutscher jüdischen Stammes,'" in *Jüdische Integration und Identität in Deutschland und Österreich 1848–1919*, edited by Walter Grab (Jahrbuch des Instituts für Deutsche Geschichte, suppl. 6), Tel Aviv 1984, 17–18.

35. *GA* VI, 303.

36. Ibid., 323.

37. The overall economic situation at the time, the position of AEG, and Walther Rathenau's personal involvement are well described in Hartmut Pogge von Strandmann, "Hochmeister des Kapitalismus," and Peter Struck, "Die Karriere Walther Rathenaus in der AEG," both in Wilderotter, *Die Extreme berühren sich*, 33–44, 45–54.

38. Quoted from Bernhard von Bülow, *Denkwürdigkeiten*, vol. 3, Berlin 1931, 40, and Etta Federn-Kohlhaas: *Walther Rathenau: Leben und Wirken*, Dresden 1927, 82.

Chapter 3. Incursions into Politics

1. *GA* VI, 364.

2. Ibid., 661.

3. August 24, 1903, ibid., 661.

4. See Ursula von Mangoldt, *Auf der Schwelle zwischen Gestern und Morgen*, Weilheim/Oberbayern 1963.

5. "Die schönste Stadt der Welt," reprinted in Walther Rathenau, *Impressionen*, Leipzig 1902, 137–63.

6. Ibid., 71–99.

7. See the correspondence with Herzl in *GA* V1, 632–37, 638, 640, 643–44, 646. For a full discussion of their relations see Rudolf Kallner, *Herzl und Rathenau: Wege jüdischer Existenz an der Wende des 20. Jahrhunderts*, Stuttgart 1976.

8. See Rathenau's letter of response (July 18, 1902) and some of Mauthner's original comments in *GA* V1, 642.

9. The essay was first reprinted in Rathenau's *Reflexionen*, Leipzig 1908, and then in *GS*, vol. 4, 9–32. The quote is on page 26.

10. November 21, 1904, *GA* V1, 712–16.

11. See Rathenau's letter to Harden, October 15, 1897, in *GA* VI, 306–9.

12. See Hans Dieter Hellige's lucid presentation in the introduction to the Rathenau-Harden correspondence, *GA* VI, especially 77–172. Compare Jeffrey Herf, *Reactionary Modernism: Technology, Culture, and Politics in Weimar and the Third Reich*, Cambridge 1984.

13. See Harry Graf Kessler, *Das Tagebuch 1880–1937*, edited by Roland S. Kamzelak and Ulrich Ott, 9 vols., Stuttgart 2009, October 12, 1906.

14. The piece, entitled "Die neue Ära," was published on February 12, 1907. It was later reprinted in Walther Rathenau, *Nachgelassene Schriften*, 2 vols., Berlin 1928, vol. 1, 15–22.

15. Kessler, *Tagebuch*, October 19, 1906.

16. Cited in *GA* II, 654, from Bülow's *Denkwürdigkeiten*, vol. 3, Berlin 1931.

17. See Rathenau's letters to his father from May 28 and 31, 1907, in *GA* V1, 788–90.

18. For the entire diary in an English translation with a very detailed and informative commentary by Pogge von Strandmann, see Rathenau, *Diaries*.

19. Ibid., 31, 34, 38, 42, entries of July 19, August 3, 5, 12, 13, and 22, 1907.

20. The memorandum was first published in Rathenau's *Reflexionen*, 143–97, and after Rathenau's death in his *Nachgelassene Schriften*, vol. 2, 9–73. Extracts in English are to be found in Rathenau, *Diaries*, 49–59.

21. Rathenau, *Diaries*, 59.

22. Ibid., 54–55.

23. Rathenau's second memorandum, "Report on the State of the Southwest African Colony," was only published in his *Nachge-*

lassene Schriften, vol. 2, 74–141; extracts in English: Rathenau, *Diaries*, 78–92. The quotes are from pages 82–83.

24. Rathenau, *Diaries*, 92.

25. Ibid., 76.

26. See the details in *GA* VI, 931–32.

27. This was written as a memorandum, but it is unclear whether Rathenau ever handed it in. It was printed as one of the appendices to his *Zur Kritik der Zeit*, Berlin 1912, 177–94.

28. See Walther Rathenau, "Deutsche Wirtschaft," *Die Zukunft*, July 7, 1906, 36–38; "Vom Wissen industrieller Krisen," ibid., July 22, 1906, 464–66; "Englands Industrie," ibid., October 13, 1906, 79–84; and "Vier Nationen," ibid., January 25, 1908, 105–16. The last three essays were soon afterwards reprinted in *Reflexionen*.

29. For the quotes see Rathenau, *Reflexionen*, 140; and "Bemerkungen über Englands Gegenwärtige Situation," 1908, in Rathenau, *Zur Kritik der Zeit*, 182.

30. Rathenau, *Diaries*, 132–33.

31. Ibid., 133–35.

32. Ibid., 173–74, 175–76.

33. Ibid., 146–48, 179–80.

34. Ibid., 164.

35. Quoted from *GS*, vol. 1, 233–49.

36. On this kind of cautious reform see James Retallack, "Ideas into Politics: Meanings of 'Stasis' in Wilhelmine Germany," in *Wilhelminism and Its Legacies: German Modernities, Imperialism, and the Meaning of Reform, 1890–1930*, edited by Geoff Eley and James Retallack, New York 2003, 235–53.

37. Rathenau to Albert Ballin, June 3, 1912, *GA* VI, 1104.

38. *GS*, vol. 1, 235.

39. Ibid., 247–49.

Chapter 4. Captain of Industry, Literary Star, Lonely Man

1. Gerald D. Feldman, *Hugo Stinnes: Biographie eines Industriellen 1870–1924*, Munich 1998, 247.

2. Ibid., 246.

3. A large collection of accounts of such meetings and conversations with Rathenau is available in *GA* II, 617–908. See also the separate edition of *Gespräche mit Rathenau*, edited by Ernst Schulin, Munich 1980, including a number of additional items.

4. Walther Rathenau, *Reflexionen*, Leipzig 1908. Regarding the price see *GA* II, 504 n. 5.

5. Ibid., 1–23.

6. Ibid., 29–37.

7. Ibid., 58–78.

8. Kessler, *Walther Rathenau*, 130.

9. For a detailed account see Dieter Heimböckel, *Walther Rathenau und die Literatur seiner Zeit*, Würzburg 1996, 161–74.

10. Ibid., 163.

11. Ibid., 167.

12. See a passage in Alfred Kerr, *Erinnerungen eines Freundes*, Amsterdam 1935, 117–18.

13. Harry Graf Kessler, *Das Tagebuch 1880–1937*, edited by Roland S. Kamzelak and Ulrich Ott, 9 vols., Stuttgart 2009, April 14, 1911.

14. Fall 1909 (no precise date on the original), *GA* VI, 915.

15. Kessler, *Tagebuch*, March 3 and April 3, 1911.

16. See Roth's "A Visit to the Rathenau Museum" (1924), in *What I Saw: Reports from Berlin 1920–33*, translated and edited by Michael Hofmann, London 2004, 183–87.

17. Kessler, *Tagebuch*, March 3, 1911.

18. Quoted in Anna Teut, *Bürgerlich Königlich: Walther Rathenau und Freienwalde*, Berlin 2007, 104.

19. Kessler, *Tagebuch*, March 28, 1911.

20. Heimböckel, *Walther Rathenau und die Literatur seiner Zeit*, 99.

21. Rathenau, *Diaries*, 110.

22. See above, p. 71.

23. Kessler, *Tagebuch*, December 13, 1906.

24. See Ernst Schulin, "Walther Rathenaus Diotima: Lili Deutsch, ihre Familie und der Kreis um Gerhart Hauptmann," in *Walther Rathenau 1867–1922: Die Extreme berühren sich*, edited by Hans Wilderotter, Berlin 1994, 55–66.

25. This and the next quote are from a letter of July 29, 1906, *GA* VI, 772–73.

26. Ibid., 869–70.

27. *GA* VI, 650.

28. See the entry of April 7, 1912, in Rathenau, *Diaries*, 155–56.

29. *GA* VI, 651–52.

30. December 21, 1913, *GA* VI, 1243.

31. Ibid., 688.

32. The first piece, "Massengüterbahnen," was first published separately in January 1909 and then reprinted as an appendix to Rathenau's *Zur Kritik der Zeit*, Berlin 1912, 161–76. The second, "Geschäftlicher Nachwuchs," first appeared in the *Neue Freie Presse*, December 25, 1909, and was later likewise reprinted in *Zur Kritik der Zeit*, 206–18.

33. Rathenau, *Zur Kritik der Zeit*, 207.

34. Ibid., 218.

35. The three "letters" first appeared in January, February, and March 1911 and were all reprinted in an appendix to Rathenau's *Zur Kritik der Zeit*, 219–43.

36. Ibid., 242.

37. *Zur Kritik der Zeit* was later reprinted as *GS*, vol. 1. I have here used the new, annotated edition, including a very useful introductory essay by Ernst Schulin, in *GA* II, 17–103.

38. Heimböckel, *Walther Rathenau und die Literatur seiner Zeit*, 182.

39. Rathenau expanded upon this theme later, in a speech on September 28, 1921. See Walther Rathenau, *Gesammelte Reden*, Berlin 1924, 264.

40. The book later appeared as *GS*, vol. 2, in 1918. Again, the best available edition now is in *GA* II, 105–295.

41. *GA* VI, 1229.

42. The text of the "Breviarium Mysticum" was never published during Rathenau's lifetime. It first appeared in a slightly shortened version in Kessler, *Walther Rathenau*, 73.

43. *GA* II, 251.

44. Ibid., 280.

45. Ibid., 295.

46. Musil, "Anmerkung zu einer Metapsychik," *Die Neue Rundschau*, 1914, 556–60.

47. July 30, 1914, *GA* V2, 1345.

48. In a letter to Gustav Schmoller, ibid., 1683.

Chapter 5: Hitting the Glass Ceiling

1. *GS*, vol. 1, 209–20.

2. Ibid., 221–32.

3. Ibid., 224.

4. "Eumenidenopfer," *GS*, vol.1, 251–63. The last quote is on page 263.

5. "Deutsche Gefahren und neue Ziele," *GS*, vol. 1, 265–78. The last quote is on page 277.

6. Ibid., 278.

7. "Zur Lage," ibid., 305.

8. Ibid., 306.

9. *GA* V2, 1351–52.

10. For the full argument see Fritz Fischer, *Germany's Aims in the First World War*, New York 1967 (the German-language version was first published in 1961).

11. See his comments in *GA* V2, 1371, 1411–12, 1425–26.

12. Letter to Wilhelm Schwaner, *GA* V2, 1361.

13. See Walther Rathenau, *Der Kaiser: Eine Betrachtung*, Berlin 1919, 28. For the quote in Bülow's memoirs, see *GA* II, 856.

14. For details see Gerhard Hecker, *Walther Rathenau und sein Verhältnis zu Militär und Krieg*, Boppart am Rhein 1983, 193–201.

15. Letter to Fanny Künstler, December 6, 1914, *GA* V2, 1401–2.

16. Letters to Fanny Künstler, November 1 and December 5, 1914, *GA* V2, 1394–95, 1401–2.

17. January 24, 1915, *GA* V2, 1413–14.

18. August 14, 1914, *GA* V2, 1356.

19. See Christine Holste, *Menschen von Potsdam—der Forte-Kreis 1910–1915: Vergesellschaftungsversuch eines oppositionellen Zeitgeistes vor dem Ersten Weltkrieg*, Stuttgart 1992, and *Der Potsdamer*

Forte-Kreis: Eine utopische Intellektuellenassoziation zur europäischen Friedenssicherung, edited by Richard Faber and Christine Holste, Würzburg 2001.

20. See Wilhelm Schwaner and Walther Rathenau, *Eine Freundschaft im Widerspruch: Der Briefwechsel 1913–1922,* edited by Gregor Hufenreuter und Christoph Knüppel, Berlin 2008, 81.

21. Ibid., 84–85.

22. Ibid., 92–93 and 93–94.

23. This is quoted from one of Schwaner's articles in the *Volkserzieher,* August 2, 1914, ibid., 109 n. 4.

24. Letter of January 23, 1916, Schwaner and Rathenau, ibid., 141–43.

25. Ibid., 134–35.

26. *GA* V2, 1346.

27. *GA* V2, 1366.

28. The speech was first printed in the *AEG-Zeitung,* then separately by Rathenau and finally on the pages of *Die Zukunft.* It is here quoted from *GS,* vol. 5, 9–21.

29. Schwaner and Rathenau, *Eine Freundschaft,* 126.

30. July 7, 1915, *GA* V2, 1442–43.

31. Schwaner and Rathenau, *Eine Freundschaft,* 126.

32. *GA* V2, 1491–92.

33. *GA* V2, 1818.

34. For details see Hecker, *Walther Rathenau und sein Verhältnis zu Militär,* 333–47.

35. The lecture later appeared in *GS,* vol. 5, 23–58.

36. *The Times,* October 11, 1915.

37. For a full description of the setting up of the KRA, the related controversies, and the role of all the persons involved, see Rathenau, *Diaries,* 187–90.

38. *GS,* vol. 5, 60–93. The quotes are on pages 79 and 90–91.

39. Ibid., 88–91.

40. Ibid., 93.

41. *GA* V2, 1598–1600, and the informative note 2 on page 1599.

42. January 15, 1917, *GA* V2, 1606–7.

43. Letter to Baron von Lustig at the War Ministry in Vienna, *GA* V2, 1621.

44. *GA* V2, 1552.

45. Quoted in Hans Tramer, "Der Beitrag der Juden zur Geist und Kultur," in *Deutsches Judentum in Krieg und Revolution 1916–1923*, edited by Werner E. Mosse, Tübingen 1971, 321. In the same volume see also Eva G. Reichmann, "Der Bewußtseinswandel der deutschen Juden," esp. 530–31.

46. November 16, 1918, *GA* V2, 2023.

47. March 28, 1921, *GA* V2, 2544.

48. See excerpts from Richard Lichtheim, *Lebenserinnerungen aus der Frühzeit des deutschen Zionismus*, Stuttgart 1970, in *GA* II, 783.

49. First published separately by the Fischer-Verlag and then reprinted in *GS*, vol. 5, 95–119.

50. For a full summary of this position see Uriel Tal, "Theologische Debatte um das 'Wesen' des Judentums," in *Juden im Wilhelminischen Deutschland 1890–1914*, edited by Werner Mosse, Tübingen 1976, 599–632.

51. *GA* V2, 1777.

52. See, for instance, a letter of December 30, 1912, *GA* V1, 1151–52, and for the quote see the undated report of a conversation with Lore Karrenbrock, in *GA* II, 788.

53. *GA* V2, 2138–39.

54. For the letter and the following quotes from it see *GA* V2, 1725–27.

55. October 29, 1918, *GA* V2, 2010.

Chapter 6: Politician Manqué, Prophet with a Vengeance

1. See Walther Rathenau, *Politische Briefe*, Dresden 1929, 47.

2. Ibid., 48.

3. See Rathenau, *Diaries*, 199–204. The quote is on page 200.

4. See the letter in Rathenau, *Politische Briefe*, 74–78, and the quotes on page 77.

5. See Gerald D. Feldman, *Army, Industry and Labor in Germany, 1914–1918*, Princeton 1966, 150.

6. For details of this episode and the quotes see Gerhard Hecker, *Walther Rathenau und sein Verhältnis zu Militär und Krieg*, Boppart am Rhein 1983, 361–67.

7. See Ernst Schulin, "Max Weber and Walther Rathenau," in *Max Weber and His Contemporaries*, edited by Wolfgang Mommsen and Jürgen Osterhammel, London 1987, 311–22.

8. Rathenau, *Politische Briefe*, 111–19.

9. See Rathenau, *Diaries*, 219–22, and *Politische Briefe*, 128–34.

10. See the detailed notes in Rathenau, *Diaries*, 222–32.

11. Letter to Captain Max Blankenburg at army headquarters, October 16, 1917, *GA* V2, 1778–80.

12. Ibid., 1780.

13. August 19, 1917, ibid., 1749.

14. See *GA* II, 740–43.

15. Letter from Captain Max Blankenburg, October 13, 1917, *GA* V2, 1777–78.

16. Rathenau's *Von kommenden Dingen* was reprinted as *GS*, vol. 2, in 1918. All the quotes here are from the English translation by Eden and Cedar Paul, *In Days to Come*, New York 1921, 57, 16, 27, 60, 155, 203, 247, 286.

17. See Ernst Schulin, "Zur Rathenaus Hauptwerken," in *GA* II, 499–595; on this book especially, 555–95; the quotes here are on page 564.

18. Ibid., 565–72.

19. June 13, 1917, *GA* V2, 1707.

20. The speech was first privately printed and distributed and then included posthumously in Walther Rathenau, *Gesammelte Reden*, Berlin 1924, 9–26.

21. Ibid., 24.

22. Quoted in Dieter Heimböckel, *Walther Rathenau und die Literatur seiner Zeit*, Würzburg 1996, 336.

23. Having been first published as a separate booklet, the essay was then reprinted in *GS*, vol. 5, 179–261. It is here dated 1917. The quote is on page 181.

24. Ibid., 261.

25. Ibid., 200.

26. Ibid., 231.

27. Letter of unknown date at the end of 1907 or beginning of 1908, *GA* V1, 869–70.

28. September 19, 1919, *GA* V2, 2255–56.

29. December 25, 1917, 1826.

30. For these views, see, for instance, Rathenau's letters of May 17, 1918 and June 5, 1918, *GA* V2, 1919–20, 1930.

31. Quoted in Hecker, *Walther Rathenau und sein Verhältnis zu Militär*, 416.

32. The latter piece was reprinted posthumously in *GS*, vol. 6, 93–214.

33. The quote is from Kessler, *Walther Rathenau*, 239.

34. See Michael Geyer, "Insurrectionary Warfare: The German Debate about a Levée en Masse in October 1918," *Journal of Modern History*, vol. 73, no. 3 (2001), 467.

35. Ibid., 428–29.

36. This article, dated October 7, was later reprinted in *GS*, vol. 6, 258–60.

37. Geyer, "Insurrectionary Warfare," 460.

38. Ibid., 470.

39. Ibid., 479.

40. Ibid., 481.

41. Ibid., 479.

42. See *GA* VI, 750.

43. On Harden's position in detail, see ibid., 747–50.

44. The article first appeared in *Die Zukunft* of December 1918, and was reprinted in *GS*, vol. 6, 273–81.

45. See Hecker, *Walther Rathenau und sein Verhältnis zu Militär*, 444.

46. See Kessler, *Walther Rathenau*, 263.

47. Rathenau, *Politische Briefe*, 88–91.

48. See Hecker, *Walther Rathenau und sein Verhältnis zu Militär*, 433.

49. Letter of October 7, 1918, *GA* V2, 1985.

50. October 12, 1918, ibid., 1992–93.

51. October 31, 1918, ibid., 2012–13.

52. October 10, 1918, ibid., 1990.

Chapter 7: Fulfillment and Catastrophe

1. Carl Legien was a prominent figure in the Socialist trade union movement and at the time its chief spokesman at the negotiations with the industrialists.

2. For the first open letter see Chapter VI, note 44 above. The second was first published in the Social Democratic daily *Vorwärts* in December 1918, then in February 1919 as a separate pamphlet, and finally in *GS*, vol. 6, 268–73. Here it is quoted from Kessler, *Walther Rathenau*, 262.

3. Reported by Theodor Leipart in a memorial book for Carl Legien and quoted in *GA* II, 763–64.

4. See Walther Rathenau, "Apologie," in *Kritik der dreifachen Revolution*, Berlin 1919, 71–107. The quote is on page 103.

5. *GA* II, 765.

6. *GA* V2, 2084.

7. December 16, 1918, in Walther Rathenau, *Briefe*, vol. 2, Dresden 1927, 88.

8. November 22, 1918, *GA* V2, 2028.

9. For the revised form of his plans for a new social, economic and political order see Walther Rathenau, *Autonome Wirtschaft*, Jena 1919.

10. Quoted in Ernst Schulin, *Walther Rathenau: Repräsentant, Kritiker und Opfer seiner Zeit*, Göttingen 1979, 98.

11. Walther Rathenau, *Politische Briefe*, Dresden 1929, 224–25.

12. *GA* V2, 2069–71.

13. See Schulin, *Walther Rathenau*, 100.

14. See his letter to the *Neue Zürche Zeitung*, January 14, 1919, in Rathenau, *Politische Briefe*, 231–33.

15. Walther Rathenau, *Der Kaiser: Eine Betrachtung*, Berlin 1919, 25–26; quotes and paraphrases here are from 41–43, 54–60.

16. The review was printed in *Die Weltbühne*, May 29, 1919, 616.

17. Rathenau, "Apologie," 80.

18. Ibid., 82.

19. Ibid., 98–99.

20. See Thomas Mann, *Tagebücher 1918–1921*, edited by Peter de Mendelssohn, Frankfurt a. M. 1979, 293–94.

21. See Kessler, *Walther Rathenau*, 136.

22. Walther Rathenau, *Die Neue Gesellschaft*, Berlin 1919. Quotes here are from the English translation by Arthur Windham, *The New Society*, New York 1921.

23. Ibid., 86.

24. Ibid., 92–93.

25. Ibid., 13.

26. Ibid., 85–87, 98, 147.

27. See the speeches in Walther Rathenau, *Gesammelte Reden*, Berlin 1924.

28. For the full text of this speech see ibid., 51–80.

29. November 11, 1918, *GA* V2, 2021.

30. See especially his letter of May 19, 1919, ibid., 2179–80.

31. Constantin Brunner, *Der Judenhaß und die Juden*, Berlin 1918.

32. February 20, 1919, *GA* V2, 2119–20.

33. For Brunner's comments on Rathenau see the notes ibid., 2672, and for the quote here Brunner's letter, March 1919, ibid., 2134–36.

34. June 8/9, 1919, ibid., 2204.

35. March 28, 1919, ibid., 2145.

36. See Harry Graf Kessler, *Das Tagebuch 1880–1937*, edited by Roland S. Kamzelak and Ulrich Ott, 9 vols., Stuttgart 2009, February 20, 1919.

37. See, for instance, his letter of December 24, 1918, in *GA* V2, 2067–68.

38. This quote is from Pogge von Strandmann's introductory comments on Rathenau's diary entries of 1920. See Rathenau, *Diaries*, 238.

39. Ibid., 248 n. 40.

40. The quote is from Kessler, *Walther Rathenau*, 276, who could not refrain from adding that Stinnes himself "had Southern French blood in his veins and looked like a Phoenician sea-captain."

41. Ibid., 244.

42. See Hans Dieter Hellige's commentary in *GA* VI, 764.

43. See Sebastian Haffner, *Geschichte eines Deutschen: Die Erinnerungen 1914–1933*, Stuttgart 2000, 47–51.

44. See his letter to Julius Frey, June 3, 1921, *GA* V2, 2571.

45. Ibid.

46. Letter to Mathilde Rathenau, June 8, 1921, *GA* V2, 2177–78.

47. *Gesammelte Reden*, 199–204.

48. Rathenau, *Diaries*, 271–72.

49. See her letter, February 13, 1919, in *Betty Scholem–Gershom Scholem: Mutter und Sohn im Briefwechsel 1917–1946*, edited by Itta Shedletzky, Munich 1989, 38–39.

50. Haffner, *Geschichte eines Deutschen*, 35.

51. June 26, 1921, *GA* V2, 2586–87.

52. See *GA* V2, 2601 n. 1, to Rathenau's reply to an earlier communication by Kerr.

53. November 12, 1921, *GA* V2, 2619–20.

54. Rathenau, *Diaries*, 278–81.

55. Ibid., 277.

56. Quoted in Gerald D. Feldman, "Der Unschlüssige Staatsmann: Rathenaus letzter Tag und die Krise der Weimarer Republik," in *Ein Mann vieler Eigenschaften: Walther Rathenau und die Kultur der Moderne*, edited by Tilmann Buddensieg et al., Berlin 1990, 94.

57. *GA* V2, 2638.

58. Letter to Lili Deutsch, April 11/12, 1922, *GA* V2, 2654–55.

59. The speech is reprinted in Walther Rathenau, *Cannes und Genua: Vier Reden zum Reparationsproblem*, Berlin 1922; reprint ed., Teddington, UK, 2007, 16–27.

60. Ibid., 40–41.

61. *GA* V2, 2654–55.

62. For details see Carole Fink, *The Genoa Conference: European Diplomacy, 1921–1922*, Chapel Hill 1984. The quotes are from her essay "'As Little a Surprise as a Murder Can Be': Aus-

ländische Reaktionen auf den Mord an Walther Rathenau," in *Walther Rathenau 1867–1922: Die Extreme berühren sich*, edited by Hans Wilderotter, Berlin 1994, 238–40.

63. On the last few weeks of Rathenau's life see especially Martin Sabrow, *Die verdrängte Verschwörung: Der Rathenaumord und die deutsche Gegenrevolution*, Frankfurt a. M. 1999, and Feldman, "Der Unschlüssige Staatsmann."

64. For the conversation with Hellmut von Gerlach see *GA* II, 854.

65. *GA* II, 872–74.

66. Ibid., 853.

67. Ibid., 854.

68. Ibid., 852.

69. Ibid., 854.

70. Ibid., 853.

71. For full details, see Sabrow, *Die verdrängte Verschwörung*, 123–30.

INDEX

Page numbers in *italics* indicate illustrations

Jewish Lives is a major series of interpretive biography designed to illuminate the imprint of eminent Jewish figures upon literature, religion, philosophy, politics, cultural and economic life, and the arts and sciences. Subjects are paired with authors to elicit lively, deeply informed books that explore the breadth and complexity of Jewish experience from antiquity through the present.

Jewish Lives is a partnership of Yale University Press and the Leon D. Black Foundation.

Anita Shapira and Steven J. Zipperstein are series editors.